DANGEROUS FLIGHTS

What Could Possibly Go Wrong?

By

Kerry McCauley

The works of Kerry McCauley:

Ferry Pilot: Nine Lives Over the North Atlantic.
Dangerous Flights: What Could Possibly Go Wrong?
Riskaholic: The Hobo Series.

Printed in Menomonie, WI, United States of America

First Printing, 2022

EBOOK: ISBN 978-1-7353390-2-3
PAPERBACK: ISBN 978-1-7353390-3-0

www.kerrymccauley.com

Cover Design by David Ter-Avanesyan/Ter33Design
Photographs by Kerry McCauley

DEDICATION

To John Driftmier
The man behind the curtain.

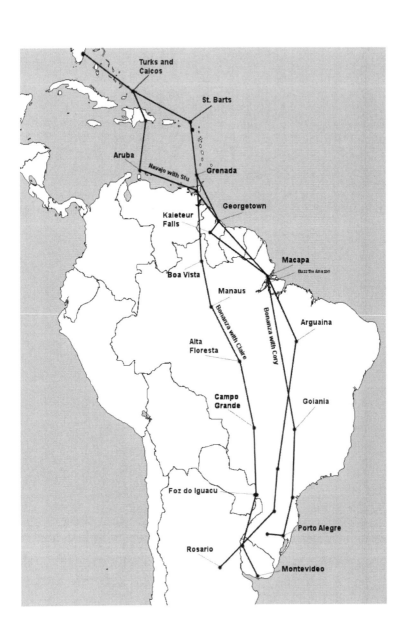

Turks and
Caicos

St. Barts

Aruba

Navajo with Stu

Grenada

Georgetown

Kaieteur
Falls

Macapa

Buzz the Amazon

Boa Vista

Manaus

Arguaina

Bonanza with Claire

Bonanza with Cory

Alta
Floresta

Campo
Grande

Goiania

Foz do Iguacu

Porto Alegre

Rosario

Montevideo

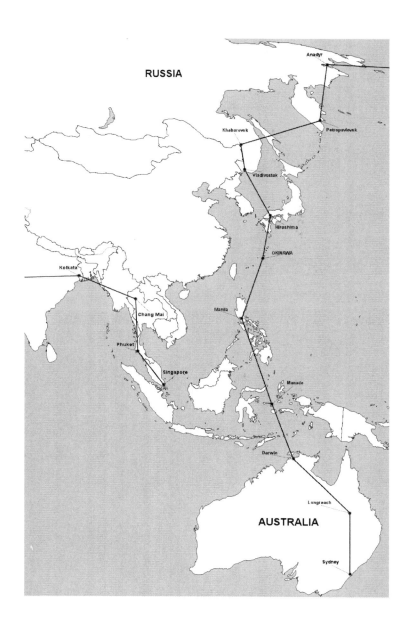

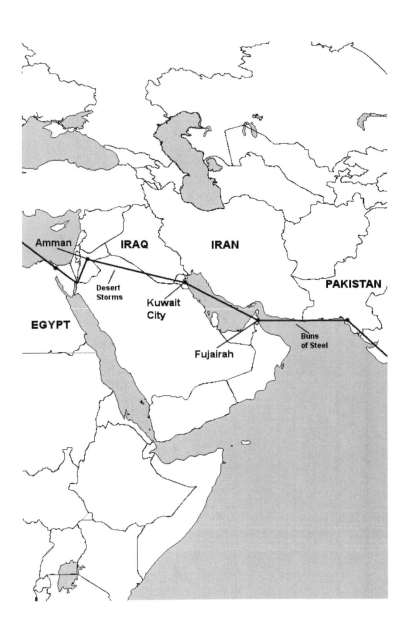

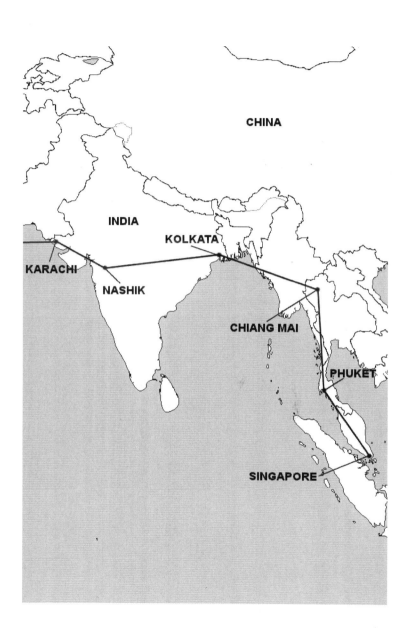

CHINA

INDIA

KARACHI

NASHIK

KOLKATA

CHIANG MAI

PHUKET

SINGAPORE

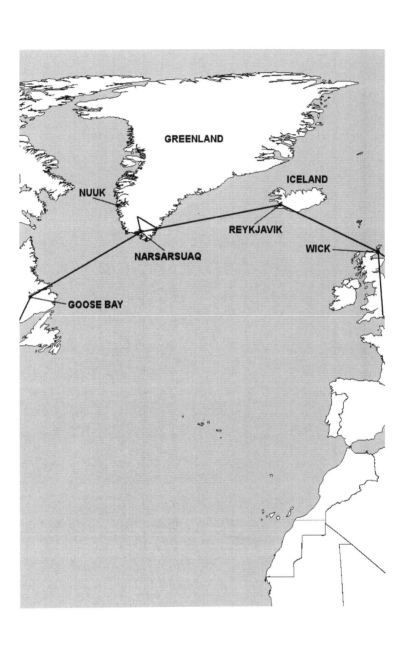

GREENLAND

ICELAND

NUUK

REYKJAVIK

WICK

NARSARSUAQ

GOOSE BAY

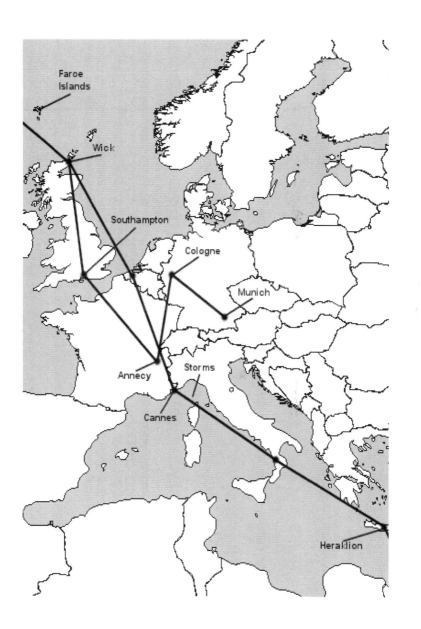

Table of Contents

PREFACE

"Anadyr Tower Phenom seven bravo foxtrot, can you please request runway lights full bright. Lights full bright at the airport please."

"Aaaah, lights are inoperative at this time."

Marcio and I looked at each other.

"Did he just say no lights?"

"No lights. Doesn't help much does it?"

"No … That's not good. We better make this first one count."

Wonderful. We were about to attempt a night landing in Northern Siberia, the cloud deck was reported to be well below our legal minimums, the visibility was almost zero and now the runway lights were out. Things just keep getting better and better.

"Seven bravo foxtrot, wind three zero zero, six meters per second."

I didn't know how to convert that to miles per hour but it sounded windy.

As we got close to the airport I saw a lone mountain top poking up through the sea of clouds below us. The fast moving clouds were flowing around the mountain, coming back together in a jumble of swirls and rents. I catch a glimpse of inky blackness beneath. *Looks pretty dark down there.* Then it's behind us as we turn in and begin the approach. Marcio reduces power and the Phenom heads for the dark gray blanket shining in the moonlight below. All light leaves us and the cockpit windows go black the second we enter the clouds. The instrument lights give off a warm glow as Marcio adjusts the autopilot while I keep track of our progress on my iPad.

I once read about an Air Force cargo plane that was forced to do a true zero zero landing one night back in the early sixties. The crew found the runway using the primitive navigation instruments of the time and landed using only the altimeter. The fog was so thick they still couldn't see anything even after coming to a stop on the runway. I was thoroughly grateful for a good autopilot and the GPS system as we rode the Phenom to whatever awaited us at the end of our approach.

"When we hit five hundred feet I want you to call down our altitude."

"Roger."

Everything is all set now. The landing gear is down and locked, flaps are set, all instruments in the green. There's no point asking for a condition update, the die is cast. Our cameraman in the back cabin hasn't said anything for a while. I briefly wonder what he's thinking? Can he detect the fear in our voices or is he blissfully unaware of our situation?

"Five hundred."

"Four hundred."

Marcio gently puts his hands on the yoke but leaves the autopilot engaged.

"Three hundred … Two hundred."

Our legal minimums. Nothing outside. We should go to full power and execute a missed approach … We don't.

LIGHTS, CAMERA, ACTION

TV production company Pixcom is urgently searching for adventurous Ferry Pilots on interesting runs for a new Discovery Channel Series. If this sounds like you or someone you know, please contact us for more information. Please note that this is not an offer of employment – we are looking for pilots already working ferrying aircraft.

I read the advertisement in the Beechcraft owners and pilots forum again. Urgently searching for adventurous Ferry Pilots on interesting runs for a new Discovery Channel Series.

Hmmm, I'm a ferry pilot. I'd like to be on TV. I'm adventurous.

The thought rolled around in my head like a Christmas tree ornament, all shiny and new. I chuckled to myself and continued to scroll down, skimming through random posts about the best type of wax to use on a Bonanza and where to fly to find the best $100 hamburger. I wasted more of my morning surfing the internet but that Discovery Channel ad kept creeping back into my mind.

I'd be perfect for that! I'm good on camera, I'm personable, I'm interesting, and gosh darn it, people like me! Okay, I'm not really any of those things, but I am a ferry pilot.

Or **was** a ferry pilot. I hadn't flown an aircraft over the ocean in ten years. But that didn't mean I wasn't a ferry pilot anymore, did it? I just hadn't done it in a while.

Screw it.

I scrolled back to the Ad, copied the email address and composed a reply. I highlighted my many years of ferry flying experience (minus the ten year layoff), my fifteen thousand skydives (not much to do with ferry flying but it seems to impress people when I tell them that) and a few other random facts that I hoped were interesting. I had my wife Cathy take a few glamour shot photos of me and sent the whole mess to the email address in the ad. I was optimistic (I mean, come on! What idiot wouldn't choose me for a TV show about ferry pilots?) but not overly optimistic. I assumed the production company would have literally thousands of pilots applying for a spot on a Discovery Channel series about flying.

A few weeks went by and I'd almost forgotten about the ad when I received an email from a Canadian TV production company called Pixcom. They wanted to set up an interview with me to see if I was a good fit for the show! *Holy cow!* I was blown away. I'd responded to the ad in the spirit of "you can't win if you don't play." I never really thought anything would come of it.

The next day I sat down for a Zoom interview with two of Pixcom's producers. They asked me about my ferry flying experience, my hobbies, my family and any other interesting things about my life that they should know. I could tell that they didn't know much about aviation because they spent way more time asking me about my skydiving experience than my flying credentials. They mostly wanted to get a feel for how I would be on camera. And I blew it. It was terrible. I was nervous and wooden. I wasn't funny and I wasn't charming. Basically, I just sucked. When I got off the line I told Cathy that I'd just blown my big chance at stardom. Oh well, I'd given it my best shot.

A month or more went by without any more contact with Pixcom so I assumed that they'd chosen some other, more engaging pilots for their stupid TV show. Then one afternoon I got a phone call from a Pixcom producer. He wanted to know if I was still interested in being on the show. I was taken by surprise but managed to tell him that, yes, I'd love to be on their TV show!

"Great!" He said "Any chance you can fly down to Florida and ferry a Piper Navajo down to Argentina two days from now?"

I was taken aback. Two days? "Ummmm, sure. I could do that."

"Excellent! I'll have my assistant send you the information right away. Welcome aboard!"

With that he hung up and left me standing there, holding my phone and wondering what in the hell just happened and what I had just agreed to. I was more than a little concerned for a number of reasons.

1. It was smack dab in the middle of the busy skydiving season and just picking up and leaving for who knows how long worried me. I had a business to run and being a major control freak meant that it drove me nuts to miss an afternoon of jumping, let alone two weeks.

Could I trust my staff to keep things going without killing too many of my customers?

2. I hadn't ferried an airplane internationally in over ten years and never to South America. What if I couldn't do it? What if I made some kind of really stupid mistake? I had no idea if any of the rules or regulations of international flying had changed over the years. I'd hate to get some kind of violation. And of course any mistakes I made would be seen by millions of people all over the world. Talk about stage fright!

3. I'd never flown a Piper Navajo before. Not only had I never flown a Navajo before, I'd never even sat in one before! Okay, I'll admit that climbing into strange aircraft and flying them around the world was my specialty back in the day, but like I mentioned before, it had been ten years since I'd done anything like that. Hell, I wasn't even current on instrument flying!

As I thought about all the reasons to be nervous, one thing continued to make me feel good about my decision, I was going to be on TV! That's right, I, Kerry McCauley, am going to be filmed flying a twin engined Piper Navajo from the United States to South America! Millions of people around the world would get to see me doing something so cool that pilots literally dream about it. That's right! Millions of people would get to see every single thing that happened on my trip to Argentina. Every single thing that happened … All of it … Including my mistakes … Especially my mistakes … Because the mistakes and disasters are what make reality shows good TV. And I'd just agreed to have every single thing I did wrong broadcast to the world from six different angles … *Crap, what have I done?*

Pixcom flew me down to Ft. Lauderdale Florida and put me up in a hotel near the airport where I spent a sleepless night worrying about the upcoming flight. The next morning I went down to breakfast to meet the team I'd be flying with. I'd been told that not only would I be flying with a cameraman from Pixcom but that I'd also be flying with another ferry pilot. When I heard the news that I'd be flying with another experienced ferry pilot I felt a whole lot better because having a co-pilot would make things soooo much easier! Not only are two pilot operations safer, but having someone else to consult in difficult situations just gives you more confidence in yourself and the decisions you make. Hopefully the other pilot was far more experienced than I was and my job would be to just smile and look good for the camera.

When I walked into the hotel restaurant I scanned the tables for my new co-pilot and cameraman. The first man I spotted was Stu Sprung. At least I assumed it was Stu. The man sitting alone just looked like a pilot. He was well built, in his mid 30s, with thin blond hair and a pair of sunglasses hanging from a silver chain around his neck. He was wearing shorts and sandals, and had kind of a beach-going hipster look to him, but it was summertime and we were in

Florida so I didn't let his attire sway my judgment of him too much. We both looked each other over like we were on a blind date. (Which I suppose we were.) I walked up, introduced myself and sat down. Stu and I had barely started talking when our director and cameraman John Driftmier walked up. I could tell he was the cameraman because ... well, he looked like a cameraman. John was tall and skinny with a head full of curly brown hair and just had that AV geek look to him. The huge video camera he was carrying was also a dead giveaway.

As the three of us sat down and got to know each other it became apparent that as the director, John was going to be the boss and we were now just actors. Stu and I also found out that in the TV game there is no messing around wasting time. We were expected to start work immediately, and that meant flying. The first thing on the agenda was getting a series of air-to-air shots. We drove to the Ft. Lauderdale Executive Airport to meet the pilot of the camera ship that would shoot the video. We would also see the plane Stu and I would be flying to Argentina.

On the way to the airport Stu and I asked each other about our flying experience. I told him that I had just over 5000 hours of flight time in my logbook and that I'd started ferry flying in 1990. Stu seemed impressed with my flying experience, especially when I told him that I'd crossed the Atlantic over 75 times. Then it was his turn. Stu told me that he had a little over 700 hours and that most of that was in helicopters. He also told me he was very happy to be paired with such an experienced ferry pilot because he'd never done a ferry flight before and had been a little nervous about the upcoming flight.

Great, a ferry flight rookie.

I was hoping that I was going to be flying with an experienced and current ferry pilot. Instead I was the old hand and my co-pilot was a rookie on his first trip! Stu and John would be counting on me entirely to get the Navajo safely from Florida to Argentina. So much for a no-pressure trip.

Once we got to the airport the first thing we did was stop in a large hangar and meet the Navajo. And it was … OK. I'd flown worse but I'd definitely flown better. (For the record, I like "better".) The Piper Navajo Chieftain is an eight passenger multi-engine plane designed for the small cargo, feeder line and corporate market. Its two Lycoming 310 hp engines push the Navajo along at a blistering 238 mph with a range of 1,165 miles. It looked like a beast of a plane. Not sleek, just capable, a workhorse. I climbed into the cockpit and squeezed myself into the left seat. I then began my old ritual of "what does that button do?" Running my eyes and fingers over the controls I slowly became familiar with the controls of the Navajo. This is one of my favorite parts of ferry flying. I love meeting new planes. New or old it's like meeting a new woman.

"Hey baby, what's your story? Where shall we go today?"

After finding most, but not all, of the important switches I grabbed the *Pilot's Operating Handbook* (*POH*) and climbed out of the plane. The *POH* is each plane's bible and has all the information a pilot needs to fly the plane. It's basically the *How to fly a Navajo for Dummies* book. I'd be studying that book intently before even starting the engines.

As Stu and I climbed out of the Navajo, John Driftmier, AKA Drifty, ushered us into a meeting with the camera ship pilot that would be filming the air-to-air flight. When we met David Gibbs I immediately liked him. David was a rough looking guy in his mid- fifties who had a devil-may-care no nonsense competence about him. He came off a little rough at first, with a "How did I ever get talked into this, you will probably kill us all." kind of attitude.

He explained that he'd be filming us from all different angles doing many different maneuvers and that would require a lot of formation flying between the Navajo and the camera ship. And just to make things even more difficult he told us that the camera ship was a helicopter! When I heard that he'd be flying a helicopter I understood his concern. Formation flying is dangerous enough if both pilots are flying similar performing aircraft. If you're going to try to fly formation with two aircraft that have vastly different stall speeds things can get interesting very quickly! And in case you're wondering, interesting is bad. I also understood his concern about the formation flying itself because the vast majority of pilots have little or no experience in formation flying and formation flying is dangerous.

When David finished his rant it was clear that he wasn't happy about the whole situation. Then it was my turn. The first thing I did was to completely agree with him. (That always makes people feel better.) Then I tried to make him feel better by telling him what an amazing pilot I was. It probably sounded like bragging but I did it in a humble way (sort of). I told David that as an old school jump pilot I'd not only done a lot of formation flying but my career was a non-standard one like his and I had the skills and attitude necessary to keep things safe. The more we chatted the better we both felt about the air-to-air shoot.

"OK, let's go do it then!" David said standing up.

"Wait, what? We're going flying now?"

"Sure, why not? The list of shots Pixcom sent me is pretty long. Probably going to take most of the day so we'd better get started."

I was in a minor jam. After telling David and everyone else that I was essentially God's gift to aviation I sure didn't want to have to tell them that I didn't know how to fly a Navajo. I at least had to spend a few minutes going over the POH and familiarize myself with the controls. Remember, when in doubt, stall.

"Sounds good David. But I just saw the Navajo for the first time ever and will need a few minutes to do a thorough pre-flight and make sure the paperwork is in order."

"Okay, that's smart. John and I will head over to the helicopter and go over the shot list while you get the plane ready. Oh, and by the way let's use 131.85 as our air-to-air frequency."

I agreed to the plan and used a pen to write the radio frequency on the palm of my left hand while we all filed out of the meeting room. As David and John walked across the ramp to the helicopter I hustled Stu over to the plane and told him to do the pre-flight while I learned how to fly a Navajo. Stu began looking the plane over, while I grabbed the book and sat down on a nearby bench to study.

Luckily I've been hopping into strange planes and flying them ever since I started ferry flying. The first thing I did was flip to the emergency section of the POH and jotted down a few of the more important highlights in my notebook, mainly emergency procedures that were unusual or different than the norm. Then I quickly flipped to the fuel system page, checked how many fuel tanks there were and how to switch between them. Finally I hit the "Normal Procedures" section and noted power settings and fuel flow rates for each setting. Lastly, I read the "Start Procedures" section. You'd be amazed how handy it can be knowing how to start the engines. This whole process took about five minutes and after I was done I was only a little nervous instead downright terrified.

I walked over to the plane where Stu was working on the pre-flight and gave him a hand. Of course by "giving Stu a hand" I meant taking over completely and doing it all over myself. I did this because:

A. Stu didn't have much experience flying anything this big, and large twins have a lot of hidden things to check, like fuel quick drains.

2. I didn't trust Stu. Not because I thought he didn't know what he was doing (although he did have only 12 hours of multi-engine time) but because I didn't trust anyone, let alone someone that I just met.

And C. I am a massive control freak. Just ask anyone.

The whole process seemed incredibly rushed. I'd just walked down for breakfast less than two hours before and now I was about to do some of the most challenging and dangerous flying I'd ever done … in a strange plane … with a co-pilot I'd never flown with before … in unfamiliar airspace … with no clear idea what exactly I was supposed to do. Wonderful, let's go flying.

The reason Pixcom had us do a day of air-to-air filming was because when the editors finally put all the film together for the episode they'd need footage of the Navajo flying over all the different terrain in order to tell the story accurately. When they wanted to show us flying over the ocean or the jungle they would need a shot of the plane over the water or trees. It would be way too expensive to have a plane follow us all the way to Argentina so it was decided to get all the shots over southern Florida.

Despite all the red flags, the day of air-to-air filming was some of the most challenging and rewarding flying I'd ever done. Of course for a completely sick and twisted individual such as myself, scary = fun. We took off and headed southwest looking for suitable backdrops for the Navajo. As I followed David and John in the helicopter I got my first good look at the camera they'd be using to film us. The camera was the size of a beach ball and was mounted on a gimbal mount sticking out from the nose of the helicopter. Drifty told me that the camera was a HD Gyro stabilized model worth well over one million dollars. John would be able to control the camera from inside the cockpit of the helicopter and could rotate it 360 degrees vertically and horizontally. I admit that was impressive but all I cared about was the fact that whatever I did in the Navajo was going to be caught on film, good or bad.

First things first, John wanted to get just a standard shot of the Navajo flying right next to the helicopter so I increased power and moved into position just off their right side. John was on the radio directing me and as soon as I got into position he called again.

"Hey Kerry, that's right where I want you but please don't look at the camera."

I looked at the whirling rotor blades spinning just a few feet from my wing tip and wondered just how in the hell he expected me to fly a nice tight formation if I couldn't look at them? Especially seeing that I was having a difficult time matching the slow speed of the helicopter.

"Uhh, how am I supposed to stay in position if I can't look at you?" I asked in exasperation.

"I don't know. Can't you just watch us out of the corner of your eye?"

Try that sometime.

Formation flying is a constant balancing act in which the pilot uses non-stop throttle and control wheel inputs to keep the relative motion of his aircraft to another as close to zero as possible. It's hard work, but fun. What's more fun was what we were doing in the Navajo that day over Florida.

"Next I want you to fly up our left side, then just as you pass us bank away steeply. But not too steeply!"

I gave Drifty a quick "Roger" and advanced the throttles, spurring the Navajo on and quickly overtaking the helicopter. I could see the camera tracking us as we approached. As we pulled abeam the camera ship I turned the yoke left in a steep (but not too steep) left bank. Making sure to not lose or gain altitude as we completed the turn.

"Great! Next I want you to fly directly under us and pull straight up after you get maybe fifty yards in front."

This should be fun!

"Pass as close underneath us as you can."

More fun!

I cranked a steep left bank to finish the turn directly behind the helicopter and went to full throttle to catch up. As we approached from behind I gave them a countdown.

"Coming up underneath in … 3 … 2 … 1. Now! Now! Now!"

After passing maybe twenty feet under the helicopter I counted One Mississippi, two Mississippi, and pulled straight up into a near vertical climb. I held this attitude for five or six seconds watching as our airspeed dropped then gently nosing over and reducing power. I tried to keep the maneuver smooth but Stu and I still floated off our seats due to the negative G forces.

"Great! That was awesome! Let's do that again, only this time don't go straight up."

"You said go straight up."

"I didn't mean straight up, straight up."

"Then don't say straight up. Be precise in your language," David said, chiming in so I didn't have to. "In aviation you say what you mean and mean what you say."

"Okay, sorry. Kerry this time fly directly under us as close as last time and after you pass us pull up about half as steep as you did before. Call it a forty-five degree climb."

"Roger."

And that's how the rest of the day went. John had us fly dozens of different formations and maneuvers close to the helicopter so he could get the shots Pixcom required. I'd come up from behind then peel off in front of them or bank away. Sometimes I'd get way out front and fly directly at them, breaking away at the last second or passing over or under them. I constantly heard the phrase "That was great! Let's do it again but get closer next time. And remember not to look at us!" It was nerve wracking flying. Both fun and terrifying at the same time. It was also damned hard work. The stress of banking and cranking that big twin around the sky plus the hot Florida sun beating down on my head had sweat pouring down my face. At one point when we were out over the Gulf getting ocean shots I commented to Stu that a fishing boat we were flying over was really big. Then I noticed that we were just five hundred feet over the water. The boat wasn't big, we were low! At that point I told Stu that his job was to keep track of our altitude. I told him that if he caught me below five hundred again he was to punch me in the mouth as hard as he could.

Probably the most fun we had that day was when John had us fly to some of the biggest, tallest cumulus clouds we could find and basically play in them for a half hour. That was a blast! I really put that big Navajo through its paces as I climbed and dove in and around the billowing mountains of white. They were maneuvers the plane was never designed for, but if that's what the boss wanted, who was I to say no?

When we stopped for fuel and to take a break David and I sat down and talked about how the day was going. We were both happy with each other's flying and how well we'd worked together. We discussed how to get the remaining shots by flying with our hands fighter-pilot style. We finished off the day by finding a big unpopulated section of woods that would probably pass for the Amazon

Jungle and made multiple passes over it. With John satisfied, David and I flew formation back to Ft. Lauderdale and called it a day.

When we landed and finally shut the Navajo down I was completely drained. The six hours in the cockpit had been one of the toughest and most challenging days I could remember. Heck, flying over the North Atlantic in the winter time was easier than that! As I was cleaning up the cockpit I noticed that the white plastic yoke had a blue discoloration on the left side. When I looked closer I saw that it was the radio frequency I had written on my left hand earlier that morning. I'd been sweating so much and gripping the yoke so hard that the ink on my hand had transferred to the plastic. It had been one hell of a first day as a TV star.

The next day was a busy one. Drifty had a full schedule of interviews scheduled for Stu and I, but we had another problem to deal with. During our air-to-air flights I had discovered that the Navajo's directional gyro compass wasn't working. The DG, as it's called, is the main instrument a pilot uses to determine his heading in flight. It's a precise and absolutely vital instrument when flying in the clouds. It basically tells you what direction you're heading. Without it, a pilot would have to use the liquid filled compass mounted on the windshield. Otherwise known as the "whiskey compass" this device is a crude substitute for the DG and bobs and shakes whenever the plane turns or moves. It's practically worthless in turbulence and any pilot forced to use it during an instrument approach would have his work cut out for him.

As a ferry pilot hired by an aircraft delivery company I didn't usually deal directly with the customers. I left that up to the company. The company in this case was CB Aviation and the owner was Cory Bengtzen who was the boss of all the pilots on the TV show. Pixcom and Cory worked directly with each other and the show was basically built around him and his company. The general concept of the show was that Cory's company gets hired to ferry airplanes around the world by their new owners. Then Cory contacts two of his pilots (Stu and me in this case) to fly the plane to its destination. Along the way the show will check in on Cory and the pilots as they deal with the never ending headaches of flying small aircraft around the world. The great thing with a show about ferry flying was that there would be a never ending series of challenges for the TV crews to film us overcoming.

Such as the DG not working. With John filming me I called Cory on speakerphone, and told him about the bad DG. Cory said he'd contact the Navajo's new owner in Argentina and ask him if he'd authorize it to be fixed. In as dramatic a fashion as I could muster I told Cory that there was no way I'd fly the Navajo to South America unless the DG got fixed. We went back and forth, discussing the issue before Cory told me he'd take care of it. Then we pretended to hang up after finishing the scene. After John told us he was happy with what we'd just filmed Cory and I talked for a few minutes about what we were going to actually do about getting the inoperative DG fixed.

That was one of the first scenes we shot for the show and it was my first lesson in how to be a TV star. It turns out there's a lot to it. The first thing we did each morning was get mic'd up. Having everything you say being recorded takes some getting used to. There are really only three things to remember when wearing a microphone all day. Always keep your batteries charged, don't talk shit about the director behind his back (he can hear you) and don't forget to turn off the mic in the bathroom. (He can hear you then, too, and would rather not.)

Being mic'd up was the easy part. It turns out that being filmed constantly every day has its own challenges. First of all, having someone follow you around with a camera all day takes some getting used to. It's difficult to act natural and have conversions when there's someone with a gigantic camera shoved in your face. It took a while not to be self conscious but after a day or so you learn how to act naturally. Despite what you might have heard, you never forget the camera's there. You just get better at acting. Because that's what it is, acting.

Drifty wouldn't exactly film every second of every day, it just wasn't possible or practical. We had set scenes we would film, such as having us sit down at a chart table and talk about the route we'd be taking that day. John would also get the camera running if it looked like we were going to do or say something interesting. But sometimes he missed. When that happened that's when we went from reality stars to actors. If one of us said or did something that Drifty thought was interesting he'd lift his gigantic camera up onto his shoulder and tell us to re-create our conversation. The first time we said what we said it was natural. The second time we were actors playing ourselves. Ever try to have the exact same conversation with someone you just had seconds before? It's incredibly difficult but Stu and I got better with practice.

Over the next few days we not only spent time getting interviews and shots of the Navajo taxiing around the ramp but setting up cameras inside and outside the plane to record the trip. We had four cameras mounted inside the cockpit and two on the wings and tail. This took a lot of time because Drifty hadn't done it before and I had to help him mount the cameras in such a way that not only would they capture the angles he wanted but not damage the plane in doing so. The camera on the top of the tail proved to be especially difficult because it was so high up that we needed a tall ladder to reach it. We made a trip to Walmart and bought a big aluminum folding ladder that just barely fit inside the plane. That stupid ladder would become a constant source of aggravation throughout the rest of the trip. We also rigged a curtain in between the cockpit and the back cabin so the audience wouldn't be able to see Drifty when the cameras were on.

The broken DG in the plane also got fixed but not without a ton of hassle and controversy. Cory had heard back from the Navajo's new owners and much to our surprise they didn't want the DG fixed! That didn't make any sense at all. We told them that there was a great avionics shop right on the field and they could get it fixed quickly and a lot cheaper than they could get it fixed in Argentina. But no, the owners said just fly it as is. That meant we had a decision to make. Cory could either pay for the repairs himself and eat the cost or I could fly it without the DG. That was a tough one. I told him that I'd be willing to fly it as is but if we ran into any really bad weather it would be dangerous and I'd have my work cut out for me. Using the whiskey compass would be next to useless but I'd brought my Garmin 696 GPS which I planned on mounting on the yoke. If it worked and held the satellites, I could use it for heading control throughout the trip. But that's a big "if " when talking about a handheld GPS. They are notorious for losing the signal at the most inconvenient of times. And even though I was pretty sure I could make it work, I decided that my first time flying an airplane on a major international TV show might not be the best time for me to be my normal cowboy, fly by seat of my pants self (probably). In the end Cory opted to pay for the repairs himself and trust that when we delivered the plane, the new owners would come to their senses and pay him back. I was happy with that decision. I like having all my instruments working when I'm about to fly a few thousand miles over oceans and jungles. I'm funny that way. Okay, "most" of my instruments anyway.

When we were finally ready to leave the three of us began loading the plane up with everything that we'd need to make the trip. Stu and I each had two small bags of clothes and that was it. I'd brought along a survival kit I'd customized for the trip but it was only the size of a football so that wasn't much of a factor. Drifty, on the other hand, was another story entirely. When he pulled up in his rental car and started unloading the stuff he wanted to bring along I was stunned. In addition to his personal bags he had at least ten big plastic Pelican cases filled with all sorts of gear he said was necessary for filming. There were big heavy tripods, extra video cameras, recording equipment, lots of lights and about one hundred pounds of batteries.

Add in the ladder and a big plastic cooler and there was a small mountain of gear on the ramp that I somehow had to fit into the plane. Lucky for us we were flying a Navajo Chieftain which had a huge useful load. If we could get the doors closed the Navajo could lift it. I hoped.

I somehow managed to cram everything into the plane without it bursting like an overcooked hot dog, so we started up and taxied to the end of the runway for departure. In a rare moment of generosity I told Stu that he could do the takeoff. I planned on switching off flying duties with Stu and thought he might as well start right away. Seeing that this was the first time we'd flown the Navajo fully loaded I probably should've done that take off myself. With a look of intense concentration Stu pushed the throttles up and the mighty Navajo roared down the runway. Well, not exactly roared, more like sauntered. The Navajo didn't pick up speed as fast as it normally had. Not surprising because we were a good fifteen hundred pounds heavier than we'd been the first, and only, time we'd flown the plane. As the Navajo slowly accelerated down the runway we quickly approached the point where I must decide whether we should abandon the take-off and jump on the brakes or fully commit to flying. I gave the engine instruments another quick glance and found nothing wrong so I held my tongue and let Stu continue.

We're heavy and it's a hot and humid day. Not surprising she's a pig.

When we reached takeoff speed Stu eased the yoked back and the Navajo struggled into the already hot morning sky. I raise the landing gear just as the stall horn chirps a small but unignorable warning.

"Nose down … nose down," I say calmly but firmly to Stu.

We need to build up more speed, and quickly. There are buildings and trees off the end of the runway rising up to greet us but we're still too slow. When you're heavy and slow you can only do what you can do and pulling up before you've increased speed will have the opposite effect you desire. It's better to make a more leisurely climb out than to risk a stall. Stu brings the nose down slightly and the airspeed climbs agreeably. We continue to climb and clear the obstacles easily as Stu makes a turn to the southeast and heads for the ocean. First stop, the Bahamas.

While not exactly a stop (our actual first stop is the Turks and Caicos), the shallow waters of the Bahamas is one of the most beautiful areas of the world to fly over. The ever shifting sands under turquoise water are a swirling pallet of color that I could stare at for hours. Three hours and twenty minutes to be exact because that's how long it takes to fly from Ft. Lauderdale to the Turks.

But we had other things to do besides gawking at the scenery. The three of us figured out how to fly as a team and film a reality show at the same time. John pointed out to us that in his opinion the main reason that we'd been hired was to be actors, and do whatever is necessary to make a good episode. The fact that we were delivering an actual planes to actual customers didn't matter much to him as long as we got good content. So before we did or said anything interesting we had to give John a head's up so he could turn on the cameras because we couldn't just leave them on the entire time we were flying.

Still, just because the cameras were off didn't mean Stu and I stopped talking. We're pilots on a long leg, of course we're going to talk. The problem came when we accidentally said something interesting and Drifty heard us on the intercom.

Then it was all, "Wait, wait, stop! That's good stuff! Let me get the cameras going then I want you to say what you said again."

Great, now we're actors again. It happened so often that Stu and I sometimes stopped talking for fear that one of us would say something interesting or funny. Eventually we got the hang of it and we'd give Drifty a heads up when we knew our conversation was about to be worthy of filming. We were usually wrong.

There was another challenge I'd have to overcome. Flying with a co-pilot. My flying career up to this point had been very different from a normal pilot's because the vast majority of my flight time was solo. Most commercial pilots fly with someone else and develop what's called good crew or cockpit resource management (CRM). It's the effective use of all available resources for flight crew personnel to assure a safe and efficient operation. It reduces error, avoids stress and increases efficiency. Which is a word salad for "plays nice with others". Unfortunately that's not my strong suit. I'm more of a loner pilot. When I fly by myself I do all the take offs and landings, I talk on the radio and take care of navigation. And if there's a difficult weather call to be made, I make it without having to take anyone else's opinion into consideration. I'm also never late for anything if I'm alone. Flying with someone was going to take some getting used to, but he was a nice guy and so far we'd gotten along well so we probably wouldn't kill each other.

I wasn't worrying about that at the time though. We were flying a sweet plane to paradise on a beautiful day. I could think of nothing that could dampen our spirits. Except the right engine oil temperature gauge. The needle on the instrument was bouncing a little and had occasionally bounced up into the red. That's not good. But the way the needle was bouncing and vibrating so much made me think/hope it was a bad gauge. The oil pressure was still good and the cylinder head temperature was still in the green so I didn't think it was necessary to shut the engine down just yet. If either of those gauges changed for the worse and started backing up the oil temp gauge, that would be a different story.

And I was having such a good day!

Another hour went by and the oil pressure gauge continued its antics without a corresponding rise in oil temperature so I assumed that our problem was most likely the gauge or sending unit and not a problem with the engine. That really took a load off my mind and allowed me to go back to enjoying the flight. Which wasn't difficult because I love flying big twin engine aircraft. There's just something more satisfying about being in control of a bigger plane with two engines. They're heavier, more complex and give me the feeling that I'm in charge of something important. Big twins are faster too. And who doesn't like to go fast?

After a nice three hour flight over the Bahamas, we started our approach to the Providenciales International Airport. I loved stopping at Providenciales. I'd landed there many times flying jump planes down to St. Croix in the US Virgin Islands when I had a small skydiving operation there in the 90's. Each winter I would fly one of my Cessna 182 jump planes down to St. Croix for a season skydiving and scuba diving before heading back up to Wisconsin each spring.

The Turks had a great airport for a quick fuel stop because the airport officials really knew what they were doing and got visiting aircraft turned around quickly. Their reputation for excellent service is what made Providenciales the number one fuel stop for aircraft flying down to the Caribbean. Combine this with the fact that I really love landing big planes and I was all set to have a thoroughly enjoyable approach. With no wind to speak of, bright sunny skies and a runway three times longer than I needed, everything was perfect as it could be. I flew straight in to final approach and moved the landing gear handle down and called out the checklist for Stu in preparation for landing.

"Pre-landing checklist. Gas … on the main tanks."

Plenty for a landing and go-around.

"Undercarriage … down"

I knew I'd moved the gear handle down and did a double take when I glanced at the indicator lights.

Crap! Only two out of three green landing gear lights are illuminated!

"The right side landing gear isn't showing down and locked!"

Although I had started the landing checklist as the landing gear was coming down I'd been watching the lights when the wheels thumped into place as is my habit. When the green landing gear lights flicked on I noticed right away that the right main light was not illuminated.

The reaction a pilot has to an unsafe landing gear indication totally depends on his experience and his natural presence under fire. First time in the box? You might get a little panicky, loose your cool and do something stupid. Been around the block a few times? Then hopefully you know better than to let your emotions get in the way of what you need to do to rectify the situation at hand. If you've got time to panic, you've got time to do something more productive.

The first thing I did was use the push to test feature on the dark light. It's never just a burned out bulb, but you've got to check anyway. Nope, the little green light came on when tested so it was not a burned out bulb.

Again, *Crap.*

"That's not good," Stu said as he watched me mess with the indicator.

"Nope," I replied as I grabbed the white plastic gear handle. It was molded into the shape of a tire for the dumb pilots who can't read the words "Landing Gear" stenciled above it.

"I'm going to recycle it and see if that helps," I said as I pulled the knob up to retract the gear.

"Tower, November 27608 is going to do a three sixty while we sort out a landing gear problem."

"Roger 608, understand you're doing a three sixty. Report when you're ready to land."

As I pushed the throttles forward and pulled the Navajo into a climbing left turn I realized that I hadn't asked for permission to do a three sixty, I'd just told them I was doing it. *Oh well, as far as I know I'm the only one out here. If they'd had a problem with it they would've said something.* Ya gotta love tower controllers in the Caribbean. They're just so laid back. "Whatever, mon! It's all good!"

As the landing gear retracted I thought about what I was going to do if I couldn't get the right main to lock in place. I did have the advantage of having had this problem before, twice before to be precise. The first time was many years prior when I was flying jumpers in a Beech Queen Air back in Wisconsin. I'd dropped the meat bombs and was setting up for landing when I had the same issue. Only two out of three lights. The right main landing gear light wouldn't light up.

Having an unsafe gear indication is a big deal. Especially if it's one of the two main wheels because if one of those collapses on landing the plane will immediately veer off the runway and into the grass. What happens after that is anyone's guess but there's a good chance the plane will cartwheel across the field, creating a spectacular and entertaining fireworks display. Can be tough on the pilot though.

Hoping to avoid the whole cartwheel, crash and burn thing I circled the dropzone and recycled the landing gear once, twice, three times. Each time hoping to be rewarded with three green lights and each time disappointed. I slapped the gear handle up again to give it one more try only this time nothing happened. The landing gear didn't retract. I moved the handle up and down a few times, trying to get something to happen, but no luck. The landing gear was stuck down. Now there was definitely something wrong.

Up until this point I had been relatively confident that the problem had been minor.

Just a faulty indicator or something. No big deal.

But now that the gear wouldn't retract there was definitely something wrong. I was now certain that the right main landing gear would collapse as soon as I touched down. And that little event was going to happen in the next few minutes because I was out of gas and out of time.

When I first noticed the landing gear problem I'd radioed down to my boss Gene (Geno) Broom and told what I was dealing with. He wanted to know if he should call the fire department and after a moment's hesitation I told him no, I had the situation under control. I think there was a little bit of denial going on there. Now that I was setting up for what I was sure to be a crash landing I regretted my decision to not call the fire department. I gave Geno the updated situation and he told me that he had found a fire extinguisher and he'd be in his truck following alongside on the parallel taxiway in case something went wrong.

When something goes wrong you mean.

I set up for landing and endeavored to make it the softest smoothest I'd ever done. I figured even if the right main wasn't actually locked into position maybe if I did a good enough job it wouldn't collapse. Of course there was a strong crosswind that day making things just that much more difficult. As I came in on short final I saw Geno's brown Toyota pickup truck start rolling down the taxiway heading for the soon to be scene of the crash. It was both reassuring and terrifying at the same time. I left a little power in as I leveled off over the runway, shooting for a soft landing rather than my usual short one. I touched down on the left main tire first and held the right side up as long as possible before letting it down as gently as I could. The weight of the plane fully settled onto the landing gear and … nothing happened. The Queen Air rolled peacefully along. Greatly relieved, I let out the breath I'd been holding.

Post non-crash analysis revealed the initial problem to be a small broken wire on the down-and-locked indicator. And why didn't the landing gear retract after I'd moved it up and down three times? Because cycling the landing gear up and down so many times in a row had overheated the motor and blown the circuit breaker. The number of times you can move the gear up and down in a short time span is clearly spelled out in the pilot's operating handbook. A fact I learned shortly after needing it.

All these thoughts were running through my mind as I banked the Navajo around in a left hand turn and moved the gear lever down once again. The landing gear motor whined as it forced the gear down with a hopefully satisfying thump. Aaaaand … crap. Still no green light on the right main landing gear indicator. Out of habit I reached down and pushed on the light to test it.

Hmm, the light didn't come on this time.

Then I twisted the light to once again make sure the dimming iris wasn't closed all the way and voila! The light green light peeked out from behind the two little metal louvers that close when twisted to block the light if the pilot finds it too bright. Why they can be twisted so far as to completely block the light is a mystery to me. Stu must have twisted it closed when we were trouble shooting the light when we first had a problem. (Yes, I'm blaming Stu. Because I know how the dimming feature works and I would never do that. Besides, this is my story and I'll tell it how I want.)

I informed the tower that we'd solved our problem and was granted permission to land. After shutdown we opened the right engine cowling and checked the oil. The level was fine and it didn't look burned or discolored in any way. The engine itself didn't seem or smell overly hot so without any other information to go on I declared our oil temperature problem to be a faulty gauge. (The gauge would continue to act up for the next half of the trip before suddenly settling down and behaving itself.)

We were deep in the "getting to know the plane you're ferrying" stage now. It's the same every time I deliver an aircraft I've never flown before. Each plane has its own quirks and peculiarities that reveal themselves as you go along. Usually in the most inopportune of times.

After determining that the landing gear and oil temperature problems were not actually problems (much to John's disappointment), we climbed back into the sweltering Navajo and took off for Santo Domingo in the Dominican Republic. It was a short leg and before long Stu and I were on the ground with a camera in our face. Not that we hadn't had four cameras pointed at us in the cockpit all day. No, this was different. Now that the day's flying was over John insisted that we each stand in front of the airplane and recount the day's events. He called it the end of day interviews and would become the daily ritual that both Stu and I hated. Why? Because the last thing I wanted to do after a long day of flying is stand around on the ramp and talk about what we'd done all day. And you have to be perfect. No flubbing or stuttering or you'll have to do it again. If it takes five tries to get it right, then that's what it takes.

We finally managed to tell the day's riveting tale to Drifty's satisfaction and were allowed to find a hotel and dinner. Afterwards the three of us walked down the street in search of some nightlife. Well, the young and single Stu was looking for nightlife. John and I being two old married guys would have preferred the library or perhaps a museum but we couldn't let our wingman go out there alone could we?

The first thing we noticed were all the old white guys with young, hot women on their arms. It seemed that the Dominican Republic was the place to go for lonely retired men. The entire area had more of a third world local flavor rather than a glitzy tourist trap. The streets were dimly lit and the buildings had an overall shabby feel. We found a small bar, ordered some drinks and started talking about the next day's flying and shooting schedule. We hadn't been there long when four young ladies came up to our corner of the bar and started talking to us. The conversation started off as just friendly banter but it was obvious who they were and what they were after. Everything changed when they tried to get us to buy them drinks and we refused. Things sort of went south from there. It turns out that hookers aren't accustomed to being told no and their sales pitch became so persistent and aggressive I suggested they'd be perfect saleswomen for a time share company. Things progressively went downhill from there so we finished our drinks and tried to extricate ourselves from the situation. As we were leaving things got worse as one of the girls went to the back of the bar where a table of young locals sat glaring at us. I couldn't hear what she was telling them but it was obvious from her yelling and pointing at us that she wasn't a fan.

Time to go!

When we hit the street we saw the girl heading back with four young Dominican men in her wake, looking serious and a little scary. Stu, Drifty and I took off in the opposite direction trying not to draw attention to ourselves but there weren't enough people on the street to get lost in. When we saw her point in our direction we picked up the pace considerably. Just running pell mell down the street didn't seem like a good idea so we ducked down a side street in an attempt to lose our pursuers. Unfortunately the street was a short one and ended right at the beach! We'd inadvertently gone to the absolutely worst place imaginable. It was dark. There was nowhere to hide. And it was deserted, i.e., no witnesses.

Wonderful.

With no choice, we took off down the beach in what we hoped was the direction of our hotel. After a while we looked back and saw that nobody was chasing us. We must have looked quite comical. Three grown men running down the beach at night with no one chasing them.

The next morning we were halfway to Aruba and feeling fine. All thoughts of pimps chasing us through the night had been replaced with another day of beautiful flying weather in the Caribbean. The leg from the

Dominican Republic to Aruba was a long four hundred miles of open ocean and under normal circumstances, well within the range of the Navajo. It was a beautiful day and I wasn't particularly worried about the flight but neither Stu or John had ever made such a long open water leg. I wondered if they were scared but I couldn't ask. It's just not done. A man puts on his mask of bravery and marches off the cliff with his brothers and that's that. You wouldn't want the guys to think less of you by questioning the wisdom of whatever stupid thing you're about to do would you?

I was mildly concerned that we were flying over four hundred miles of open ocean without so much as a single life jacket let alone a raft. While we were in Florida getting ready for the trip I'd searched the internet for a cheap used raft we could talk Pixcom into buying for us but had come up dry. Brand new rafts were over two thousand dollars and Pixcom said that was too expensive. Besides, the Navajo has two engines. What are the odds that both of them fail while we're out over the ocean? Why didn't we at least get life jackets? Good question. I guess a lot of it was due to just good old fashioned blind faith and optimism. I still wasn't happy.

If you look at a map of the Caribbean you might ask yourself, "If these guys are heading to Rosario, Argentina, what in the world are they doing in Aruba?" Good question. Why? Because Pixcom told us to, that's why. One thing I was learning on this trip was that being a ferry pilot and filming a TV show about ferry pilots were two completely different things. Where a ferry pilot is supposed to be fast and efficient (cheap), the TV show pilot's job is to be entertaining and provide the editors with massive amounts of footage they can sift through in order to put together a one hour episode. That means you have to film ten times more footage than anyone thinks will ever be needed. Which also means that everything takes two to three times longer than it usually does. Do you need to walk across the ramp to the MET office? Hang on, gotta let Drifty get fifty yards ahead of you so he can film it. Taking a taxi to the airport in the morning? First you have to explain to the cab driver that he has to drop John off at the front door, then do a loop around the parking lot before letting the pilots off so they can be filmed getting out of the taxi. (Bonus points if the driver doesn't speak English.) And once you're done filming a scene you need to get everyone within a five mile radius to sign a waiver. So yeah, progress was sometimes measured with a calendar.

Which brings us back to question, why were we in Aruba? Because Pixcom had a special field trip planned for us. We were going scuba diving! That sounded good to Stu and me. We were being paid by the day, and if they wanted to pay us to go scuba diving in Aruba who were we to argue?

Of course everything we do has to make some kind of sense or tie in with ferry flying somehow. So Stu and I would be scuba diving on a sunken airplane off the coast of Aruba to highlight what happened when you had to ditch. But we couldn't just go scuba diving in the middle of a ferry flight. What kind of sense would that make to the audience? We had to come up with some kind of story or excuse that people would believe. Stu came up with the idea of saying that the airport at our next stop in Trinidad and Tobago would be closed for some kind of holiday. That would be the reason we had a day off to go scuba diving. To help sell the story we enlisted the help of a beautiful young woman that worked at the airport. John had her tell me on camera about the fictitious airport closing. I wasn't sure anyone would buy that story but it was all we had.

The scuba diving trip was both a lot of fun, and a near catastrophe. The dive boat took us out to the plane and the three of us and a divemaster dropped down sixty feet to the big commuter plane that had been sunk as a tourist attraction. It was pretty cool swimming around and inside the plane, but we were there to work. Have you ever had a director try to give you direction while underwater? Try it sometime, it's great fun. There was a lot of pointing and confusion and in the end Stu and I just swam around doing what we thought would look interesting while Drifty filmed us with a GoPro in a waterproof case. When we all started getting low on air the divemaster motioned for us to follow him back to the boat. We'd only gone a short distance before I noticed that Drifty wasn't with us. I motioned to the divemaster that I'd go get him and headed back to the plane.

It took a few minutes to find the wayward director but I finally saw him still filming the tail of the plane. When I reached him I had him tell me how much air he had left. John checked his gauge and signaled that he only had three hundred pounds of air left! That wasn't nearly enough. We still had to get back to the boat and do the safety stop to avoid getting the bends. I checked my air pressure gauge and saw that I had eight hundred pounds left, more than enough to share with John when he eventually ran out. I led John on a slow ascent as we made our way back to the boat so we'd be able to skip the safety stop and save time. Halfway to the boat John tugged on my arm and indicated that he'd run out of air. I gave him my spare regulator and we shared the air in my tank all the way back to the boat.

That night the three of us were having dinner and re-telling stories of our scuba diving adventure and laughing until we cried. Then John made an observation.

"Kerry, it would be great if you could somehow show as much energy and humor in the end of the day interviews as you do when we go out to dinner each night."

I understood what he was talking about because I had been struggling to be interesting and funny when John filmed me at the end of each day.

"I don't know John, it's hard to be witty and full of energy after flying all day."

"You're witty and full of energy now. Hell, you're hilarious right now!"

"Of course I am. I've had a couple of beers. I'm always hilarious after having a few beers!"

John was quiet for a moment, obviously thinking about the problem.

"Maybe we should shoot your interview after you've had a few beers!"

"Sure, that would work. But you like to shoot the interviews right after we land, standing next to the airplane. It would take too long to go into town, have a couple of drinks at the bar and then get a ride back to the airport."

"Why don't we bring beer along with us? You could drink one or two while I film Stu, then I could do your interview!"

Stu and I looked at each other. Drink beer on the ramp? Unheard of! Well, maybe not unheard of, but surely frowned upon. The more we thought about it the more sense it made. Drinking beer on the ramp might get us some strange looks but it definitely wasn't illegal.

"What the hell, let's give it a try! I'll do anything for the team! And seeing that it's for the good of the show, that means I'll be getting paid to drink beer!" This gig had really turned into my dream job!

Back in the air the next day, John broached another delicate subject. It seemed that he and the producers at Pixcom were a little worried that the flights might be too boring to make good TV. The producers at Pixcom had a lot of experience with reality shows and the usual problem was that not enough real drama happened for them to film. That's why when you watch those shows they tend to make mountains out of mole hills. They take any little thing that happens and make a big deal out of it. They have to, otherwise they wouldn't have a show.

Unfortunately John's big idea to make the show more interesting was to fake some drama. He told me that he wanted us to pretend that we were running low on fuel while we were flying over the Amazon Jungle. I couldn't believe my ears. Didn't they know how bad that would make me look? "Hey everybody in the world, here's Kerry McCauley, world famous ferry pilot about to run out of gas over the Amazon because he's a moron!"

I told John in no uncertain terms that there was **no way** I would do that. I told him that it would make me look stupid and damage my reputation as a ferry pilot. But John was persistent. He called producers and had them pressure me into accepting John's idea. They said that I was under contract and had to basically do whatever they said. I probably could have fought it more but I was afraid that if I wasn't a team player they might replace me on the next flight. And I didn't want to be replaced. I was having too much fun! Plus, I wanted to make a good show and what if nothing else happened on the trip? What if it really was boring? I wasn't super worried about that because something always happens on ferry flights, but still.

Miracle of miracles, the three of us are on airport property just after sunrise instead of our usual late morning arrival. We'd agreed the night before to get up before dawn and get an early start and had somehow managed to pull it off.

Team Navajo burned through the Aruba to Trinidad and Tobago leg with ease. It started with an unusually early takeoff into the kind of sunrise one can only get over the Caribbean. I loved the sunrise and the fantastic colors that were painted across the horizon, but what I really loved that morning was the early start to the day. By this point of the trip I'd learned to tolerate the slow pace and general lack of progress but it still grated on me.

Ferry flying is different from any other kind of flying. Besides the obvious challenges of ocean crossings, there are constant delays that get in the way of the go, go, go, mentality you normally have. A good ferry pilot quickly learns patience in the game or he will become one miserable son of a bitch. Pete Demos, the owner of Orient Air, who taught me everything I know about ferry flying, was a perfect example of someone who struggled with patience. Everything bothered Pete. He would literally lose his mind over small matters that were out of his control and I could see how it sucked all the joy out ferry flying for him. I actually think watching him get angry over little things helped me develop my own sense of patience. I loved ferry flying and decided that the problems that I encountered were just challenges to overcome instead of things that made me angry.

But if I thought a normal ferry flight took a lot of patience I soon found out that filming a TV series about ferry flying took ten times more. This was because every … single … thing had to be captured on camera! It was maddening. Even the simple act of climbing into the airplane and going flying took forever. First Stu and I would have to wait for Drifty to run ahead of us so he could film us walking to the plane. Then we had to get a short segment of us talking about what we were about to do. Then John had to get all the GoPro cameras mounted on the wings, belly and tail ready. Once we were inside he would then have to change the batteries and memory cards for the cameras mounted in the cockpit. All this took forever while Stu and I cooked inside a plane that had been baking in the hot equatorial sun. The black polyester CB Aviation shirts we were forced to wear didn't help much either. We were usually drenched in sweat by the time we were allowed to start the plane.

So the early morning takeoff from Aruba was a rare treat. We'd finally put up some decent miles that day.

The fuel stop in Trinidad and Tobago went about as quickly as could be expected. The soon-to-be famous TV stars (us) were paraded around the airport like prize pigs. We got to meet the governor, the guys working in the tower, the janitor and even Miss Trinidad and Tobago. Pictures were taken and autographs signed while Stu and I just wanted to get in the plane and go. I suspected we'd have to get used to that if the show became a hit.

Once we were back in the air we pointed the Navajo at South America. I was excited. I'd never been to South America before and was really looking forward to it. Our first stop was going to be Georgetown, Guyana and blocking the way were my old friends, the daily thunderstorms of the inter-tropical convergence zone.

The ITCZ is a belt of converging trade winds and rising air that encircles the Earth near the Equator. The rising air produces tall cumulus clouds, frequent thunderstorms, and heavy rainfall. I'd battled these storms in Africa and Asia before and wasn't looking forward to trying to get through the ones I saw building over Guyana. As we crossed the coast Stu and I tightened our seat belts and started looking for a crack in the wall of storms.

As we got closer I looked over at Stu and he appeared as calm as I was. We were doing what all flight crews do when confronted with a difficult or dangerous situation. We were playing the old never let them see you sweat game. It's the calm and cool outward appearance a man has to show his partner that says "I'm not scared because I've been through far worse than this before." It's usually done by staring straight ahead and not talking very much. It is allowed to casually check the map but it must be done with the same casual indifference as if he were just out for a pleasure flight on a sunny Sunday afternoon. You are allowed to ask "What do you think?" but it has to be done in such a way as if to say "I'm not concerned, mind you. I'm just making conversation."

I didn't know for sure, but I suspected that Stu hadn't been faced with weather such as this before. Over the previous few days we'd gotten to know each other and what kind of flying experience we had. If he'd battled major thunderstorms before I'm sure he would have mentioned it.

Stu had a little over eight hundred hours in his log book and most of that was in helicopters. He'd told me all about his time spent flying the camera ship for the Baja 1000 off road race. I was impressed when he told me how he filmed the competitors by flying his helicopter down in the weeds behind and next to the motorcycles as they raced down the Baja peninsula. It was impressive flying and required excellent stick and rudder skills but was totally different than punching through hard IFR conditions and challenging weather. If he'd not done any flying like that before he was about to get a crash course.

The closer we got to the wall of cumulus clouds the higher and darker they became. We both pointed out possible routes and cracks we could sneak through as we picked our way through. I'd love to tell you about our epic battle we had with the storms. How heavy rain, hail and lightning battered the Navajo for hours on end. But I can't because it didn't happen that way. We flew through some moderate rain, got bounced around rather violently and had to weave our way around a lot of big storm cells but the sky between the cells was mostly clear. There was one big cell off the end of Georgetown's runway that forced us to do some fancy flying but after a sharp turn to final and a steep descent we made it into Georgetown.

The sun was already high in the eastern sky by the time we got back in the air the next day. We'd gotten a late start out of Georgetown because the woman at Pixcom who was coordinating our hotels tried to save a few bucks by booking us a hotel thirty miles from the airport. It might have looked good on paper but it forced us to take a two hour taxi ride in the morning down the only road that ran through the center of the crowded city. It was an interesting ride but it put us way behind schedule.

We eventually got back into the air and on our way to Macapa, Brazil. The seven hundred mile leg would take us over one of the most dangerous and inhospitable jungles on Earth, the Amazon.

One of the things I had to constantly remind everyone was that even though we were filming a TV show with a dozen cameras mounted all over the plane that didn't make the flying any less dangerous. It was easy to get caught up in the TV aspect of our mission and forget what it was that we were actually doing.

Even in this day of GPS navigation, electronic maps and satellite phones, flying small general aviation aircraft around the world is still incredibly dangerous and something that shouldn't be taken lightly. That fact is something that most modern pilots have a hard time grasping. Most pilots, even ferry pilots, don't give much thought to what to do if they survive a crash in a remote part of the world. They think that just because the modern world we live in is bubble wrap safe, nothing bad can happen to them, and for the most part, they are correct. For example, if you crash anywhere in the United States or Europe you can count on being rescued relatively quickly. But there are still many parts of the world where the Starbucks coffee shops are few and far between. Areas where the map should still read "Here there be dragons!" Areas that rescue might be days, not hours, away. If it comes at all.

This is usually because the area you're flying over is vast and there is no radar coverage. If you don't get a Mayday call out before you go down, no one will know you're in trouble until you don't show up at your destination. They'll never know what happened or where you are. You're just "overdue". Unfortunately most of these areas are surrounded by countries with little or no professional rescue services. If you crash in the ocean off the coast of Gabon in Africa, I wouldn't count on someone coming out to look for you anytime soon.

Or the problem can be a combination of the two. If you go down in international waters and the nearest countries are all relatively poor they're not going to be fighting each other to see who gets to spend time and money to go out looking for you. That's why a ferry pilot needs to think about all aspects of survival when he's on a trip.

The first, and arguably the most, important thing to think about is communications. No one will come looking for you if you don't tell them that you're in trouble. To help with that I always fly as high as possible. The higher you are the more range your radio has and the more likely someone will pick up your mayday transmission.

Flying at a higher altitude also has the added benefit of giving you more time to prepare for the crash or ditching. Such things as, securing loose items in the cockpit, making sure your survival kit is handy, popping the door open so it doesn't jam shut in the crash and putting your survival suit on if you're over water. Flying high also gives you more options on where to put down. If your engine dies at fifteen thousand feet you can literally glide for twenty miles, but if you're scudding along at five hundred feet when your engine goes silent you're going to land right there!

Then you have to actually survive the crash. It doesn't matter if the best rescue team in the world knows exactly where you are if all they're going to find is a body.

There are three kinds of terrain a pilot might be faced with when attempting a crash landing (and let's face it, if you're landing off the airport, it's a crash landing), your options are going to be trees, rough terrain or water. Yes, you might get lucky and lose your engine over open farmland but I'm not going to waste time talking about how to land in an alfalfa field. I also won't bother trying to rank which terrain is the worst because there are too many variables. One hundred foot tall triple canopy jungle is vastly different than ten foot pine trees. Just like a calm suburban lake is a lot different than the North Atlantic.

So let's go over what I think about how to crash, survive and get rescued from each option.

Rough terrain: The number one thing I think about when I'm crashing into a surface that's not smooth, level ground is to take Bob Hoover's advice and "Fly the thing as far into the crash as possible." Which is to say, **Don't stall!** You'll want to hit whatever it is you're crashing into as slow as possible, so full flaps, minimum controllable airspeed and into the wind if you can, but for God's sake maintain flying speed and control as long as possible. It might sound like no brainer advice but the stall, spin, crash scenario kills more pilots than any other. This advice applies to all crash landings. The next big decision you might have to make is if you're in a retractable gear aircraft should you leave the gear up or down? It's an endless debate but a lot of pilots think that leaving the landing gear up prevents the plane from nosing over. I think the opposite. Unless I'm going down in water or swamp I think putting the gear down is best. Besides the possibility of having some breaking and steering control, shearing the gear off will dissipate some energy and that's the goal. One last thing to think about is if you have to hit some sort of object it's best to hit it with one wing rather than head on. Hitting an obstacle with a wing will immediately absorb some of the energy and you will pivot around spinning to a stop. Much better than head on. If you're alone in the plane I'd hit the object with the left wing root so you spin left and put the right side into the crash first. Of course that's an advanced maneuver and you probably shouldn't try it at home.

Trees: If you're going down in the trees you have two options. If able, you can try to fly in between two trees in an attempt to rip the wings off. If successful, that will dissipate the most energy and also reduce the risk of fire because that's usually where the fuel is. (Remember, fire bad.) The other tree landing option is to land in the treetops as softly as possible. Remember, if you do that well you might be stuck in the treetops with no way to get down. I again want to emphasize the don't-stall point because I've heard some pilots say that they'd try to stall the plane into the trees tail first. The theory is as you drop backwards into the trees you'll have the tail and seat backs to protect them as you slide vertically into the forest. Yeah, good luck with that. What would most likely happen would be that after you pull up into a vertical climb, the front of the aircraft will drop and you'll go nose first, straight into the ground. (Boom, crash, dead.)

Ocean: The first and most important issue in surviving an ocean ditching is to avoid getting knocked out by impact with the water. All your careful planning and preparation will be for nothing if you go down with the ship because you're unconscious. Step one in avoiding getting knocked out is simple, make sure you put your shoulder harness on before you hit the water. It might sound like an obvious one but a lot of pilots will take the shoulder harness off during a long cross country flight and it would be easy to forget that little detail. That oversight would mean your head will smash into the instrument panel one millisecond after the plane hits the water. You'll also have to get your survival suit on and zipped up before impact. Getting that accomplished in the cockpit of a small airplane can be challenging. Some pilots fly with their survival suit in its storage bag, which in my opinion is terribly optimistic because they take forever to squeeze into. That's why I fly with the suit on but only up to my waist. That way all I have to do is put my arms in and zip it up.

Remember, before you zip the suit up all the way you'll need to fill it with any survival equipment you really, really, really want to make sure gets into the raft with you. This is one of the big differences between going down in the ocean and crashing on land. If you crash on land and the plane doesn't burn you can take your time and dig through the wreckage for whatever might come in handy in helping you survive until rescued. In a ditching situation whatever you don't grab joins the plane at the bottom of the ocean. Some of the things I'll zip up in my suit are: personal locator beacon (PLB), signal laser, handheld radio, GPS, and as much water as I can fit. If you still have room you can add a few foil space blankets and a Snickers bar or two. If you still have room maybe a flask, you know, for crew morale.

Of course you'd better be done needing to do anything with your fingers like switch frequencies because once your arms and hands are in the suit it's like wearing two oven mitts. Even putting your seat belt back on can be a challenge.

Once you're all ready to hit the water then you need to decide "how" to hit the water. Ditching a small plane in the ocean is a tricky thing. Do it well and you might be able to just step out onto the wing, inflate the raft and load it up with all the crap you think you might need. Do a bad job and you could crush the front of the aircraft and the soft, squishy parts that sit there – you. There are two big goals when ditching a plane. Land parallel to the swells and hit the water as soft as possible, so don't stall.

Good job! You're in the water! Now get out! Hope you remembered to pop the door before you hit so it doesn't jam shut. And for god's sake don't forget to grab the raft because if you don't have a raft you might as well not bother.

If you managed to survive the crash or ditching you're now on to the next step, surviving long enough to be rescued. That also might be harder than it sounds. Most pilots die because of injuries received in the crash. But if you're lucky enough to get through the crash relatively unharmed there are three things you need to survive. Food, water and shelter. Usually the most important thing is shelter. It takes days to die from dehydration and weeks to starve to death, but you can freeze to death or succumb to hypothermia in just hours. Unfortunately a ferry pilot can't usually bring along a tent or sleeping bag. The most you can bring is a space blanket or a small rain poncho.

Food is usually not much of a problem because every ferry pilot I know has a big bag of snacks in the cockpit with them. (Or is that only me?) Don't worry about finding or catching food. You won't, so don't waste energy trying. I haven't heard of plane crash survivors starving to death since that soccer team crashed in the Andes back in the 70's. But if you're worried about it try and find a fat co-pilot to fly with.

Water? Now that can be a problem. Mostly because a lot of pilots fly a little dehydrated. Why? So they don't have to pee into a Gatorade bottle in flight, that's why. But that means they start out with a handicap in a survival situation. And if you don't have an adequate supply of water in the plane it's unlikely you'll find a source of fresh, drinkable water at the crash site.

Now if you think all these factors make survival difficult after a "normal" crash, it's ten times harder if you have to ditch in a cold ocean environment like the North Atlantic. A North Atlantic ditching situation makes everything more difficult. To start with, just the act of ditching is made harder if you happen to be forced down in wintertime The short winter days increase the odds of having to attempt a night ditching, which is pretty much suicide. Plus, the North Atlantic is almost never calm. Twenty to thirty foot ocean swells are common so good luck getting the plane down in one piece, let alone getting out and getting into the raft. Imagine trying to get out of an upside down plane that's being tossed around by thirty foot waves and is quickly filling with water, at night! Good fun.

So what does all this cheery information have to do with us? Because even though we're filming a TV show, it was still a very real ferry flight with some very real dangers. Like flying over the Amazon. The dangerous part of going down in the Amazon is mainly just surviving the crash itself because trees that make up the triple canopy jungle are up to three hundred feet tall. That means when your aircraft hits tree tops and stops flying it still has three hundred feet to fall before hitting the jungle floor. (Ouch!) The only other option when flying over miles and miles of impenetrable jungle is to hope for a stream or river to crash into.

I wasn't worried about the dangers of surviving a crash landing in the Amazon though. What was bothering me was this was the leg I was supposed to run low on fuel. Being forced to pretend to be a dumb ass pilot on a TV series that would be seen by millions of people was still bugging me. But the show must go on!

"If this head wind gets any worse, we could be in real trouble!" I was supposedly talking to Stu but in reality I was saying my lines for the camera. Stu and I put on a good show, consulting the map, going over our options, and generally sounding concerned. We even put one of the cockpit cameras up to the airspeed indicators to show the audience just how slow we were going. Never mind that it has nothing to do with our ground speed.

"Macapa approach, Navajo November 27608 requesting priority landing. Low fuel emergency." This radio call was also pure theater. Our next bit of showmanship was to run one of the aux tanks dry and let the engine sputter a little before switching to a tank with plenty of fuel in it. I have to admit that Stu and I did a great job of playing our role of pilots in distress. Once I was resigned to my role in this little play I put my all into making it believable.

Coming in on final I reached over and shut off the Navajo's air conditioner. This was the first plane I'd flown with such an unheard of luxury and I don't know how we would've survived without it. Unfortunately the pre-landing checklist called for it to be shut down for all takeoffs and landings. It ran off engine power and it wouldn't do to have the air conditioner robbing you of some power when you really needed it. As soon as we landed I popped the pilot's window open and was greeted by a blast of tropical heat. Macapa lies almost directly on the equator and it's hot down there. Stiflingly hot, face melting hot, Amazon hot. I turned the air conditioner back on while we taxied to the ramp.

We taxied to the ramp, shut down and I started drinking beer. Remember, I was under the director's orders. I'd had two beers after landing in Georgetown the day before and we all agreed that it had been a resounding success. I was witty and full of energy when it was my turn to be interviewed just like John had hoped. I did make a slip or two so Drifty suggested I cut my prescribed intake from two beers to one and a half. We were definitely taking a scientific approach to the humor enhancement project.

That night while we were having dinner on the banks of the Amazon River I got that same old feeling I used to get when I first started ferry flying. That feeling that I was just about the luckiest man in the world. I still couldn't believe they paid me to do this.

The next morning we were out on the ramp bright and early. We had to be wheels up no later than 8:00 am because the airport was closed from 8:00 until noon. When I went to file the flight plan I met a Brazilian ferry pilot named Jonas. When I told him where we were going and what fuel stops we'd be making he suggested I follow him to a small uncontrolled airport instead. He told me that as long as we had cash we could fuel up and leave very quickly. That was music to my ears. I was already sick of dealing with large airports and their forest killing mountains of paperwork. An added bonus would be that because we weren't crossing any borders we'd be able to fly using visual flight rules (VFR). I really liked the sound of that! Flying VFR would allow us a lot more flexibility in where and how we flew the Navajo. A very helpful thing when you're filming a TV show and might want to deviate from your course from time to time. I would also allow me to turn off the radio and just enjoy the flight without some damn controller constantly calling me and ruining my Zen.

Now that I knew we were free to fly and film where and what we wanted to, I looked at the map for inspiration … And found it.

The cameras had new batteries and the morning interviews were done. Landing fees paid, weather checked and flight plans filed. Nothing left to do on an already hot and steamy Amazon morning but go flying!

The runway at Macapa Brazil points almost directly at the Amazon River. As I brought the landing gear up I quickly told the tower that I was departing the area to the south and wished them a good morning. The man in the tower told me to have a good flight and I was free. With the cameras still rolling I stopped my climb and pointed the nose of the Navajo down at the misty waters of the Amazon.

When I'd looked at the map earlier I'd noticed that our route of flight took us almost directly along one of the many branches and tributaries of the Amazon River. What better time and place to do a little low level than first thing in the morning over the largest river in the world? And what better excuse to goof off than it would make for some amazing video for our TV show?

Oh … my … God! It was perfect! We started off over a wide and muddy part of the river that was covered with thick patchy fog and mist that gave everything a strange and mysterious feel. The visibility varied from one to three miles. Enough to see where I was going but it was still challenging.

As I weaved between the lower and thicker patches of fog I spotted a large fishing boat plying its way across the calm water. With a grin I altered course and pointed my nose gun at the bridge of the enemy ship. OK, I didn't have a nose gun, but I did have a camera mounted on the center of the instrument panel. I hoped the camera would get good strafing video like the gun camera footage from WWII. As I bore down on the unsuspecting target I couldn't help but yell TAKA! TAKA! TAKA! On the intercom. (Yes, I think we've already established that I'm very immature.) At the last second I pulled up, banked away sharply and fled down river at full power. There might have been some giggling in the Navajo and some spilled coffee on the boat when they saw the big twin engined plane suddenly appear out of the mist, flash over them and disappear just as quickly.

Shortly after leaving the fishing boat behind the mist disappeared, allowing bright sunshine to illuminate a bright green wall of jungle pushed up to the river's edge. It was an unbelievable sight. The morning air was clear and calm and the surface of the river was smooth as glass. Up ahead a narrow tributary branching off the main channel appeared. On a whim I put the Navajo into a hard right bank to see what lay inside. The new section of river was perhaps two hundred feet wide and the tall unbroken jungle grew right to the river's edge. With only a few tendrils of smokey mist curling up from the river to block my view I dropped us down to fifty feet, chasing our shadow along the winding river course.

My attention took on a laser beam focus as I looked ahead for random killer power lines that might block our path or a bend in the river that might exceed the Navajo's ability to make the turn. While I endeavored to not to tie the low altitude flight record John and Stu were having a blast, taking pictures and chattering like school children.

"Look at that! ... Check this out! Wow! ... Was that an alligator? So cool!"

A sharp bend in the river approached and I made sure to keep the wingtip out of the water as I lay Navajo on its side in a tight bank. Before I even had fully leveled the wings Stu cried out.

"Check that out!" Pointing upriver.

There, just ahead was a small wooden hut perched on the riverbank. It had a grass roof and a long dock jutting out into the river. As we got closer we could see the small figure of a boy standing on the end of the dock and someone else in a long dugout canoe in the water alongside.

I yelled for both John and Stu to quickly get a picture as we bore down on the idyllic scene. As we flashed by at one hundred fifty knots the young boy ran to the end of the dock waving his arms wildly in greeting. I risked a quick wave back before getting back to business of not killing us.

"Tell me you got that! I yelled.

Both John and Stu assured me that they had indeed managed to capture that one perfect moment on film. We spent another thirty hair raising minutes skimming the smooth water in the emerald green death star trench before pulling up hard into the clear morning sky.

The rest of the day was easy and fun. The impenetrable jungle started to show more and more signs of civilization. Small farms and clear cut fields dotted the landscape and even the occasional road slashed through the thick green carpet. We called our new friend and guide Jonas on the radio and were able to locate the little "V" tail Bonanza he was ferrying and do a little formation flying as we followed him to our next fuel stop.

That evening we landed at Foz do Iguacu, Brazil and after my beer and a half interview, we drove an hour outside of town to a beautiful hotel overlooking a magnificent series of waterfalls. After shooting a scene in front of the waterfalls, John went to check the hotel prices while Stu and I got the bags. We needn't have bothered. John came back with the bad news that the hotel was much too nice for the likes of us. Pixcom thought we'd be just fine someplace cheaper. It was a salty crew that rode the taxi back into town.

We finished the trip the next day at Rosario, Argentina. The new owners had originally wanted the Navajo delivered to a private grass strip outside of town. That sounded like they wanted to avoid paying import taxes so I declined their offer. Which was a polite way of saying "No freaking way!" I wasn't interested in risking jail just to save them a little money.

That afternoon we went to a small airport to shoot the final interviews for the show. John found an old hanger to use and we filmed an endless recap of our trip that ran late into the evening.

At one point I was wandering around the dark and deserted airport, waiting for Drifty to finish up with Stu when I looked up at the night sky. The stars looked different and I was momentarily confused until I realized that I was in the southern hemisphere. I'd never been that far south before and was amazed at how different and alien the night sky was. Then I found the Southern Cross blazing above me. As I stood and stared at the constellation for a long time it really brought home the fact that I was truly on a grand adventure far from home. Then the line from a Stephen Stills song started playing in my head. "When you see the Southern Cross for the first time, you understand now why you came this way."

BOSS CORY

"OK, Go!" John yelled with a wave, his head down and pressed against the camera viewfinder.

Stu and I started walking awkwardly across the ramp to an equally awkward aircraft broker who was about to be on camera for the first time. The man was standing next to a 1986 Beechcraft A36 Bonanza that was our next mission for CB Aviation and Pixcom.

The Navajo trip had been a success and the powers at Pixcom had decided to keep going forward with the show. They were also apparently happy with me and Stu because we hadn't been given the boot yet. They didn't have a name for the show yet, which made things difficult but the working title was "Air Devils" I wasn't crazy about that name but it was all we had until someone with imagination came up with something better.

Despite not having a name, the show seemed to be gaining momentum. Pixcom hired two new pilots and another director which gave them three teams filming around the world. Stu and I had been tasked with the mission of ferrying the A-36 down to Porto Alegre, Brazil. We were also lucky enough to have John Driftmier as our director again. All three of us were happy with the assignment because we'd worked well together on the Navajo trip and enjoyed each other's company. At least I was happy. If John and Stu were unhappy about flying with me again they hid it well. We were also happy to be flying through the Caribbean again.

Oh no! Please don't make us fly a cool airplane to a bunch of beautiful tropical islands again! I don't know if my liver can take any more rum and fruit punch!

Filming a reality show was still a lot of hard work, but Stu and I were a lot better now than we'd been going into the last trip.

We made it through the pre-trip filming quickly and the air-to-air filming day with David Gibbs was again both extremely challenging and fun at the same time. Now that we'd all done this before things were clicking better.

Once we were almost ready to leave the US and head south, I started looking at the weather forecast for our first few legs through the Bahamas and down through the Caribbean. I didn't know why I was bothering. The weather is always the same. Sunny skies, light winds with afternoon showers and the occasional hurricane. Not much to worry about. I mean, what are the odds we run into a hurricane? Pretty good it turns out.

I couldn't believe my eyes. There, just east of the Virgin Islands was the unmistakable shape of a hurricane on the satellite image. Seriously? I looked at the track the hurricane center was projecting and of course it was about as bad as it could possibly be. The hurricane was supposed to travel west until it hit the islands, then hang a right and follow the islands north all the way to Florida. Exactly the opposite course we'd be taking.

But it wasn't supposed to hit the islands for two or three days so if we got a move on we might be able to beat it … might. Of course we couldn't just hop in the plane and go. That would be too easy. No, we had a TV show to film and if there's a race with a hurricane we've got to spend an hour filming Stu and I talking about it first. It was just another maddening delay that we'd come to expect. On to the next delay!

We wrapped up that scene as fast as we could, filed the flight plan, topped off the fuel tanks and told John to grab the rest of his gear so we could load the plane and go. Stu and I dumped our small suitcases and backpacks next to the plane and started doing the pre-flight. Then John pulled up with a rental car full of gear. And I mean full!

"Jesus, Drifty! You think you've got enough stuff?" I asked as he unloaded box after box to the growing pile next to the plane.

"I don't have any more that I did last time!"

"Maybe. But last time we had a much bigger plane! You might not have noticed, but the Bonanza is a lot smaller. We'll never get all that gear into the plane!"

Stu and I tried to explain the weight and balance restrictions of the Bonanza but Drifty was adamant, he had to bring everything he'd packed and that was that. I could see there was no sense arguing with him so I decided to give him a demonstration. I started grabbing boxes filled with camera gear and loading them into the plane. The cabin filled quickly and there were still a few odds and ends on the ramp when the tail of the Bonanza started to slowly sink as the nose wheel came off the ground. I anticipated this and caught the tail before it hit the ramp. I hoped he didn't notice that I'd placed most of the heavier items in the back of the plane. I had to make sure the tail dropped or he might not believe that we would be way overweight if we loaded everything he'd brought.

"See? There's too much weight in the tail. Just because we can get all your crap in the plane doesn't mean it will fly."

John finally accepted the fact that he couldn't take everything. He then began the long process of removing everything he didn't absolutely need to film the trip. This is the process I go through every time I ferry an aircraft. Especially if it has extra ferry tanks installed inside the cockpit. I go to such extreme measures to shed weight that I count the pairs of socks and underwear I think I'll need, then cut that number in half.

When we loaded the plane again it was still probably over its max allowable weight, but at least the tail wasn't dragging on the ground anymore.

We left South Carolina and headed south, planning on spending the night in Florida before tackling the Caribbean. Both Stu and I were frustrated with the slow start and pace of the trip so far. We also knew better than to be so impatient that early in the trip but it was natural to chafe at the ball and chain that was John and his ever present camera. Stu was a lot more upset at the lack of progress than I was because he had a deadline looming over his head.

Before becoming a pilot, Stu had been a firefighter in New York. He left before the 9/11 attacks but had worked with some of the men who lost their lives that day. Ever since that fateful day, Stu had been going back to New York on the anniversary to honor his fallen brothers. This year was going to be the 10th anniversary of the attack and he had made a solemn vow to attend the memorial. The problem was that September 11th was only seven days away. That meant that Stu had to be on a plane headed to New York in six days. That gave us five days to fly a Bonanza from Florida to southern Brazil. That normally wouldn't have been a problem. But dragging Drifty along with us every step of the way would slow us **way** down. It was possible we'd make Stu's deadline but it was going to be close.

The legs from Florida to the Turks and then onto St. Martin went flawlessly. Like every flight everywhere, if nothing goes wrong it's just a pleasure to be in the cockpit on a sunny day, listening to music and wondering why everyone isn't a pilot. (Stupid mortals.)

Once we were on the ground at St. Martin it was time to set up the trip's first field trip. I was going to get checked out at one of the world's ten most dangerous airports, St. Barts.

The St. Barts airport, also known as Saint Barthelemy, serves one of the most exclusive Caribbean islands that cater to the rich and famous. It's a small island with limited space, so when the time came to build a landing strip they were forced to shoehorn the tiny little airport into the only space they could find, a not very level strip of land in between the only road on the island and the beach. What makes landing at St. Bart's so difficult is that the runway is a short 2,100 feet (short for most aircraft) and that it is on a hill that slopes down to the beach. This combination of short runway and a downhill slope makes it extremely difficult to get a plane down and stopped before sliding into the ocean. Over the years the runway has proven so difficult the local authorities have required any pilot wanting to land there get a special checkout from a local flight instructor.

This sounded like just the sort of thing that would make for an interesting segment on the show so John called up the instructor who does the training at St. Barts and made an appointment for me the next day. We made arrangements to meet him at the St. Martin airport and then fly the twenty miles over to St. Barts together. When I mentioned that there were three of us he told me that he'd rather leave one of us behind because the runway is so short and getting out of there with a full airplane can be tricky. When I told Stu that he'd have to stay behind he was devastated. Instead of sitting in the back of a small airplane all day while it did multiple takeoffs and landings he would be forced to spend the day on the beaches of St. Martin, drinking tropical drinks with little umbrellas in them and admiring the scenery. But Stu was nothing if not a team player and he told Drifty and me that he'd somehow manage to get over it.

The next morning John and I met my instructor for the day, Yves Blanchet. Yves was a heavy-set Frenchman who had the enviable job of flight instructing in St. Martin. He had a non-French happy-go-lucky air about him and I enjoyed listening to him as he explained how to not run off the end of the runway and give the Bonanza a salt bath in the Caribbean after landing at St. Barts. He showed me photos of the island and runway and talked about how critical it was to be dead on perfect when setting up for landing. He had two main points that he hammered into me. One was that if your set up was poor you had to abandon it and try again. If you were too high and fast on final there was almost no way of salvaging the approach. The other more important lesson was that if you didn't touch down on the first third of the runway you **MUST** go around. Yves told me that most pilots who ended up sliding off the end of the runway and into the water were ones who actually had a good approach to landing but weren't able to get the wheels to make contact with the runway until they were too far down the runway. The reason for that is simple. With the sloping downhill runway, if you level out to try and make a nice soft smooth landing, the runway will continue to drop away from you as you float peacefully along. Then, by the time you finally run out of airspeed and fall onto the ground, you're so far down the runway you're forced to slam on the brakes in a futile attempt to get the plane stopped before dropping off the edge and into the sand or water.

Once Yves was convinced that I had the basic concepts down we hopped into the Bonanza with Drifty and took off for my first landing at St. Barts. The twenty mile flight from St. Martin to St. Barts took only a few minutes and before I knew it Yves was coaching me onto the final approach to the runway at St. Barts. As I looked over the nose of the Bonanza I couldn't help but feel a little intimidated. The short runway looked even tinier in person than in photographs. I wasn't all that worried though, because the short grass runway at my skydiving school in Wisconsin is only three hundred feet longer than St. Barts and has a raised set of train tracks on one end and a set of power lines on the other so I was used to landing short. But

I didn't have an ocean on one end of my runway so St. Barts was still intimidating.

As I got close to the hill that blocked the approach to the runway I noticed a young man on a moped pull up and stop on the road that ran across the top of the hill. I could see him turn to watch us, not realizing that his head just became an obstacle that I might or might not clear. Yves told me that in order to get your wheels down on the first third of the runway you needed to fly as close to the top of the road as you can before following the slope of the hill down to the runway. You heard him, He said "fly as close to the road as you can." When I saw the young man stop and look my way I just couldn't help but smile and lower the nose of the Bonanza ever so slightly. The young man's eyes got wider and wider and I bore down on him and I could see Yves hand twitching as he fought the natural instinct to grab the yoke. At the last second I pulled up a tiny bit and the young man ducked as we roared by just a few feet from where his head had been moments ago. It might have seemed like a dangerous stunt to a normal pilot but I've done that exact approach to landing literally thousands of times at my grass strip in Wisconsin. The raised train tracks on the north end of my runway have a brushy line of trees that grow up above the tracks on either side. Whenever I land from that direction I always see just how close I can get the wheels of my plane to the thin branches that stick up on either side. It's good fun but also really good practice at precision flying. After doing that approach a few thousand times over the past twenty years I'd gotten rather good at it.

Once we'd passed the top of the hill I lowered the nose of the Bonanza just a little. Enough that we continued to skim down the grassy slope, but not enough to pick up speed. Extra speed was the killer that would cause the plane to float down the runway farther than I wanted. As the end of the runway flashed under us I took out the last tiny bit of power I still had in and brought the nose up slightly into a half flare. I didn't want to level out completely because that would in effect cause us to gain altitude due to the runway's slope. I held that attitude and just a few seconds later the wheels of the Bonanza squeaked onto the runway. I was well short of the go around point and was about to hit the brakes when John spoke up.

"Kerry, keep going all the way to the end and make it look like you just barely got stopped in time!"

Great, here we go again.

I suppressed a snide comment about stuffing the plane's nose in the sand if he wanted and kept my speed up. I knew John had the cameras running so I played along.

"Come on baby! Stop! Stop! Stop!" I yelled as the end of the runway got closer.

"Whew! Made it!"

I was getting this acting stuff down pat.

I let the plane roll to the end of the runway and noticed a lot of black streaks on the concrete leading up to the edge of the runway. As I turned around I realized that they were tire marks from pilots who'd locked their brakes trying to get stopped before running off the end of the runway and into the water.

We taxied up to the base of the control tower, shut down and got out. John had arranged for us to meet with the guys in the tower and talk about what accidents they might have seen. We climbed the metal stairs to the control tower and met the two senior controllers inside. The men told us that on average one plane a year overshoots the runway and ends up in the water and three or four land so hard they pop one or two of their main landing gear tires. After seeing that approach and landing up close I believed them.

After interviewing the controllers, John set up his camera on the ramp to film us while Yves and I got in the Bonanza and did the rest of the landings required to obtain the special endorsement that would allow me to land in St. Barts for one year. The final four landings went smoothly including the uphill landing that we made from the ocean side. It's a tricky landing that he doesn't let everyone do because a go around is impossible with the hill at the other end of the runway. But I hadn't scared him too much after buzzing the boy on the first landing so he let me have a go at it. I have to say that landing uphill was more intimidating than expected. From the ocean side the runway is located in a narrow bay. On the base to final leg of the landing pattern you're forced to make a short, last minute turn because there is a hill on the other side of the bay that blocks a long final approach. Once you're on final, you're committed. Rising terrain on all three sides of the approach makes chickening out and going around an unwise decision. There was still a little residual adrenaline flowing through my hands as we stopped to pick up Drifty for the ride back to St. Martin.

That night John and I took a break from teasing Stu about being unable to meet any women on the beach that day to talk about Stu's upcoming deadline. After spending the day flying at St. Barts we only had four days left to get him to Porto Alegre and on a plane to New York.

"That's going to be close," I said, propping my feet up on the balcony ledge that overlooked the beach.

"Something always happens on these trips. Always. Especially if there's a deadline."

"What's the last day you can leave Porto Alegre? Is there any wiggle room? Can you be one day late?" John asked.

"No, I can't be late. The memorial ceremony is on the 11th. I'm pretty sure they're not going to hold it up for a day because I'm running late."

"OK, not a big deal. We'll just do the best we can and hope we get lucky."

"And if he has to leave early? Do I get to finish the trip by myself?"

"I'll call the office. I'm sure that will be okay with them."

The next morning we were moving along the taxiway in the Bonanza on our way to the end of the runway for takeoff. I was unusually excited that morning. Perhaps it was because we were headed to Grenada and I'd heard that it was one of the most beautiful islands in the Caribbean chain. Or possibly because of the simple reason that it was just going to be one of those perfect flying days that pilots only dream of.

I'd been awakened by morning doves cooing and the sound of waves crashing on the beach through the open patio door in my hotel room. I got up, walked out onto the patio and spent a minute taking in the beauty of the perfectly manicured hotel grounds and the ocean beyond. Then I grabbed a quick shower, threw on a pair of khaki cargo shorts, a black CB Aviation polo shirt and headed down to breakfast. I saw that Stu was already there so I grabbed a heaping plate of everything from the buffet and joined him. The setting was perfect. White linen table cloths, a cool ocean breeze blowing in from multiple open patio doors and attentive waiters ready to refill your coffee cup whenever it dropped below the full level. Which I unfortunately couldn't take advantage of because today was a flying day and it wouldn't do to get too full of liquid this early in the day. As I sat down, Stu smiled up at me and grunted a greeting with a mouth full of eggs. His eyes were bright and I could tell he was thinking the same thing I was. How in the world do two shlubs like us luck into this gig? Pixcom usually tried to save money by putting us up in the cheapest hotels they could find. But cheap hotels are few and far between in St. Martin, so our stay had been a comfortable one.

It was one of those mornings in ferry flying where you were aware of how lucky you were that someone else was paying the bill for you to be hanging out in this exotic location instead of you. Forgotten for the moment were the bad days in ferry flying. The nail biting nights over the North Atlantic with ice forming on the wings and the fuel level dropping. Or the bitter cold mornings in Greenland, hand pumping avgas into your plane from a fifty-five gallon fuel drum. No, my only concern this morning was whether or not my waistline could handle a third pastry.

Drifty walked up with his meager plate of food and sat down. He was his usual ten minutes late for breakfast because he'd been up in his room working. John had tons of work to do each night after we were done flying. He had to give the bosses at Pixcom a call to keep them in the loop and coordinate our next few days of shooting. He had to charge the batteries for the cameras and check the footage we'd shot that day and he had to give his wife a call to reassure her that Kerry hadn't flown them into the side of a volcano yet. I was very glad that I didn't have to do all that at the end of each busy day.

After breakfast we grabbed our gear and a taxi and headed to the airport. The taxi rides to and from the airports are one of the high points of my day when I'm ferry flying. They're usually the only glimpse of the local culture of whatever city or country I'm visiting. It can be very frustrating to travel the world and only see the tiny view from the taxi cab to the hotel and back. Yes, if it's a clear day you can see hundreds of square miles of fascinating landscape once you're airborne, but it's not the same thing. And if it's a cloudy IFR day you might not see anything at all.

We got to the airport, did the usual "walking to the airplane, getting ready to go flying" shots and climbed aboard. After startup I called ground control to pick up our clearance to Grenada while Stu taxied us off the ramp and down toward the end of the runway. It was an absolutely perfect day for flying so I'd filed our flight plan to take us direct to Grenada instead of following the islands. From St. Martin the chain of islands that led to South America were laid out in a half moon shape.

Following the chain of islands was an extremely safe way to fly a small plane to South America. The islands were on average only twenty mile to thirty miles apart, so if you flew at the perfectly reasonable altitude of ten thousand feet you were almost never out of gliding range from some point of land. Very comforting. And even if you did go down and have to ditch, the water was so warm you should have no problem surviving until help arrived. Providing you had a raft of course, which we didn't … again.

Instead, I opted to cut the corner and go directly to Grenada. By going direct instead of following the curve of islands I'd shave almost one hundred miles off our flight, saving both time and money, which is what a good ferry pilot is supposed to do. We would be out of gliding distance to land for most of the trip but never more than ninety miles out. With the warm water and short distances involved I deemed it well worth the risk.

When ground control called me back with my clearance it wasn't the nice easy "Direct Grenada" route that I'd filed for. Instead the controller read off a long and complicated route that obviously took us down the island chain. I diligently copied the routing down and repeated it. When I was done I asked the controller the reason for the change and all I got back was that direct routing was not allowed. Dang it! Oh well, at least we still had enough fuel to make it comfortably. Still, being inefficient bugs me. It's my ass on the line here, I should be able to risk it if I wanted.

But you can't fight the man, so we taxied to the end of the runway and got ready for takeoff. The runway at St. Martin is relatively famous because there is a road and a beach right off the end of the runway and all that separates spectators from the aircraft lining up for takeoff is a flimsy chain link fence. There are lots of videos online of beach goers hanging on to the fence while a large passenger jet takes off. It's a stupid thing to do and many people have been hurt when they lost their grip and were blown away by the jet's takeoff thrust. Of course Stu and I had to give it a try while we were there. When in Rome. Anyway, I was a little insulted that there wasn't anybody hanging onto the fence when we went to full power in the Bonanza but it was to be expected. All we could do is give them a light breeze.

The flight down the island chain was amazing as usual but It bugged me that we couldn't go direct and I whined about it for at least a hundred miles. In the end it was probably for the best because it gave John something to film as we passed over each island. He especially liked when we were able to swoop down low over St. Vincent and see the damage caused by the island's volcano that had erupted a few years before.

The landing and subsequent overnight stay in Grenada was remarkable only because of its tropical splendor. Another beautiful green island with white sand beaches, a first class hotel and an early end to the day, ho hum. Even though we'd gotten an early start to the day, filming requirements and the normal delays of ferry flying robbed us of the chance for a second leg that day. By this time Stu had mostly accepted the fact that it was unlikely that he'd be able to complete the trip. Spending another night in paradise instead of the hell hole that was Georgetown seemed like an acceptable trade off to him.

The next day we were on our way to Georgetown, Guyana. We'd managed to get another early start out of Grenada and if we didn't screw around too much getting fuel in Georgetown we stood a reasonable chance of making it a two leg day and spending the night in Macapa. The flight was uneventful and fast, and soon we were back on the ground dividing up tasks to get us back in the air as soon as possible. I rushed off to pay the landing fees and file the flight plane while Stu took care of fueling. Nascar eat your heart out! Stu also needed to call the CB Aviation office and make sure that the customs office had been informed and was aware that we were on our way.

By the time I was done with landing fees and flight planning it was still early in the day. Barring any unforeseen difficulties we would make Macapa that afternoon and Porto Alegre two days after. It was looking like Stu had a shot at finishing the entire trip after all!

"CUE THE UNFORESEEN DIFFICULTIES!" ... **Aaaaaand ... Action!**

As I walked back to the Bonanza with a fresh flight plan in hand I was greeted by a long faced co-pilot with a cell phone in his hand.

"You're not going to believe this one!" He said.

"Oh God, what now?"

"Customs in Macapa closed early today and will be closed all day tomorrow. Apparently it's some kind of holiday tomorrow and the whole country is closed!"

Crap.

My shoulders slumped as I tried not to look at the camera.

"That's it! I'm done! There's no way I can finish the trip now!"

I tried to think of a solution but came up dry. The possibility of some stupid delay had been hanging over our heads for days and it finally happened. I pictured the rest of our route in my head and did some mental calculations.

Georgetown to Macapa – four hours.

Macapa to Goiania – four hours thirty minutes.

Goiania to Curitiba – two hours forty-five minutes.

Curitiba to Porto Alegre – two hours thirty minutes.

Total – thirteen hours forty-five minutes.

In theory we could make it from Georgetown to Porto Alegre, Brazil in just one day. Heck, I'd flown longer legs than that in Africa by myself. If you add three hours at each stop for fuel and customs the total is just over twenty five hours. With both Stu and I trading off flying and sleeping it could be done in just one day. Two at the most. But we couldn't do that. Our job wasn't to ferry a plane to Brazil. Our job was to film a TV show. We couldn't just abandon that just because Stu had a date. It didn't matter at that moment anyway. We were done flying for the day and that meant some beer to drink and an interview to do.

Later that evening Stu and I were hanging around the dingy hotel pool, swimming and talking about the day and what to do next. I was trying to get some exercise in because I'd just turned fifty years old and even though making six or seven hundred skydives each summer was keeping me in shape (shut up, round is a shape), I was still unhappy with how my small belly looked on camera. Remember, the camera adds ten pounds … right? It didn't help that Stu was twenty years younger and in great shape.

After swimming Stu and I sat down at a small table by the pool and ordered drinks. (Staying hydrated is important to any exercise routine.) As we waited a swarthy man in his mid-sixties walked up, introduced himself and asked if we were pilots. He'd overheard our conversation and told us he was a pilot himself. We invited him to join us and we did what pilots do. Talk flying.

After hearing our story and why we were in Georgetown he proceeded to tell us his own claim to fame. In 1978 he was the first pilot to fly into Jonestown after the famous massacre. His eyes got a far away look as he recounted seeing dozens of bodies scattered around the airport where multiple people were shot including a United States congressman. Still fearing for their lives, the pilot and a government worker loaded a few survivors and the body of the congressman onto their aircraft and hurriedly took off for Georgetown. Stu and I sat in amazement as the old pilot told us his tale of death and adventure. When he was done, he immediately switched gears and told us about an amazing sight that was in the middle of the Amazon Jungle that we just had to go see. I pulled up a map of the Amazon on my iPad and the pilot showed us where the site was. It wasn't too far out of our way so we decided that we'd have to add it to our flight plan the next day.

The next morning we were back in the air. Somehow the gang at CB Aviation had gotten customs in Macapa to let us land despite it being a holiday. But it was too little too late for Stu. He'd have to leave for New York right away if he was going to make it to the memorial on time.

John and I were disappointed but we'd just have to finish the trip a man short. That was tomorrow's problem though. Today we were headed west, into the heart of the Amazon Jungle, looking for the surprise our new pilot friend in Georgetown told us about.

After flying over unbroken triple canopy rainforest for an hour we came to a long steep ridge line rising up from the jungle floor. We turned left to follow the ridge and soon we came to a break where a deep gorge had sliced through the rock. I banked us to the right and entered the narrow gorge, following its twists and turns before it widened into a deep canyon with steep vine covered cliffs hemming us in on either side. A small river snaking its way through the canyon floor was visible through breaks in the trees. The prehistoric scene was like something out of "The Lost World". Following the Georgetown pilot's instructions we wove our way up the canyon, getting deeper and deeper into the dark green slash in the earth. Then we rounded a particularly sharp bend and there it was ... Kaieteur Falls.

It was amazing! Kaieteur Falls is the world's largest single drop waterfall by volume of water flowing over it. The falls are three hundred seventy-one feet wide and the drop is almost eight hundred feet!

I circled the Bonanza around the falls as Stu and John took pictures and shot video. The massive amount of water roaring over the falls produced a large cloud of mist at the bottom that turned into a spectacular rainbow that framed the falls perfectly. It was an amazing scene that left us speechless. Anywhere else in the world and this would be a major tourist attraction with dozens of restaurants, hotels and a theme park. But out here in the middle of the Amazon Jungle, Kaieteur Falls sits undisturbed. A hidden jewel in the wilderness.

Before we left I flew out over the canyon again, turned around and flew directly at the edge of the falls. When we sped over the rim of the falls our height over the ground went from eight hundred feet to ten feet in an instant. It was an incredible sensation and one of the top highlights of my flying career!

I'd love to say the rest of the flight over the Amazon to Macapa was a memorable one with magical sights and feelings to last a lifetime but honestly, I can't remember hardly a thing about it. I know there was an endless carpet of thick green jungle and probably a river or two but the experience of Kaieteur Falls overshadowed everything else that day.

On the ramp at Macapa my liquid inspiration had to wait. Pixcom wanted us to phone CB Aviation for an update. They told us that they were flying Cory directly from a ferry trip to Poland down to Brazil to "help" me finish the trip! When I heard that news I put on one hell of a performance for the camera!

"I don't need any help finishing this trip! I've been ferry flying for twenty years! Almost all of them solo! I've done WAY more difficult than this one!" Blah, Blah, Blah … I pretended to be upset that I had to wait two days for Cory to arrive but in reality I was happy. I was getting paid per day whether I flew or not. Sitting around Macapa was just a two day paid holiday for me! Take your time Cory, I'll wait.

5:00 a.m. in the hotel lobby. The last two days have indeed been a vacation. John tried valiantly to fill the days with interviews and shots of me walking back and forth to the airplane but even he got sick of it after a while.

The word from Pixcom was Cory had arrived late last night after having flown straight from Poland. I imagined he'd be fresh as a daisy and ready for a full day's flying.

5:20 a.m. Still no sign of Cory. I'm not worried yet but we needed to get a move on. The runway closes at 8:00 a.m. and if we don't get off the ground by then we'll be stuck in Macapa another day. Don't get me wrong, I love Macapa, I was just ready to move on after being stuck there for two days.

5:28 a.m. A bleary eyed Cory Bengtzen stumbles down the steps to the hotel lobby and introduces himself. Cory is my height, fit, in his late thirties, with a goatee and curly blond hair held firmly in place with a liberal coating of gel. A former car dealership owner who decided to change gears and move into aviation, Cory immediately struck me as someone who had big plans and the drive to get them done. But this morning he was tired, late and desperately in need of some strong coffee. Too bad. The hotel restaurant wasn't open yet and we didn't even have time to go searching. We had to jump in the waiting taxi and race to the airport. It was a flying day!

6:05 a.m. The three of us unload our small mountain of luggage and camera gear onto a large baggage cart and start pushing it across the ramp. Cory and I walk slowly so Drifty can get ahead of us and shoot some video of us getting ready for our first trip together. Acting tired for the camera was not difficult.

6:20 a.m. Cory runs the baggage cart back to the terminal while I survey the mountain of gear I need to somehow cram into the Bonanza. I'm convinced that John's collection of camera equipment has grown over the last two days. I'm not sure how I'll fit it all in.

6:45 a.m. I send Cory off to pay the landing fees while I check weather and file the flight plan.

7:10 a.m. The administrative crap is done. It's time to go flying! But not before we each get the obligatory interviews and fire up the GoPros. Hurry up John!

7:35 a.m. Everything is ready with time to spare. Let's get this show on the road. I love it when a plan comes together!

7:40 a.m. Crap! The plane won't start! The battery is completely dead. The plan did not come together.

7:42 a.m. I send Cory running across the ramp, looking for some way to jump start the engine while I get to work opening up the engine cowling. Drifty is beside himself, trying to film both of us at the same time. He wants us to not do anything unless he can film it. I tell him no, that won't work. We don't have time. He'll have to pick which one of us might be more interesting. He runs off after Cory.

7:45 a.m. The engine cowling is off. The A-36 has a split cowling that unlatches and swings up and opens easily. Thank you Mr. Beech!

7:47 a.m. I don't understand it. There is no reason the battery should be dead. The terminal connections are tight and the master switch hadn't been inadvertently left on. Maybe John left a light on in the back of the plane? Some planes have a baggage light that can be turned on even though the master switch is off. Doesn't matter now. All that matters is getting the plane started and off the ground by 8:00 a.m.

7:51 a.m. Cory comes running back with a set of jumper cables. He thinks the line boy told him that there's no start cart available but he's not one hundred percent sure because he doesn't speak Portuguese.

7:52 a.m. Jumper cables aren't much good without electricity. I look around the ramp for a solution and see two men walking towards a Cessna parked on the row across from us.

7:53 a.m. I run over to the men and explain that we need a jump start. They don't speak English and I don't speak Portuguese. Luckily I'm fluent in international charades. With much gesturing and throat slashing motions they get the idea that we need a jump. I point to my watch. Tick Tock, time is of the essence.

7:55 a.m. Their airplane is a Cessna 206 and the battery comes out easily. The men run across the ramp with a bucket of electricity for us.

7:56 a.m. I climb into the cockpit while Cory hooks up the jumper cables. Drifty is loving the drama. This is great TV!

7:57 a.m. I turn the master on, twist the ignition key and the Bonanza springs to life! Cory unhooks the jumper cables and closes the cowling while standing next to the spinning propeller. I radio ground control for permission to taxi before he's done.

7:58 a.m. Cory hops on the wing and I start moving while he opens the door and climbs aboard. I hope John made it.

7:59 a.m. The end of the runway is over one mile away. I taxi so fast the plane almost becomes airborne.

8:00 a.m. I don't bother going all the way to the end of the runway, instead electing to do an intersection takeoff. The Bonanza's excellent performance allows us to take off using only half the runway. Tower gives me clearance. Full throttle on the roll. The second we lift off, the tower closes the runway. The time on my GPS reads 8:01 a.m.

8:02 a.m. Buzz the Amazon River.

The mad scramble to get out of Macapa on time was a great team building exercise for me and Cory but we weren't done getting to know each other just yet. Cory and I were about to get a crash course on what kind of pilots we each were. Maybe "crash course" isn't the best way to describe it.

As soon as we left the airport area I once again pointed the nose of my plane at the Amazon River. I didn't say why. I was curious to see what Cory would say. To his credit, he didn't say anything until we dropped below five hundred feet.

"Something I should know?"

"Oh, sorry, I forgot, you're new here. This is the part of the trip where we buzz the Amazon."

"Cool."

Cory's nonchalant reaction, whether real or not, was just what I was hoping for. If Cory had been a nervous Nelly, the rest of the trip would have been a long one. The low level Amazon flight was similar to the one we did in the Navajo and after a few minutes I gave Cory the controls to see how he'd do. With under three hundred hours in his log book Cory was a relatively new pilot and I wanted him to get as much experience as possible. He was also the boss, so giving him some stick time would be a good way of sucking up. Cory was practically giggling as he followed the winding course of the river. Another sure sign that I'd like flying with him.

After a good amount of low level training we left the river behind us and headed for Goiania, Brazil, our first fuel stop. As we flew along we used the time to get to know each other. Cory told me about some struggles he'd had in his personal life recently and I told him about what it was like ferry flying back in the good old days. It was amazing how fast we bonded and became a crew. So of course I proceeded to screw that up.

As we approached Goiania we were set up for a straight in landing on the south runway. It was a short runway with a slight downhill slope, challenging but doable. Cory got us set up to land but he was a little high and fast so I had him go around and land in the other direction on the north runway. I didn't blame Cory for coming in a little hot. He'd never flown a Bonanza before and it can be a hard plane to slow down. Cory's approach was picture perfect on our next attempt and my hands only twitched a couple of times while they lay on my lap, ready to spring into action and save the day if the need arose. Have I mentioned that I'm a massive control freak? Keeping my hands off the controls and my mouth shut while someone else is flying is nearly impossible for me.

When Cory began the flare for landing he let go of the throttle and grabbed the yoke with both hands. It normally wouldn't have been a big deal except that he had left the throttle at about twenty percent power. I knew this would cause us to float farther down the runway than I was comfortable with, so without thinking, I grabbed the throttle and chopped the power. As soon as I did, the Bonanza stopped flying and fell the last eight inches onto the runway. It was more of an arrival than a landing. It wasn't a bad landing but I could tell that Cory was pissed. But what was I supposed to do? At the speed we were going and with that much power left in we'd land long and fast on the short runway. The risk of running off the end of the runway or being forced to lock up the brakes was real and I couldn't accept that risk. The safety of the plane was my responsibility and I did what I thought I had to do in the moment.

Of course Cory didn't see it that way. In his mind, he had the landing made and I screwed it up by grabbing the controls. None of that mattered though. What mattered was that the incident was great TV! John was in reality show director's heaven. He interviewed each of us at length, trying to get angry and emotional responses from us.

"Cory, how did it make you feel when Kerry grabbed the throttle and messed up your landing? Was he essentially calling you a bad pilot?"

"Kerry, how bad of a pilot do you think Cory is? Do you think you'll be grabbing the controls a lot?"

Those weren't John's actual questions but that was the gist of it. His probing questions might have been good TV but they weren't helping Cory heal the sudden rift in our relationship and become a team again. Cory and I needed to handle it like guys.

"Sorry man."

"That's okay. Don't worry about it."

There, done.

I probably could've handled the landing better. But I'm not a flight instructor and unused to giving last second landing advice to other pilots. I just reacted. Drifty loved it. I became the ferry pilot who grabs the controls.

Great.

But all the drama of the control grabbing incident would have to wait. John had a more pressing, and immediate, issue to film. We solved the mystery of the dead battery. When I shut down the Bonanza and turned off the master switch the lights in the cockpit stayed illuminated.

What the hell?

I flipped the master electrical switch on and off a dozen times but it had no effect. The electrical power from the battery stayed on. That's what must have happened when I shut the plane down in Macapa. I just hadn't noticed that the power stayed on that time and had walked away while the battery slowly went dead.

Great, mystery solved, but the power was still on and unless we wanted to have a dead battery every day I had to find a way to stop the electrical bleeding. I hopped out, opened the engine cowling and disconnected the battery with my multi-tool. Sometimes the simplest solutions are the best ones. Although I wasn't looking forward to delivering the plane to its new owner with such an inconvenient method of turning the power on and off.

With a new problem to fix, Cory and I went over to a nearby hangar and soon had a cluster of local pilots giving us suggestions of how to fix the power switch problem. We tried everything we could think of but gave up in the end. We'd just have to fly it as is and hope for the best.

Unbelievably when we stopped for fuel the next day the master switch worked and shut the power off. Cory and I were pretty happy about that little bit of luck. If we could manage to keep the switch working just a few more times it would then be someone else's problem.

Two days later we crossed the barbed wire fence that marked the end of the Brazilian doctor's grass landing strip on his ranch. Keeping the nose of the Bonanza as high as I could I gingerly taxied up to the massive house next to the strip, stopped the plane and shut the engine down.

The doctor was very happy and appreciative to get his new airplane but almost before we got out of the plane he had a question that he just had to have an answer to immediately.

"Please tell me, why when you left Georgetown did you fly west for so long before turning south?"

It turns out that he had been watching our progress with an online program that allowed him to track our plane via radar. He'd been beside himself seeing the Bonanza head the wrong way for so long that morning.

"Oh, that. Sorry but we'd heard about Kaieteur Falls and just had to make a quick detour to go and see it," I told him with the guilty look of a teenager who'd been caught borrowing his father's car for a joy ride.

I was worried that he'd be angry that we'd put a little extra time on his new plane but he didn't care at all. He was just happy to have the mystery solved. The doctor then showed his appreciation by treating us to a traditional Brazilian barbecue followed by a horseback tour of his ranch. It was a fantastic end to a ferry flight.

But as they say, the job's not over till the paperwork's done, or in our case until the final interviews are filmed. The final interviews are the absolute worst part of the trip. They usually take a full day and involve John asking us questions about each and every little thing that happened during the trip. Over the course of the day he'll ask each of us dozens of questions and he insists the answers be perfect. No slurred words, no awkward pauses or mispronunciations. No mistakes! It might take ten attempts to say your answer acceptably. My biggest problem was saying the word "decision". It was my Kryptonite, and once it got stuck in my head, I couldn't say it correctly to save my life. It didn't help that it was the word I used the most.

And if you think doing interviews first thing in the morning sounds difficult, try doing them with one of the worst hangovers you've ever had. The three of us probably should've celebrated the completion of the trip the night after the interviews, not before.

THE JET AGE

"All I need to know is if I advance or retard the throttles too aggressively will I break the jet?"

The man I was directing this perfectly reasonable question to was Captain Marcio Lucchese, a Brazilian American airline pilot who was joining me on my next ferry flying adventure for Pixcom. Or should I say I was joining him? In addition to being a first officer for Delta airlines, Marcio was a ferry pilot who specialized in delivering Phenom business jets. Somehow Pixcom found him and convinced him to join our merry band of second-rate TV stars. I don't know if Pixcom liked him because of his larger-than-life personality, his exotic foreign accent or the fact that he was the captain of a jet that needed to be ferried from Australia to Las Vegas. Either way they picked me to be his co-pilot, so I was off to The Land Down Under.

I was excited about this trip for a number of reasons. First of all, seeing this was my third trip for Pixcom I was firmly established as one of the main pilots on the show and who knew how popular or successful it might become? Was this the next *Deadliest Catch*? All I knew was that Pixcom was dumping a ton of money into the show and I was going to be a TV star! Maybe … sort of. The next reason I was pumped about the trip was that we were starting off in Australia and I'd never been to Australia before. I had a globe at home that I used to keep track of everywhere in the world that I'd flown as a ferry pilot. The globe was crisscrossed with long black lines from my twenty-five years of flying all sorts of aircraft around the world but none yet touched Australia. That was about to change. And the final reason I was excited was that I was going to be flying a jet!

Of course every trip has a beginning and the beginning of my trip sucked. In order to get to Australia from Wisconsin you need to take a long plane ride followed by a really long plane ride. My really long plane ride was going to be an ass busting nineteen hours long. *Ugh.* When I boarded the jet and took my window seat I was happy to see that the aisle seat was occupied by a very beautiful young woman. I couldn't ask for a better seatmate except maybe a kindly old grandmother with a big box of homemade cookies. As the time to depart got closer and closer it was starting to look like we might be lucky enough to have an empty middle seat between us. Then a large dark shadow came down the aisle, blocking out everything. My heart sank as an extremely large young man stopped our row and squeezed himself into the middle seat. *Great.*

It wouldn't have mattered so much except for the fact that he blocked all view of the girl in the aisle seat and the fact that he had the worst body odor I'd ever smelled. It was so awful I could hardly breathe. I spent the entire flight with my head pressed up against the window. Not a great way to start the trip.

Day 1.

After landing in Sydney I met Marcio at the airport and was immediately impressed. Not only did he have a big air of confidence and friendliness about him, he was also a very big guy! At six foot four inches he literally towered above me. The fact that the in person Marcio seemed to live up to his impressive resume as a pilot made me very happy because believe it or not, I was looking forward to flying as a co-pilot. Yes, I know, I'm a complete control freak, I admit it. Especially in the cockpit. I like to be in charge. But being in charge can also be draining. Having to make every hard decision on a flight can wear on a man after a while. Ever since getting my private pilot's license I'd been the pilot in command of almost every flight I'd been on. For six thousand three hundred and nine hours I'd been the one responsible for every little decision made in the cockpit and on the ground. And most of the time I'd been the only one in the plane. Ferry flying is mostly a solo affair. The job is to move aircraft around the world as quickly and inexpensively as possible. That means there's no money for a second pilot. No one to help on a difficult instrument approach, no one to keep you awake or share the flying and no one to ask "What do you think?"

On this trip though, I'd be flying with a current ferry pilot who knew everything about the aircraft we were flying while I knew nothing since I'd never flown a jet before. Plus he was an airline pilot! I know I've looked down at their job as boring but there's no disputing their skill level. I was planning on letting Marcio do all the hard work while I played Angry Birds on my iPad. This trip was going to be a piece of cake! … At least that was my plan.

Rounding out the team on this trip was good old John Driftmier. This would be our third trip together and we had become close friends. Each of the previous two trips had lasted about two weeks and I can't think of a better way to really get to know someone than to spend virtually every waking moment with them for weeks at a time. Although just spending time with someone isn't sufficient to achieve the level of bonding we'd achieved. No, those days need to be filled with incredible adventures, challenges and danger. The more intense the experience the closer the bond. Prior to being on the show with Stu, Cory and Drifty I thought the only place to get to know someone that intensely and really become brothers like that was in the military.

Once introductions were made the first thing we did was go meet the Phenom 100 that would be our home for the next two weeks. I was as excited as a kid on Christmas morning as we walked into the hangar. Of course I couldn't show it. Gotta play the cool and seasoned ferry pilot.

"Huh, nice jet. When's lunch?" But inside I was bubbling over with anticipation. "A jet! A jet! I get to fly a jet!"

Climbing into a new plane for the first time is an almost sexual experience. You slide into the cockpit, put your hands on the yoke and lovingly run your eyes over the instrument panel as if to say "Hey baby, where shall we go today?" Sliding into the cockpit of the Phenom was like that, only this time it was like meeting a supermodel. The plush leather seat fit my body like a glove and the instrument panel was a futuristic collection of computer screens and LED displays. Even the ram's head yoke was hi-tech and ergonomically pleasing to hold. It was an amazing display of technology and I was as lost as a caveman in the Space Shuttle.

The Phenom was like nothing I'd ever flown before. Up until that point all my flying had been in older planes with steam gauges and very simple autopilots. Now I was faced with computers and hi-tech gizmos. Getting to know a new plane might have a steep learning curve but that comes with the territory if you want to be a ferry pilot. Take the engine start procedure for example. In all the other turbine powered aircraft I'd flown up until that point the engine start sequence is: Starter-engage. Then, when the RPM reaches a certain point then advance the fuel flow lever to introduce fuel to the engine. While you watch the RPMs increase be sure to monitor the exhaust gas temperature to make sure it doesn't climb too high, too fast and give you a hot start and destroy the engine. If that happens, cut the fuel and continue motoring the engine to prevent a hot start that might destroy the outrageously expensive engine. In the Phenom the start sequence is – push the start button. The end. The Phenom's onboard computer completes the start procedure and aborts automatically if anything is outside parameters. Simple, now go flying. I took the pilot's operating manual back to the hotel with me that night. I had a lot of studying to do.

Day 2.

A cheerful voice with an amazingly sexy accent gave me my morning wake up call. It was air-to-air day! Air-to-air with a jet, and from what I understand, a helicopter. *This should be interesting.* I would have tried to find something a little faster but nobody asked me. I met Marcio for breakfast and filled him in on what he could expect to do that day and he looked rather surprised. The maneuvering required in shooting the air-to-air footage was exactly the opposite kind of flying he was used to doing in the airlines.

We met the helicopter pilot at the airport and I conducted the safety and operation briefing for the day. One big question I had for both the helicopter pilot and Marcio was how fast and how slow they each could fly, respectively. The helicopter pilot said he could get his bird up to one hundred forty-five knots while Marcio told me he wouldn't be comfortable maneuvering any slower than one hundred thirty. That gave us fifteen knots to play with. Not much but it would have to do.

After the briefing Marcio and I climbed aboard the Phenom and took off. The takeoff was amazing! When Marcio advanced the throttles the jet ripped down the runway like it was shot out of a cannon. This time I didn't even try to play it cool and hide the grin on my face. The helicopter had taken off first and before long we'd caught up with our target. Then came the tricky part, formation flying between a helicopter and a jet.

As we closed with the bright red helicopter Marcio put one notch of flaps out, brought the power to idle and shot right past. *This is going to be tricky*. When Marcio circled around for another attempt to form up he asked the helicopter pilot to fly as fast as he could to make it easier to match speeds. This time we were more successful and pulled up next to the helicopter and stayed there. Sort of.

As we got close to the helicopter I was alarmed to see that Marcio was using the autopilot to attempt to keep us in formation. I stress the word "attempt." He was using the heading bug to move us left and right and the altitude select knob to move us up and down and it wasn't working at all. While the helicopter was flying smooth and steady, we were wallowing all over the place. The problem was twofold. The first problem was that the autopilot was just not nimble enough to keep up with the constant heading and altitude changes necessary to fly in formation with another aircraft. The other problem was that Marcio had exactly zero experience in formation flying. And if you're talking about difficult formation flying, trying to do it with a helicopter and a jet is as hard as it gets.

After the third or forth near-collision I couldn't hold my tongue any longer. I suggested to Marcio that maybe he should try hand flying it. He wasn't really open to the suggestion. He said that you don't hand fly jets, you use the autopilot for everything and formation flying should be no different. He just needed some practice. I let him try and kill us for another few minutes before speaking up again.

"Marcio, can I take the controls for a minute and show you a few things?"

Marcio reluctantly relinquished the controls and I grabbed the yoke and flipped off the autopilot. It took me a few seconds to get the jet stabilized but soon we were hanging just off and to the left of the helicopter with a minimum of effort. I was actually surprised how well the jet handled at such low speed. Marcio looked at me in amazement.

"Don't feel bad," I said without taking my eyes off the helicopter. "I've had a lot of formation flying experience lately. This is my third air-to-air session in the last two months. Plus, I used to do a lot of formation flying back when I flew jump planes."

From that point on I was the one flying the jet that morning. When we got to the practice area we started doing the normal air-to-air maneuvers and **WOW!** Was that fun!

I thought putting the Navajo and the Bonanza through their paces had been a good time but that was nothing like doing it in the Phenom. I swooped and dove, banked hard and did high speed passes all around the camera ship. It was amazing. John was in the helicopter giving us directions and from his voice on the radio I could tell he was loving the shots we were getting. At one point we came upon a cluster of tall, billowing cumulus clouds and John just told me to play in them while he filmed. If I thought buzzing around the helicopter was fun it was nothing compared to what I did with those clouds.

To finish up the day we flew into Sydney harbor and did laps around the inside while the helicopter hovered in the middle and took video of us flying past the iconic Sydney opera house. There was a little confusion getting into the busy airspace of the harbor at first. Coming in we'd somehow missed a frequency change and didn't hear ATC tell the helicopter pilot to clear out and come back in five minutes. When the helicopter suddenly banked hard and took off for apparently no reason, we were confused. We held our course for a minute, getting more and more nervous. As soon as I got into the harbor I knew something was wrong. Instead of being empty, the harbor was full of helicopters and float planes buzzing around. I was trying to keep my eyes on everything at once but it was difficult doing that and flying a jet at two hundred knots. Things were getting crazy and out of hand. The last straw was when a helicopter I hadn't seen went whizzing by less than a thousand feet away.

"That's it, I'm out of here!" I said as I banked the Phenom away from the center of the harbor, raced toward the entrance and escaped.

The helicopter pilot finally got clearance and we flew back in and got the shots. That was it for the day and Marcio took us back to the airport. We were both drained as we poured ourselves out of the Phenom. Marcio had had one heck of a first day as a TV pilot.

Day 3.

Once the fun flying was over, then came the work of getting the Phenom ready for the trip and seeing if Marcio was any good on camera. This was not a small thing because even though a pilot might be a master craftsman in the cockpit he still might not be able to string two sentences together when you shoved a camera in his face. We needn't have worried, Marcio was a big expressive Brazilian with personality as large as he was. He even came with a cool nickname, "Poppy." I knew John was happy as soon as Marcio started talking. He was a natural. His cool Brazilian accent and tendency to wave his hands around when he talked didn't hurt either.

Then came time to mount the cameras in and on the plane. This was easier said than done because the only good way to mount the cameras in the cockpit was with tape. Trying to find suitable places to stick large patches of sticky duct or Gaffers tape on an aircraft's glare shield is difficult at best. During the Bonanza trip John had run out of good Gaffers tape, which leaves no residue, and had substituted black duct tape. This was a big mistake. Whenever the plane was sitting on the ramp in the Caribbean or Brazil the cabin temperature would climb to well over one hundred degrees. These high temperatures melted the adhesive on the tape and made it almost impossible to get off. Needless to say the owner wasn't very happy about that and I had to spend an entire evening scraping the melted glue off with my fingernails.

We didn't want to make the same mistake with a multi million dollar jet so mounting the cameras inside the cockpit took a lot longer than normal. A bigger challenge was trying to mount a GoPro camera on the outside of the jet. On the Navajo and Bonanza we mounted a GoPro on each wingtip giving us a good view of the plane and cockpit from the outside. It's a lot harder to secure a camera on an aircraft that travels at three hundred fifty knots than one that goes one hundred ninety. We consulted a local mechanic and he wasn't comfortable mounting any cameras on the outside of the jet at all. Even when I pointed out that we could easily bolt one to the tail tie down ring. It was a heavy, metal skid point that had the perfect sized hole in it to mount the bracket to. I told him that even in the unlikely event that the bolt broke the camera would just fall harmlessly away behind the jet. There was no danger to the plane whatsoever. The mechanic agreed in principle but still wouldn't sign off on mounting the camera to the tail. He did, however, make a mounting bracket that fit the tail skid perfectly and would "theoretically" work just fine. He mounted the camera on the plane and was satisfied that it was secure. Then he took it off, handed it to me and said. "Under no circumstances should you mount this to the tail of this jet, making sure you use the lock washers I included."

"Thank you. I'll make sure that the bolt is really tight when I don't mount the camera."

I asked John if we should tell Pixcom about our illegal camera mounting system but he figured it best not to bother them with that pesky little detail.

Day 4.

Northbound for Darwin at thirty-six thousand feet. The sun is gone, but enough orange light lingers in the sky to match the desert below. The first stars appear in the east and I'm expecting a magnificent show once the western sky finally darkens. I'm tired and the cockpit is quiet. I marvel at the complete lack of movement or vibration in the Phenom. If I close my eyes it's as quiet and still as it would be if the plane was parked in the hangar.

It's been a long day of flying. The Phenom is a great aircraft with two major shortcomings. It has short legs and is rather slow for a jet. On the smaller end of the business jet scale, the Phenom's range is only a little over one thousand nautical miles and its cruise speed is under five hundred knots. With these limitations we were looking at a lot of short legs on our trip from Sydney to Las Vegas. Our "planned" route will be Sydney to Darwin, with a fuel stop in there someplace. Then Indonesia, the Philippians, Okinawa, Russia, Russia, Russia, Alaska, Washington-and finally, Vegas baby!

Our first obstacle was Australia itself. The distance from Sydney to Darwin is a solid 1,700 nautical miles right across the center of Australia. Way too far for the Phenom to do in one gulp. After looking at the winds aloft Marcio picked Longreach, Queensland as our fuel stop. Leaving Sydney, the big city gave way to suburbs which quickly turned into miles and miles of farmland, grassy plains and large patches of forest. The green was soon gone though as we flew over what I assumed was the outback. Remember when I said the grasslands outside Sydney went on for miles and miles? Well, the desert of the outback goes on for miles and miles and miles. Seriously, how did the aborigines survive out there? And why did the white settlers move out there? Sure, it's beautiful from thirty-six thousand feet. But down there in the hot, I assume it's hot, barren wasteland it had to be a brutal existence. And even if you do manage to somehow scratch out a living, what do you do for fun with the nearest city so far away? I had the same thought I'd had many times in the past. It was a beautiful place to fly over but I wouldn't want to live there.

Marcio told me before we left that we'd take turns on takeoffs and landings. He'd done the landing coming back from the air-to-air day. That meant this landing was mine. I had to do well. Landing airplanes is my specialty, and I not only wanted to impress Marcio and John but I had my own personal standards to uphold. A crappy landing would put me in a bad mood for the rest of the day or longer. Marcio gave me surprisingly few, if any, landing tips. I guess having observed my performance during air-to-airs had given him a false sense of security. Yes, I can fly the Phenom, but can I land it? Any idiot can fly an airplane once it's far enough away from the hard stuff. It's only that last little bit that counts.

I check the runway diagram against the wind report for the airport and see that I'll be landing in a moderate left crosswind. Something to keep in mind once I get close, but first I had to get set up for landing in an aircraft that has an approach speed much higher than anything I'd ever flown before.

As we approach Longreach, the airport is just over the nose, a long brown line in the dirt brown countryside. The runway had been hard to pick out and I'm closer than I'd like. I'm already behind the aircraft and feeling rushed. I bank the jet right to put us on, what appears to me, a very wide left base leg. I'm intentionally keeping the pattern wider than I think is necessary to avoid the shame of overrunning final and having to go around for another try. My normal sight picture is out the window. I have no idea how wide the base leg should be or how long a final approach normally is. One mile? Two? Five? Marcio is still not offering any clues, he's busy doing something on his iPad and only glances out the windscreen occasionally, blissfully unaware of my struggles and self doubt.

I see the shadows of the few scattered clouds moving across the field from my right to left. This means I'll have a tailwind on the base leg. I'll have to keep that in mind when it comes time to turn final. We make the turn to base leg and Marcio finally puts his iPad down and pays attention to what I'm doing. The gear and flaps are down and I make the turn to final in a not so terrible manner, pleased that I'm lined up exactly with the runway centerline. The nose of the jet is cocked to the left to compensate for the crosswind. I instinctively pull some power off and let the jet descend, shooting for the end of the runway. It's only six thousand feet long and at the speed we're going it seems terribly short.

"Pull up … pull up," Marcio says in a low smooth tone. When giving new pilots landing advice the urgency of the commands correlates exactly to how the Captain wants his First officer to react. A calm low command means "a little" a shouted urgent command means "A lot!"

"Keep your speed up and aim for the touchdown zone."

Marcio had seen me aiming for the end of the runway which is where I usually land instead of the touchdown zone aiming point which is one thousand feet down the runway. The aiming point is set that far down the runway to give pilots a buffer in case they make a mistake and come up short. I personally hate landing that far down the runway because it seems foolish to waste that much runway. Yes, I'm cocky and confident in my ability to not come up short and land in the dirt. But that's not how my Captain wants it done.

"Remember, you don't flare a jet like those little Cessnas you fly. If you do that you'll float in ground effect all the way down the runway. Just bring the nose up a little so you touch down on the mains."

I try to picture what he's talking about in my mind and have a hard time grasping it. *If I don't flare to arrest the descent won't I hit too hard?* With nothing to base his advice on I figure I'll just wing it when it comes time to land.

We swoop across the edge of the runway and my propeller driven mind screams

"You're going too fast!" I see Marcio's hands leave his lap out of the corner of my eye as I ease the yoke back but take no notice, I'm busy.

The Phenom levels out and I hold it off the runway. And it won't stop flying. I've flared too much and now we're floating along in ground effect. Marcio wisely doesn't say a word. Too late now anyway. The speed finally falls off enough to let us sink the last few feet to the ground. At the last second I kick the right rudder pedal to align the nose with the centerline as we thump onto the runway. I realize my heart is beating a mile a minute as I turn onto the taxiway at the end of the runway.

"I told you not to flare it like a Cessna … Other than that, it was a pretty good landing!"

Marcio's approval means more than I care to admit. I haven't felt like this since my initial flight training all those years ago.

Our last night in Australia was underwhelming. A night landing allowed us to see virtually nothing of the city, and we found a hotel and restaurant close to the airport so there was no reason to go into town. Except for everyone's Australian accent, Darwin could have passed for any small town in the US. As disappointing as it was, it was a typical overnight stop for a ferry pilot.

Day 5.

Whenever I fly in Europe I can't help but think about the fact that I'm flying in the same skies that were witness to some of the greatest aerial battles of WWII. As we left Australia and headed north into the South Pacific the names on the map reminded me of the great naval battles of WWII. Now we were the ones doing the island hopping. Our first stop was in Manado, Indonesia, where Marcio would try using his favorite Ronaldo soccer shirt to curry favor with the soccer obsessed locals. I usually wear a uniform shirt with Captain stripes to command respect in the third world, so I was interested to see how his plan worked out. The stunt was mostly for the cameras but when we went to pay for the fuel he got a thumbs up from one of the clerks, who was a Ronaldo fan.

Apparently the shirt only works part of the time. When we went to the airport office to pay the landing fees the manager had some bad news for us. He told us that because we didn't have the correct paperwork and we didn't hire a local handler we would be subject to an investigation which could result in large fines or imprisonment. Marcio immediately objected, claiming he had called the day before coming and that someone told him hiring a handler wasn't necessary but that didn't faze the manager. As the two of them went back and forth I noticed the manager kept saying might, could and possibly. It appeared to me that there might be some flexibility on the issue. That's when Marcio called on his good friend Ben Franklin to help him out. Marcio slipped the manager a fifty dollar bill and suggested he take his wife out for a nice dinner. The bill disappeared and in no time we had the proper stamps and were on our way to the Philippians.

The sun went down and so did Marcio and John. It was our third leg of the day and we were all bone tired. I lifted my sore rear end off the seat for a moment, trying to restore some kind of feeling in it without taking my eyes off the radar screen. I'd been watching a line of green and red blobs march down the screen for the last ten minutes and decided to alter course to the right a few degrees to avoid one of the larger cells. From what I could tell the rest of the storms were below our current altitude.

I looked at Marcio, fast asleep in the left hand seat and thought how easily my career might have mirrored his. If I'd gone that route after finishing my earlier ferry flying career instead of going into professional skydiving I'd have probably have made Captain by now. Being an airline pilot wouldn't have been so bad, better than a real job, and doing the occasional ferry flight to keep my adventure lust satisfied might have kept me sane … Might have.

Weaving through the scattered storms was kind of fun, sort of like a video game. At this point I was really glad I was in a jet flying high above all but the tallest cells. I thought about what it would be like down there, battling the elements in a small plane. I'd been there before, many times, bouncing around the cockpit, trying to keep the wings level while rain pounded the plane and lightning flashed all around.

I looked around the cockpit and marveled at the difference. In the Phenom everything was quiet and still. Music was playing softly in my headset and the multifunction displays bathed everything in a soft, warm electric glow. Marcio, sleeping like a baby, looked like one of those giant stuffed bears you win at the fair and tossed in a corner of a child's bedroom. It was so peaceful and serene I'd be a fool to want anything else.

Was I crazy? Because I wanted to be down there. *I wanted to be down there? Why in the hell did I want to be down there?* I had to think about that for a minute. I knew the easy answer. I was not right in the head. People had been telling me that for as long as I can remember. But that wasn't it. I'm not a manic depressive, self destructive crazy person. (Of course a crazy person doesn't know they're crazy.) My desire to be down there doing battle with the thunderstorms that night wasn't because I had a mental problem. Then why?

The more I thought about it, the more I came to realize that I wanted to be down there because that was what I was meant to do. Not fight thunderstorms exactly, but to do battle with … something … anything. I was meant to respond to emergencies and hardship. I'm never more alive than when I'm dealing with a life-or-death situation. I suppose that's because I'm good at it. And I know that because I've been tested a lot.

Like every skill, and it is a skill, the ability to perform well in an emergency situation is a combination of natural ability and experience. You can't do anything about the natural ability aspect but you can put yourself in situations or pursue activities where you are more likely to gain experience. Things like scuba diving, skydiving, mountain climbing or flying small used airplanes around the world. There's a much greater chance of an emergency situation popping up on a skydive than at the golf course, or in a brand new jet. (It turns out I was wrong on that last point.)

Day 6.

Okinawa, Japan. It may sound strange but the first thing I was looking forward to doing in Japan was using the bathroom in my hotel room. I'd heard about the legendary Hi-tech Japanese toilets for years and was dying to try one out. Oh … My … God! It was everything I'd dreamed it would be! It had everything. The control panel had more buttons on it than Captain Kirk's chair on the Enterprise. With it you could control such functions as seat heater, warm water jets (Low, medium and high!), air dryer, choice of seven different fragrance sprays and entertainment center complete with DVD player. I even liked the color. The only problem was that the controls were labeled in Japanese and it took me a while to figure out what did what. I did find out that you didn't need to be seated for the warm water jets to work.

After I was done playing in the bathroom I met the boys in the lobby and we started filming our field trip for the day. We were going to participate in the world's biggest Tug of War. The Naha Tug of War is an annual festival that dates back to the 17th century. Once a year two hundred thousand people gather in the town of Naha to spend the morning tugging on a gigantic rope weighing over forty metric tons! Made out of hemp, the rope is over five feet in diameter and comes equipped with thousands of smaller ropes sticking out from each side that the participants pull on. It's a crazy event with dozens of men and women wearing all kinds of traditional garb walking along on top of the rope banging drums and chanting cadence to attempt to get each side to pull together.

Marcio and I joined in and pulled along with everyone but aside from a lot of shaking, the rope didn't seem to move much. After thirty minutes the contest was over and our side was declared the winner! (It's my story and I'll tell it how I want.) Afterwards everyone cuts chunks of rope off to bring good luck for the coming year. That evening our guide took us to a famous sushi restaurant for what I was told was a very exclusive and expensive meal. It was OK. My barbarian tastes were more in the mood for pizza though.

Day 7.

Looking down at the city of Hiroshima, Japan revealed no sign that man-made hellfire had once been unleashed there. I tried to spot the Genbaku dome, the only structure left standing after the bombing, but all I saw was one big city. We were there only as a fuel stop, and because we'd already cleared outbound customs in Okinawa, we were not allowed anywhere but the immediate vicinity of the plane while it was being fueled. I suppose that made sense but nobody told my bladder. I walked up to the airport official in charge of making sure we stayed put, informed him of my situation and asked to use the restroom. My request was politely but firmly refused.

"No problem," I told him. "Just point me to the spot on the empty ramp or side of the building that you'd like me to urinate on and I'll be done in a flash."

The look of revulsion and exasperation on his face revealed an epic conflict going on in his head. Neither option appealed to him, but one was apparently more distasteful than the other and he ushered us inside. John and Marcio joined me because in the flying game you never pass up a chance to take a piss. Our next stop would be in Russia.

Under the guise of an innocent reality show film crew, the Pixcom intelligence agency sent in their top agents to take pictures of the secret Russian airbase in Vladivostok.

Team leader – John Driftmier. Codename "Drifty"

- Audio Visual specialist.

- Fluent in English and some French.

- Lulls the enemy into a false sense of security with his non-athletic appearance and being Canadian.

Captain Marcio Lucchese. Codename "Poppy"

- Master autopilot manipulator.

- Fluent in English, Spanish and Portuguese.

- Expert in knife, fork and spoon.
First Officer Kerry McCauley. Codename "Scary"
- Expert gravity tester.
- Fluent in English and Pig Latin. Can speak in almost any accent, as long as it's Irish.
- Able to put anyone to sleep instantly with long and boring stories.

Flying into Vladivostok, Russia was weird. When I was in the Army we'd spent most of our time training to fight the Russian bear. Now I was flying into one of their most important Air force bases, pretty as you please. We did have one major source of stress, as we'd forgotten to remove the GoPro from the tail of the Phenom before leaving Japan. It wouldn't have been a big deal except for the fact that the Russians had specifically told us that no cameras or filming would be allowed at the airbase. Personally, I didn't know why we were so worried. I'm sure that the Russians wouldn't care if we broke their number one security rule. And even if they got angry they still couldn't send us to Siberia, because we were already there.

As we approached Vladivostok ATC cautioned us not to overfly the submarine base. The controller sounded very stern and serious. I was left wondering what would happen if we "accidentally" flew over the base. I can't imagine they'd shoot us down but you never know.

I noticed two things the second we touched down. The first were the dozens of military jets and helicopters parked on both sides of the runway. Or should I say abandoned? Most were parked out in the open with tall weeds growing up all around them. It was obvious that most of them hadn't moved in a very long time. There were a few more modern looking jets parked in hardened hangars that had a layer of thick grass on the roof as camouflage. Even these planes didn't look like they'd had any attention in a while.

As we taxied by I couldn't help but note that back in the 1980's I'd actually had an Army-issued deck of playing cards with the silhouettes of these aircraft on them. I'd gotten good at telling the difference between a "Hip" and a "Hind" helicopter but was glad I never had to use that skill for real.

The other thing we noticed was that the runway and taxiways were crap. As soon as we touched down a series of bone jarring bumps and thumps rocked the Phenom, causing Marcio to get on the brakes harder than normal to minimize the damage. There were a few Portuguese swear words from my Captain as he steered us around the worst parts of the runway.

Ground control directed us to a remote parking spot and told us to remain in the aircraft. *Great, it's not like we've been flying for four hours or anything.* The Phenom unfortunately didn't come equipped with a Japanese toilet. I didn't know if all Russians sounded like that naturally, but the controller who told us to stay put sure sounded angry.

The Russians left us cooling our heels in the Phenom for over an hour. Finally a group of stern looking Russian officers (Soldiers? Bellhops?). Came marching across the tarmac towards us. There were five of them, all wearing those goofy over-sized green bus-drivers hats and sour looks on their faces.

"Well, that doesn't look good," I said as the Russian contingent marched up to the plane.

I told Drifty to double check that all his cameras were indeed off and to resist his natural urge to film the Russians.

"But this would be the best footage of the trip!"

"I know, but if they confiscate all your equipment you're not bringing anything back!"

Our discussion was interrupted by a loud pounding on the side of the Phenom. It took all my willpower not to say "Who is it?" I unlatched the door and let it swing down revealing a cluster of stern faces. Apparently Russians look stern a lot. I tried my usual happy, friendly, eager to help routine but that just seemed to make them more suspicious. The first thing they wanted to see was the paperwork (the Russians love their paperwork) while two of the customs agents (KGB officers? Guards?) took Marcio to the tail of the plane and pointed at the GoPro mounted there and demanded an explanation. Marcio gave them a long winded and winding story that basically boiled down to "We forgot." The senior comrade in charge wasn't impressed with that excuse. He accused us of intentionally filming restricted areas and was really getting up a full head of steam until I pointed out that the camera only took ten minutes of footage after take-off before the batteries froze and went dead at the high altitudes we flew at. I then went and grabbed my laptop, plugged the GoPro into it and brought up the footage. It clearly only showed the take-off from Hiroshima and the climb to altitude before it went dark. This seemed to calm him down a little.

While Marcio and I were dealing with the head honcho, John was having problems of his own. Another one of the agents had climbed aboard the Phenom and he nearly lost his mind when he saw what was inside. Lined up against one wall of the plane was a bank of computers, camera displays and assorted hardware. If you were going to make the inside of a jet look like a spy plane this is exactly how you would have it laid out. The young agent turned from the display and in an accusing voice.

"John no. You James Bond!" … And he was entirely serious. He was literally calling John an American spy. Never mind that James Bond was British and John was Canadian.

At first John thought he was joking but one look on his face cleared that misconception up in a hurry. John then turned on all the cameras and showed the young Russian that all the cameras in the plane pointed inside the cockpit at the two pilots' seats. It took some doing but eventually Drifty convinced him that he wasn't a spy.

After that, the agents started in on the paperwork like they worked for the IRS. They'd grab a sheet of paper, read it carefully, show it to each other, compare it to some other random sheet of paper, shake their heads, then reach for the next one. While this was going on I grabbed my 35mm camera and aimlessly wandered about fifty feet away from the jet playing the bored co-pilot. I had the camera hidden in my jacket pocket and turned it on without looking or taking it out. Confident that everyone's attention was focused on the paperwork I discreetly took the camera out of my pocket and fired off a few shots from the hip. If they were going to treat us like spies I might as well act the part.

Encouraged by my success, I took a few more pictures from different angles. I walked back to the plane with a smug smile on my face. I would have made a great spy!

After a while the Russians sent for a bus to take John to the customs offices for further interrogation. John grabbed his big video camera and boarded the big airport bus with more enthusiasm than the situation warranted. Suspicious, I watched as the bus turned around and drove past us heading back the way it came. As the bus passed us, I could see John standing behind a large window facing us and holding the camera low on his hip. It was totally obvious that he was trying to secretly film us. After the bus passed I looked over at one of the agents who had obviously seen what John was doing and he just shook his head. John would not make a good spy.

That evening when the three of us sat down for dinner the waiter set a bottle of vodka down on the table along with the menus. He set it there as casually as a waiter in the United States would place a pitcher of water on the table. None of us were really vodka drinkers but we each poured a shot to celebrate our trip so far. Boy, was that smooth! It wasn't like any vodka I'd ever had before. Dinner came and before we knew it the bottle of vodka was empty. Not being vodka drinkers none of us had any idea how such a thing could have happened.

After dinner we retired to the bar where the locals were drinking, dancing with uncharacteristic smiles on their faces. Shortly after sitting down, two women sat down at the table next to ours. One of them was rather plain, the other was a knockout! She looked to be in her late twenties with long dark hair and the classic, beautiful Russian face complete with standard issue frown. She was sitting right next to John, and I bet him the next round that he couldn't get her to dance with him. John was having none of it and when he threw the challenge back in my face, I couldn't back down. Feeling like I was back in high school I got up and asked her to dance. Unfortunately she agreed and I walked her out to the dance floor and proceeded to make a fool of myself trying to dance to some Russian techno music. While we were dancing the woman had a big smile on her face but as soon as the music stopped the smile disappeared and she walked off the dance floor without so much as a glance back at me.

Weird, was I that bad?

I went back to the table and after John and Marcio stopped laughing, collected the money for the next round from John and went up to the bar. As I was waiting to be served a Russian man in the classic matching velvet tracksuit walked up to me and said.

"Eight hundred American dollars."

I was taken aback. I didn't know this man and had no idea what he was talking about. I was instantly wary.

"Excuse me? I don't know what you mean," I said, trying to gauge the man and what his angle might be.

"For the woman. Eight hundred."

Oh, I get it now.

"Sorry, not interested. Just getting another drink then my friends and I are leaving." What had I gotten myself into?

Thankfully, he grunted something non-threatening and disappeared back into the crowd. I went back to the table and discreetly told Marcio and John what had happened.

They thought it was hilarious. After a while Marcio being Marcio got to talking to the other woman at the table and found out that she was her friend's agent. She told us that she was a model who mostly worked in Europe but was home on holiday. As proof she gave us her card with a picture of the beautiful woman posing in a fur coat. When I turned the card over there was another picture of the woman in a different pose. Only she wasn't wearing the fur coat in this one, or anything else. Busy little entrepreneur she was.

Day 8.

Frost. The wings of the phenom were covered with lift killing frost and we couldn't take off until it was removed. Marcio had never had to deal with this situation before and was at a loss. He hadn't seen a lot of frost growing up and learning to fly in Brazil. We had two choices; call for an expensive de-ice truck to take care of the frost or wait for it to melt off. We checked and found out that the de-ice truck was unavailable and from the looks of things it could take as long as two or three hours to melt the frost off the wings. We didn't have that kind of time.

"Get your credit card out," I said.

"I already asked. They don't have a de-ice truck we can use."

"Not to pay for de-icing Poppy. Here, let me show you how we do it in Wisconsin."

With that I took a credit card out of my wallet and began carefully scraping the frost off the surface of the wing I was standing next to.

"You're joking right? This can't be a serious thing. It will take all day to get rid of the frost that way."

"Longer if you don't help. Just be careful you don't scratch the paint."

With a skeptical look Marcio began helping me and soon we each had a growing patch of clean wing in front of us. John helped by filming the process which really made things go no faster at all. The sun finally came out and helped a bit and after forty-five minutes we were back in the plane and on our way to Khabarovsk, Russia.

Passing through twelve thousand feet an alarm suddenly sounded.

"CABIN … CABIN … CABIN!" yelled Bitchin' Betty's mechanical voice over our headsets.

Both Marcio's and my ears started popping as the air pressure in the cockpit suddenly dropped.

"Put your mask on!" Marcio yelled as he leaned forward and started working on the pressurization controls.

I whipped my sunglasses and headset off, pulled the oxygen mask out of its holder and put it on. As soon as I had my headset back on Marcio told me to take the controls and stop the climb. I quickly grabbed the yoke, pushed the autopilot disconnect button and pushed down. As we topped out at sixteen thousand feet Russian ATC called and wanted to know why we had stopped climbing. Hesitant to admit to any kind of aircraft malfunction I told them to stand by and looked to Marcio for guidance. I knew that declaring an emergency in Russia would start a chain reaction of paperwork and government involvement that I would do anything to avoid.

"Tell them that we have a minor pressurization problem and will resume climbing shortly."

I passed on the message to ATC while hand flying the jet.

"Slow down!" Marcio said as our speed built up. I had leveled us off but hadn't reduced power right away.

"Slow down!"

My first power reduction wasn't enough to arrest our speed increase.

"And turn the autopilot on."

Before I could react, he reached over, dialed in the heading and altitude options, engaged the autopilot and pulled both throttles back to idle.

Fine.

I pouted for a moment as Marcio had literally grabbed the controls from me. Now I knew how Cory had felt. I put my hurt feelings aside and fended off two more calls from ATC while Marcio continued to try and get the pressurization system working properly. The controller was getting more and more impatient because an Airbus was inbound and if we didn't climb soon he was going to cancel our clearance.

Marcio finally gets the cabin pressure back up to normal by bumping it up manually. He told me that he thinks that … STALL! … STALL! … STALL! A robotic voice yells as the Phenom's nose dropped into a dive. I instantly grab the yoke but don't pull back immediately.

"*What the hell?!*"

Need information first. A quick glance at the speed tape on the HSI tells the story.

TOO SLOW!

Throttles full forward.

Keep the nose down for another second.

Speed climbing.

Start pulling out. Not too aggressively, don't want a secondary stall.

Speed building quickly, good, we've only lost two hundred feet.

Shit.

I immediately realized what happened. When Marcio took the controls away from me he'd brought the throttles back to idle because we were going too fast. But it had still been my job to monitor our speed because he'd told me to take the controls.

Crap, I'd just stalled a jet. I just stalled a jet … on TV.

Great.

"You got too slow," was all Marcio said.

I was surprised. Most Captains would've been screaming bloody murder the entire time. Which wouldn't have helped in the slightest. And anyway, I was doing enough yelling as myself for the both of us. I'd committed the cardinal sin of aviation. I'd allowed myself to get distracted. While I was supposed to be monitoring everything including our airspeed, I instead was watching Marcio fiddle with the pressurization controls. It was an easy trap to fall for, especially in a jet where the sound of the engines is always very low.

It was an ugly incident and I felt like crap. I tried not to beat myself up too much but the phrase "How could you be so stupid?" kept echoing in my mind.

Again, Drifty thought it was great TV.

An hour later another problem popped up.

Everything was calm and quiet as we cruised over the frozen Siberian landscape when I noticed a lot of moving around and swearing coming from the back of the plane. Suddenly John stuck his head up in between us in the cockpit.

"Have either of you seen the big blue bag?"

Marcio and I looked at each other.

"Nope."

"Not me."

"SHIT!! It's not back here! Is it maybe in the trunk?" Referring to the unpressurized baggage compartment in the tail of the jet. We usually only put our suitcases back there because it's unheated. We never put John's camera gear back there. When we reminded him of that he swore again. This wasn't good. Because the bag he was talking about was one that the two of us had been hauling around the world for the last four months. I didn't know exactly what was in it but I knew that it had a lot of important camera gear in it. Little did I know just how important it was.

John disappeared into the back once again and we could see him search the small cabin once again before coming back upfront.

"We need to go back!"

Marcio turned around and looked at our obviously distraught director.

"That's not possible. Even if we had the fuel you can't change a flight plan like that in Russia."

"But we have to! The cards are in that bag!"

"The cards? You mean THE cards?"

"Yes, the cards. All the cards!"

Oh shit. The cards John was talking about were the computer memory cards that had all the footage we had recorded on the trip so far. If those cards were lost the entire trip would be for nothing. I didn't even want to think about how much money Pixcom had spent so far but I was sure it was a big number. John was understandably upset but there was nothing we could do until we landed.

After we landed in Khabarovsk John hardly waited for us to shut down the engines before he was outside and opening the baggage door. By the time I got back there John had all the bags spread out on the ramp. The blue bag was not there. John was beside himself. He kept checking and rechecking the cabin and baggage compartment, hoping to find the missing bag.

I knew exactly what had happened. Every time we leave the plane for the night we take nine or ten bags to the hotel with us. When you constantly move that many bags in and out of taxis, shuttles, hotel rooms and lobbies it's inevitable that you're going to miss one sooner or later. When we'd waited for a bus to take us to the plane that morning we'd stacked all the bags against a long low concrete wall in front of the control tower. When we loaded the bus the blue bag must have somehow been missed.

The bag was gone, but maybe it could be found? While Marcio got the plane fueled John got on his phone and called the airport manager at Vladivostok hoping for a miracle. I didn't have much hope. Besides the cards, the bag contained a lot of expensive camera and computer equipment. Anyone who found it would probably keep it. Especially the Russians.

It turns out I was wrong. Unbelievably the airport had his bag! John almost collapsed with relief. Now he had to figure out how to get it. His first thought was for us to hop right back in the jet and retrieve it. Marcio nixed that idea right away. Flying a jet eight hours round trip would cost thousands of dollars in fuel and landing fees. Not to mention the time on the Phenom which rented out at over one thousand dollars an hour. John did some checking and was lucky enough to find a commercial flight to Vladivostok that evening that would get him back the next day. Thank God! Crisis averted.

Day 9.

Dangerous? What we were doing was dangerous, but it was unavoidable. It's not like we were going to walk to the airport. We were in a taxi on the way to the airport to meet John who had successfully retrieved his blue bag but I was pretty sure we were going to die on the way. As a ferry pilot I get to experience traffic and drivers all over the world. And if scary driving was an Olympic sport, the Russians would win the gold every year because it was obvious they were doping. On the way to the airport we saw wrecked vehicles lining the road everywhere, including one particularly gruesome accident where the cab of the truck was completely caved in with the driver's arm hanging out. Shortly after passing that little bit of morning fun a fighter jet came roaring by at treetop level. Marcio looked out the window.

"Look at that MiG!"

So of course we all did, including the driver who leaned his head up against the window for a better look. This made me extremely nervous because he was driving very fast and the road was full of crazy drivers weaving back and forth, cutting each other off. I yelled at the driver to watch the road as he turned back to us.

"Not MiG. Sukhoi."

Thanks Yuri. Now watch the damn road.

Our much relieved and embarrassed director came walking across the ramp with the handle of the wayward blue bag clutched firmly in his hand.

"Watcha got there Drifty? Souvenir from the gift shop?"

"Shut up Kerry."

"New makeup case?"

"Shut up Kerry."

I could've gone on and on but we were in a hurry to make our slot time. One thing I did insist on though was that we do a deliberate bag count every time we moved. As we had found out, it was easy to get distracted when John's trying to film, Marcio and I are trying to act and some random bellhop is loading the bags.

Our next stop was Petropavlovsk, Russia. At a distance of one thousand miles Petropavlovsk was right at the range limit for the Phenom. Not usually a big deal but our route would take us over a five hundred mile stretch of water known as the Sea of Okhotsk. No survival suits, no raft. I did have my rescue beacon which, if we went down, would mark the location of our demise quite nicely.

But once again we avoided rolling snake eyes and soon the Kamchatka peninsula came into view with the famous Koryaksky volcano smoking away in the distance. As we taxied up to the general aviation ramp, I noticed an adorable little blue and white Russian style church. I'd never seen a church located directly on the ramp before and we later found out that it was there to give worried family members someplace to pray when an aircraft goes missing.

which apparently is quite often due to the terrible weather in the region. The next thing I noticed was Natasha. Natasha was a beautiful dark-haired Siberian woman who was hired to assist us in Petropavlovsk. At least I think she was beautiful. She had a perpetual scowl on her face that made it difficult to tell.

Not smiling is a common trait in Russian women. Many of them are exceptionally beautiful but a smile rarely makes an appearance. And when they do smile it never quite seems to reach their eyes. I remember pointing this out to a Russian woman in Reykjavik once and her response was classic.

"Ach! You Americans! Always smiling, for no reason!"

"That's because we don't live in Siberia!" I replied, laughing.

She was not amused.

Natasha took us up to the weather office where an actual smiling young woman printed out the weather forecast for our next leg to Anadyr. Anadyr was located in far northeast Siberia and was our last stop in Russia before crossing the Bering Sea to Alaska.

The weather girl told us that the weather en-route to Anadyr was good but the forecast for the airport called for low clouds, very poor visibility and high winds. If the forecast was accurate, the cloud base would be right at the two hundred foot limit when we arrived. The trend only got worse after that. Much worse.

Both Marcio and I looked at the forecast and said, "Nope, not doing that."

It wasn't worth the risk because Anadyr was located way out in the middle of nowhere Siberia, hundreds of miles from the next nearest airport. It was one of those "Point of no return" routes that committed you to making a press on or turn back decision hundreds of miles from the destination. Once you crossed that line you wouldn't have enough fuel to return to your starting point and were committed to landing successfully at your destination or crashing. It was definitely not a situation you wanted to get into with a terrible forecast at the destination airport. It looked like we'd be spending the night in Petropavlovsk.

"There is one thing you should know. This time of year when the low clouds and fog move into this area from Central Siberia it can sometimes last for one month, or more. I'm not telling you what to do. It's just that I've seen this pattern many times and thought you should know."

Natasha, always a ray of sunshine.

That little bit of information made a big difference. It was one thing to spend a day or two relaxing in some small town in central Siberia, while you wait for the weather to improve. It would be another thing entirely if we were stuck in that little town for a month or more. We all had lives and families to get back to. I also had a dropzone to run, Marcio had to go back to work at Delta and John had another trip he needed to film. Plus, I didn't want to spend a month in Siberia! Of course if we went for it and got killed … well, that wouldn't be very productive either.

"Get-home-itis" has probably killed more pilots than all other factors combined. The desire to "get there" regardless of the conditions is something that pilots are cautioned about from the beginning of their flight training. I don't know how many times I've heard the saying "It's better to be on the ground wishing you're in the air than in the air wishing you were on the ground." Unfortunately, that attitude doesn't go along well with being a ferry pilot. A ferry pilot doesn't have the luxury of waiting on the ground for nice weather. His job is to get the plane to its destination as quickly and as cheaply as possible. That means you're expected to keep pushing on unless you think you will die in the process. And even then you're supposed to go take a look.

Marcio and I looked at the forecast, checked the distances to Anadyr and the only other airport in the area and did fuel calculations. No matter how we looked at it, the answer was the same. If we went for it, it would be close. The point of no return was almost five hundred miles from Anadyr and the only airport we could divert to was hundreds of miles west in the direction the weather was coming from and not much help.

Then, much to my surprise, Marcio told me to make the call. He said that flying jets had never put him in that situation before and he would defer to my experience.

So much for my vacation from hard decisions.

Fighting my own case of "get-there-itis," I suggested a compromise.

Let's take-off and head that way and we'll keep getting weather updates for Anadyr as we go. When we approach the point of no return we'll decide what to do then. If the weather looks good, we'll keep going. If it looks like shit, we'll turn back."

Marcio liked that idea so we scrambled to take-off as soon as we could. Drifty had been filming the entire briefing and decision making process and wanted to take a few minutes and interview each of us about how we felt about the situation. I nixed the idea, telling him that every minute we delayed meant a greater chance of us not making it. John persisted though, and I almost had to grab him by the belt and throw him in the plane to get us out of there.

Once we were in the air and moving things didn't look so bad. The skies were sunny and bright and the updates from Anadyr were good. It was starting to look like we'd been all worked up over nothing. The first report had a cloud ceiling of eight hundred feet and five miles visibility. The conditions were unchanged thirty minutes later. Then ATC called us and reported that the ceiling had dropped to six hundred fifty feet. Still not too bad, but the downward trend had started.

Decision time. The point of no return was fast approaching and we could stall no longer. The cloud base at Anadyr was holding at a little over six hundred feet which was acceptable but we still had two hours to go. I looked at the moving map on the instrument panel and pondered. The Phenom's navigation software had an amazing range feature built into it. A maximum range circle was constantly displayed that showed us how far we could fly based on our remaining fuel, power settings and winds aloft. It was perfect for our situation. As I looked, the edge of the range circle behind us moved a little closer to Petropavlovsk. As soon as Petropavlovsk was outside the circle we wouldn't have enough fuel to return.

"What do you think Poppy? Keep going or head back?"

"I don't know. It looks Okay. What do you think?"

"Well, if the trend continues we should be able to make it in. But if things get worse we could be in trouble." Marcio was silent, waiting for me to make a decision.

"Let's go for it. We still have Pevek airport as a possible alternate."

With the decision made things were less stressful in the cockpit. It's amazing how much better you feel once you've made up your mind and picked a course of action. Five minutes later the range circle passed over Petropavlovsk and we were committed. Twenty minutes after that, we were screwed.

"I called for an update. It was six hundred fifty feet, it's now three hundred ninety feet. It got pretty bad in twenty minutes."

"Twenty minutes, huh?" Marcio said, not liking the rapid change and trend.

Then ATC called with a weather update for Anadyr. (That's never good.)

"November 777 Bravo Foxtrot. Anadyr now overcast at ninety meters."

Both of us heard that and I did a quick conversion. "That's two hundred ninety feet."

"That's pretty low."

"And the trend is dropping fast."

"I'm thinking about going somewhere else. That's not going to work."

We had an alternate airport in our flight plan, so I called ATC and told them that we'd like to divert.

"November seven bravo foxtrot, Aerodrome uniform hotel mike papa is closed."

"That's just great. Just close our alternate airport. Nice."

I wasn't terribly surprised. Our alternate airport at Pevek was northwest of Anadyr and would be getting the bad weather sooner that Anadyr.

"What do you want to do, man? What do you think?"

"We don't have the option of turning around. I think we should go faster so we get there before it gets any worse. No sense flying slow and saving fuel now."

Marcio agreed. The longer it took us to get there the worse the conditions would be when we arrived. He bumped the power up to high cruise while the reports from Anadyr kept coming in.

Two hundred fifty feet and two miles visibility.

Two hundred feet and one mile visibility.

Two hundred feet and one half mile.

There it was, our legal minimums to shoot the approach and land at Anadyr and we were still forty-five minutes out. It would only get worse.

Marcio and I wanted to be left alone with our thoughts while we prepared for what was coming. John had different ideas. With the utmost confidence in his pilots (misplaced) he went about filming a TV show. He couldn't do real interviews with us but he did make us talk about the situation we were in. We gave him a few minutes of dialog but our hearts weren't in it. I hoped we looked calm and cool on camera while we casually talked about our possible impending doom.

I thought about what we might do differently if the cloud base was really low when we arrived. What if it was zero, zero? A totally blind landing? How would we handle that? The only thing I could think of was that maybe we should burn our fuel down to a minimum state before we landed. That way if we crashed in zero visibility conditions there would be less fuel for the fire. I hated the thought of being burned alive. Or dead for that matter.

Thirty minutes out, one hundred ninety feet and one quarter mile visibility. Below minimums.

We'd been flying over some very interesting terrain for the last hour but I had a hard time caring. Thick forests had given way a craggy mountain range and what looked like a dormant volcano. The first signs of the low cloud layer appeared and covered everything in its path leaving only a few peaks sticking up in the fading light.

In the descent now. One hundred fifty feet one quarter mile, mist.

"We'll have fuel for three, possibly four approaches when we get there."

"If we're in a good stabilized approach I'll continue to the runway no matter if we can see it or not. It will only get worse if we go around and try it again."

I agree with my Captain's plan and study the approach plate on my iPad.

"Anadyr Tower, Phenom seven bravo foxtrot, can you please request runway lights full bright. Lights full bright at the airport please."

"Aaaah, lights are inoperative."

Marcio and I looked at each other.

"Did he just say no lights?"

"No lights. Doesn't help much does it?"

"No … That's not good. We better make this first one count."

Wonderful, we were about to attempt a night landing in almost zero visibility conditions and the runway lights were out. Things just keep getting better and better.

"Seven bravo foxtrot, wind three zero zero, six meters per second."

I didn't know how to convert that to miles per hour but it sounded windy.

As we got close to the airport I saw a lone mountain top poking up through the sea of clouds below us. The fast moving clouds were flowing around the mountain, coming back together in a jumble of swirls and rents. I catch a glimpse of inky blackness beneath. Then it's behind us as we turn in and begin the approach. All light leaves us as soon as we enter the clouds. The instrument lights give off a warm glow as Marcio adjusts the autopilot while I keep track of our progress on my iPad.

I once read about an Air Force cargo plane that was forced to do a true zero-zero landing back in the nineteen fifties. The crew never saw the runway and landed using only the primitive navigation instruments of the time and flared using only the altimeter. I was thoroughly grateful for a good autopilot and the GPS system as we rode the Phenom to whatever awaited us at the end of our approach.

"When we hit five hundred feet I want you to call down our altitude."

"Roger."

Everything is all set now. The landing gear is down and locked, flaps are set, all instruments in the green. There's no point asking for a condition update, the die is cast. John hasn't said anything for a while. I briefly wonder what he's thinking?

"Five hundred."

"Four hundred." Marcio gently puts his hands on the yoke but leaves the autopilot engaged.

"Three hundred … Two hundred." Our legal minimums. Nothing outside. We should go to full power and execute a missed approach … We don't.

"One fifty." Nothing … Fuzzy white runway lights suddenly flash on in the mist! Someone's been working overtime! More lights appear as we drop another few feet.

"I see the runway," I say as I transition to the instruments in case Marcio can't see them when he looks up to land.

"Okay, yep, got it."

Marcio stabs off the autopilot and gently raises the nose of the Phenom. Then the white centerline appears in the hazy beam of our landing light.

"It looks like we're going to live today."

"I think so."

Marcio aligns the nose of the Phenom with the rudder, brings the throttles to idle and we touch down with a slight bump. We are down.

"The beer is going to taste soooo good tonight! Flaps coming to zero."

"This would have been a real bitch without any lights!"

"Was the issue ever in doubt? Maybe … just a little."

And just like that, it was over. No big deal. Taxiing in was challenging. The runway and taxiway lights were a collection of multi-colored orbs, appearing magically in front of us as Marcio tried to keep from hitting any. Sheets of heavy mist raced past the twin beams of our taxi lights like ghostly apparitions as the wind increased. I estimated the visibility at around two hundred feet, sometimes less. As we crept along, searching for the ramp, conditions altered between terrible and horrible.

After we finally found the ramp and parked Marcio shut the engines down. The silence was like a physical thing hanging over the cockpit like a heavy blanket. The contrast between the peace of success and the chaos of battle is always remarkable. Neither of us moved or said anything. Would have spoiled the moment. We're only allowed a few seconds of reflection before the indestructible, unflappable pilots were expected to reappear.

"Well, that was exciting."

Marcio chuckled, offered me a fist bump and levered his big frame out of his seat. To his credit Drifty was already out on the ramp filming as we climbed out of the phenom. All three of us had a beer and a half before we did the end of day interviews.

As we were finishing up, our handler came up and introduced himself. His name was Boris. Yes, his name was Boris and our last handler was Natasha. You can't make this stuff up. Boris was a big, barrel-chested man wearing a long heavy Soviet-style greatcoat and the classic Crazy Ivan fur hat perched on his chubby bald head. Boris was extremely friendly and eager to please. He also spoke almost no English which made him super helpful.

Boris took us into the terminal, and wow, what a terminal! Out at the end of the world I was expecting a dumpy run down shack. Instead, the Anadyr airport terminal was shiny, new and huge. It was also completely empty, without a soul around. Like someone bought a

brand new terminal and just plopped it down in the middle
of Siberia hoping someone would show up. I was
pleasantly surprised and went off to make sure their
restrooms were just as nice. They were spotless, but before
I sat down in one of the dozen brand new stalls I checked
for toilet paper. (I'm not new.) Empty. As was the next,
and the next after that. In fact not one of the in the men's or
women's rooms had as much as a single square of toilet
paper in it. The same for paper towels. A search of the
entire empty terminal turned up nothing but an old cleaning
rag behind the counter of an empty food stand. I cut the rag
into four squares with my Gerber multi tool and completed
my mission.

Boris took us to the hotel, which I hoped would be as
nice as the terminal. It was not. Our guide led through an
enclosed walkway into a squat, drab concrete building. It
was like stepping back in time. We went from a shiny new
terminal to a beat up, run down ghost of the old Soviet
Union. A threadbare carpet led down a narrow hallway
with dozens of identical lifeless doors lining each side like
prison cells. We were each shown to a room that was
probably worse than most American prison cells. The
windowless rooms housed a single sagging bed, a night
stand with a lamp and a wobbly wooden chair. Luxury at
its finest.

Oh well, at least it was dinner time and we were
starving. Boris understood our international charades and
led John and me to the airport store while Marcio went
back to the Phenom to fetch some toilet paper. The airport
store was a delight. Mostly empty shelves, illuminated by a
single flickering fluorescent light, produced a half-crushed

box of crackers, a few small sausages and a brick of colorless cheese. Three bottles of red drink rounded out our gourmet shopping experience as a large babushka woman took our money and offered no change.

John and I beat Marcio back to the room, so I got out my multi tool again and cut up the sausage and cheese for dinner. Only it wasn't cheese, it was butter. Great. I cut it up anyway and put it on a few crackers like it was cheese. When Marcio came back we presented him with the plate of "cheese" and crackers. Both John and I could hardly keep a straight face when our fine food loving Captain took his first bite. The look of disgust on his face was priceless.

Day 10.

Thirty-nine thousand feet over the Bering Sea. A dot on the windscreen grew at an alarming rate. I grabbed my camera and tried to get ready in time, but the 747 roared directly over us before I was ready. Having another jet fly directly over you is not unusual in the days of precise GPS tracking. It was pretty damn cool to see another jet screaming right at you with a seven hundred mile an hour closing speed.

Soon the coast of Alaska came into view. We were on our way to Anchorage, and due to the combination of a late start and burning through time zones it was already late afternoon. As we began our descent I could see Mt. McKinley off to our left glowing bright orange in the setting sun. Seeing that reminded me that I really need to climb that mountain someday.

It was my turn to land, and when I was set up on final I could see a high speed taxiway halfway down the runway that I thought I could make. It was a beautiful evening with the wind blowing right down the runway and I naturally planned on touching down on the very end of the runway in order to make the taxiway and save us from rolling all the way to the end and the long taxi back. Plus, I always take it as a personal challenge and point of pride to try and land as short as possible. As I set up and dropped below the normal glide slope that would take me to the landing zone one thousand feet past the end of the runway Marcio told me to pull up because I was coming in too low. I'd been expecting that so I told him that I was planning on landing short so we could make the first taxiway. He didn't care about making the taxiway and told me to aim for the touchdown zone instead.

"So I'm supposed to just waste the first thousand feet of runway."

"Yes. Professional jet pilots always aim for the touchdown zone. That gives them a large buffer in case they come up short."

"OK, but I'm not an idiot. I won't come up short. I'm good enough to touch down exactly where I'm shooting for."

This wasn't the first time Marcio and I had disagreed on how to fly the jet. The first thing we'd disagreed on was that he wanted me to turn on the autopilot as soon as we climbed through five hundred feet on take-off. No exceptions! I didn't want to do that though. I like flying, and I really liked flying the Phenom. To me, flying airplanes means hands on the controls, not monitoring the autopilot while it does all the fun stuff. But Marcio was the Captain, so I did what he told me and watched the high speed taxiway flash by as I landed where he told me. I could've made it easily.

Day 11.

We were on the downhill run to Las Vegas and all three of us are ready to be done with this trip. The whole adventure had been hard on us, both mentally and physically. We're getting a lucky break with the weather and have nothing but clear skies for the final push to Sin City. It had been Marcio's turn to land at a fuel stop outside of Seattle and that meant that it was my turn to fly, and more importantly, to land. It's a small thing but making the last landing makes it feel like it's my trip. Despite the fact that all my landings had been good, Marcio couldn't help but talk me through the landing that will be in front of the new owners.

"You're a little fast; no, I guess you're OK. Don't forget the yaw damper. Just a little low, that's better."

"Do you want to do the landing?"

"No. It's your turn. Keep going."

Well, shut up then. I get it though. I'm a terrible backseat pilot too. I grease the landing (it's my story) and taxi up to the ramp where a line of limousines and men in expensive suits are waiting. Marcio and I get out and each have a glass of champagne thrust into our hands. During the series of congratulations and well-done's, one of the owners complimented Marcio on his perfect landing. But Marcio set him straight on who was at the controls. That had to hurt.

Later that night Marcio, John and I walked out to the patio of the bar we were at to allow Marcio to smoke his cigar. We struck up a conversation with another cigar smoker and it turned out that he was an agent for two of the fishermen on *Deadliest Catch*. What luck! He was the exact man we needed to talk to about our hopefully up-coming fame and fortune.

We talked for a while about the financial realities of the type of TV show we were producing and possible salary negotiations for the upcoming season. It didn't sound like any of us were getting rich anytime soon but if we managed to stick around for a couple of seasons there was at least the chance of being famous enough for it to be annoying. I got the agent's phone number and promised to call him if we got a second season.

We then chatted about the show and all the peculiarities of filming something so unique. The agent had some good stories about the filming of *Deadliest Catch* and how dangerous crab fishing in Alaska was. When I heard that I thought about how many close calls I'd had ferry flying over the years and how lucky I was to still be alive.

"Fishing in Alaska might be dangerous, but it's got nothing on ferry flying," I said somberly, "and when you add in the extra challenges of filming it get doubly so."

John, Marcio and the agent looked at me with questioning eyes.

"Flying single engine planes around the world is difficult enough. The need to film things that aren't necessary, plus the pressure to make unrealistic schedules, just makes things more difficult. Then there's the added weight of two extra bodies and a ton of camera gear. Hell, most of the time we're overweight, and if we have any problems on takeoff or run into icing we're going to be in real trouble."

I hadn't really planned on talking about these things with Marcio and John in this setting but these things had been bothering me and I kind of just kept talking without thinking.

"Then there are the complicated air-to-air shoots that, while fun, are incredibly dangerous."

Then I went to the natural conclusion that had been bothering me for some time.

"As a matter of fact, I predict that someone is going to get killed on this show within the next couple of years."

Neither John or Marcio said anything. Even though this was John's third trip, he still hadn't been faced with any real crazy emergencies. If he kept flying with us, that would change. On the other hand, Marcio was an experienced ferry pilot, but he specialized in delivering jets. Not the same thing. And even though we'd been flying a jet on this trip, we'd still managed to get ourselves into one hell of a jam.

After a few minutes our conversation turned back to happier topics, but there was no denying my blunt statement had put a pall on the evening. I don't know about John and Marcio, but I sure hoped my prediction would be proved wrong.

ILLUSTRATIONS

Amazon Buzz Job

Air-to-Air Crew

Caribbean Hurricane

St. Barts

Kaieteur Falls

Cory, John and Kerry

Hula Girl at the Ranch

Trouble in Vladivostok

Marcio, Natasha and Kerry

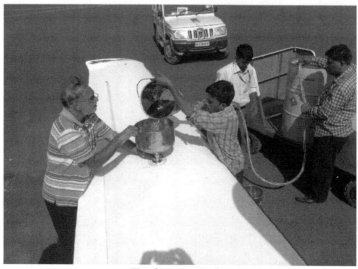

Fueling in India

Lightning Storm Over the Med

Ocean Survival Training

John Driftmier

Narsarsuaq

Air-to-Airs

Pilot Cams

Tight Fit

Claire McCauley

Kerry and Claire

Finish Line

David Gibbs, Tyson, Claire and Kerry

Pilots of Dangerous Flights

Making a Gasket

Close Match

Airborne Fuel Truck

Kerry and Lee

Vacuum Pumps In-Op

Engine Out

CAPTAIN STU

"Ladies and gentlemen, Singapore Airlines would like to welcome you to Singapore! We would like to remind you that illegal drugs are strictly forbidden, and the punishment for possession carries the death penalty. Thank you for choosing Singapore Airlines and have a wonderful stay."

Wow, nice friendly greeting. I think that the warning about drugs should come at the beginning of the flight though. You know, before some poor schmuck tries to smuggle something into the country in his underwear.

I dragged my tired rear end off the plane and over to baggage claim. The twenty-six hour flight from Minneapolis had really taken it out of me. It didn't matter though. I'd have plenty of time to sleep on the twenty minute drive to the airport where John and Stu were already waiting for me. I'd been told by Pixcom that we'd begin shooting as soon as I arrived, so I should make sure to get enough sleep on the flight in. *Sure, no problem, I'll make sure to do that sitting in coach.*

The taxi dropped me off in front of an old blue metal hangar with massive sliding doors on both ends. As I walked up to the hangar I noticed a peculiar pattern of holes in the entire door. When I looked closer I could see that they were bullet holes and damage from bomb fragments. The sharp jagged edges had been melted smooth with an acetylene torch and covered with many coats of paint making them oddly pleasing to run your hands over.

The last time anyone had attacked Singapore was when the Japanese had defeated the British and captured the island in 1942. I was standing there admiring the little slice of history when I heard my name called.

"Kerry! Get your lazy butt over here, buddy!"

I turned around and saw three of my best friends waiting for me. Stu, John and the camera, God I'd missed those guys! After hugs all around Stu introduced me to our latest challenge.

"Meet the SR-22 Cirrus!" Stu said with pride.

The Cirrus is a single-engine, four-place aircraft with fixed landing gear, state of the art avionics and one very unique feature, a parachute. The Cirrus Aircraft Company is famous for being the first company to commercially produce an airplane with its own parachute. I was very familiar with the system because a few of my skydiving friends helped design it and I helped test it. Back when the company was developing the parachute they would come out to my skydiving school in western Wisconsin to test their latest designs. First the engineers would strap the parachute to a large metal drum filled with lead. Then I would take it up in our de Havilland Beaver jump plane and toss it out to see how well it worked. Sometimes the parachute worked as designed and sometimes we had a big hole in the ground to fill in. The company moved their testing site to the desert after an incident when they dropped the test load on a winter's day that was a little too windy. The parachute worked just fine but after it hit the ground it stayed inflated and the wind blew it across two miles of Wisconsin farmland and one highway while I circled above in the Beaver waiting to see what it destroyed.

Stu was excited about our new toy. He had some experience in the Cirrus and thought it was a fantastic leap in aviation technology. Me? I was less enthusiastic. Where he saw a great modern airplane I saw another small plane with fixed landing gear (slow) and a single engine. (Dangerous over the ocean.) Don't get me wrong, I'm not an airplane snob. It's just that if given a choice I'll take bigger, faster and more engines, thank you very much. Especially when flying halfway around the world. Because that's where we were headed. We'd been hired to ferry the Cirrus back to the United States where it originally came from. Why was a Cirrus going from Singapore back to the US? I didn't know and I didn't care. Somebody got a good enough deal to cover the ferry cost I suppose. All I knew was we were going to have to fly it over a lot of water to get there, including the North Atlantic. I was crossing the North Atlantic with a single engine … again.

When I retired from ferry flying back in 1999, I'd thought I was done risking my life over that big stretch of cold water. But then Pixcom dragged me back into the game and here I was, about to do it again. Will I never learn? Too late to worry about it now. Time to go to work.

John told me the first thing we had to do was call Cory back at CB Aviation in Utah. His company had been contracted to ferry the Cirrus and he had some information for us. John had his camera rolling as we made the call.

"Hey Cory, it's Kerry. I heard you wanted to talk to me about something."

"Hi Kerry, yes. I've been thinking about your trip back to Ohio in the Cirrus. Let me ask you, have you ever flown a Cirrus before?"

"No, can't say that I have. But climbing into strange planes and flying them around the world is my specialty. I won't have any problems."

I know you won't. But Stu has flown the Cirrus before."

I didn't like where this was going.

"So?"

"So, I'd like Stu to be Captain on this trip."

"What? Stu has exactly one and a half ferry flights under his belt and no ocean crossings. I have almost one hundred!"

This conversation went back and forth but I wasn't as upset as I sounded. I knew Cory was doing this because Pixcom wanted to create drama and controversy. I knew that in reality I'd be the one making the hard calls and we'd all just be playing our parts in this little play. On the other hand this was still an incredibly difficult and dangerous trip. Hell, Singapore and Ohio were almost exactly on opposite sides of the planet from each other. This trip was as long as a trip could possibly be taken without purposely taking the long way around the world. Having Stu as Captain might be good TV, but it had the potential for a power struggle at a critical moment which could spell disaster.

From the TV producer's point of view it was a genius move.

"Let's make Kerry the control freak Stu's co-pilot!"

"Oh my God! Can you imagine? He'll hate that!"

"I know! Make sure John brings along extra memory cards because sparks are going to fly!"

When I told Stu he was going to be captain he was happy and actually thought it made sense.

"The Cirrus is a complicated system. It would probably take you a long time to figure it out."

"Are you kidding? I've been hopping in strange planes and figuring them out for twenty years. And I just got back from the Phenom trip. That jet had much more complicated systems than the Cirrus! Plus, being Captain is a lot more responsibility than just knowing which buttons to push to engage the autopilot."

As I was arguing with Stu, John was filming everything and eating it up. The decision to make Stu the Captain was already good TV!

The three days spent filming and getting ready for the trip were a lot of fun. The second night we were there was October 31st and even though Halloween is usually considered an American holiday, the people of Singapore seemed to be getting into the spirit of things. (Get it?) The downtown area was all lit up with orange and black lights and the bars were packed with costumed revelers.

As fun as Singapore was, I was restless to get the show on the road. This was my fourth trip in as many months and I was getting tired of being on the road and away from Cathy and the kids. Plus, it was deer hunting season back in Wisconsin and I wanted to get out into the woods.

First we had to get all the B-roll. Drifty filmed Stu and me doing all sorts of random pilot things. Walking towards the Cirrus, walking away from the Cirrus, sitting in the Cirrus, wishing we'd never seen the damn Cirrus.

We worked in that blue metal hangar for three days getting ready for the trip. I must have passed through those bullet-ridden doors a hundred times and each time my eyes and hands were drawn to the chaotic pattern of light shining through. There was just something pleasing about running my hand across the mini volcanoes in the metal. The big inch-thick metal doors were seemingly impregnable. But the Japanese 20 mm cannon shells had gone through them like butter. As I stood there running my hands over the shell holes I couldn't help but imagine the British airmen and mechanics scrambling for cover as the zeros bored in on their strafing runs. WWII still seemed like ancient history to me but there were still thousands of people in Singapore who remembered that attack.

I later found out later that the hangar was scheduled to be torn down to make way for a newer, more modern one. I wondered what would happen to the doors. It seemed a shame if they were melted for scrap. I fantasized about buying them and having them shipped back to Wisconsin. *I wonder if they'll fit in the back of the Cirrus?*

Northbound, twelve thousand feet over Thailand. So far Thailand is one of the most beautiful parts of the world I've flown over. A thick carpet of jungle stretches from coast to coast, covering mountains and valleys with an occasional black river slicing through. As we fly along, each pocket of standing water reflects sunlight like thousands of yellow jewels flashing on and off as the sun reflects from each in turn. Our first fuel stop is Phuket, and as we approach the city we drop down over the coast to shoot video of the famous Phi Phi islands. Dotting the sea off the coastline, the small islands look like dozens of tall Chinese junks floating on the water, giving the area an exotic feel.

After landing, we park where we are told and wait for someone to come get us. And wait … and wait. I'd thought it strange when ground control parked our little plane among the big commercial jets with no further instructions but we'd done what we were told. We couldn't wait forever so the three of us took off on our own, walking in between the jumbo jets, looking for an open door to the terminal. I was expecting armed guards to surround us at any moment. Three unescorted men wandering around the tarmac were sure to draw attention. We weren't even wearing those stupid fluorescent green safety vests.

After finding most doors locked we finally found one that was open which of course led straight into the security office. Our reception was less than friendly. The guys with guns wanted to know where in the hell we'd come from and peppered us with questions. I think they were mostly pissed that it was their job to prevent guys just like us from wandering around their supposedly secure airport. Things were getting a little heated when Drifty spotted a ukulele resting on top of a filing cabinet. Right in the middle of us getting yelled at John asked if he could see the instrument. Everyone was momentarily taken aback. Not knowing what else to do, one of the guards handed it to him. The room was silent for a moment then John began to play. It was a most surreal setting. One minute there was a room full of yelling, pointing and carrying on. The next we were all standing around listening to Drifty in concert. It was weird but it worked. The guards relaxed and started smiling. Pretty soon Drifty was talking music and ukuleles with the owner and Stu was getting directions to the MET office. I guess music really does tame the savage beast.

We ended the day in the city of Chiang Mia, Thailand, on the banks of the Ping River. After shutdown we shot end of the day interviews. Stu and I had a hard time coming up with anything more interesting to talk about than what happened to our director in Phuket. Even three beers couldn't top that story.

An evening in the Chiang Mia night market is a treasure trove of filming opportunities. First on the list is a Tuk Tuk taxi ride. Cheesy, maybe, Cliche, certainly, but you can't film pilots in Thailand without one. Then John followed us around as we wandered the market, looking at cheap trinkets, knives and swords and all manner of junk. One stall grabbed Stu's attention. It's filled with bats, butterflies and insects of all kinds, mounted on picture frames. A woman is cooking … giant water beetles? She's impressed by the camera and offers Stu a tasty six inch long green bug.

"Hundred bucks, Stu!"

"Pass!"

I don't think he'd put that thing in his mouth for five hundred bucks. We all had a good laugh. Then my leap before you look impulse kicked in and I took the beetle from the woman, put it in my mouth, bit down and pulled. The cooked bug guts squirted into my mouth like toothpaste from a toothpaste tube. I thought Stu was going to puke but John loved it. Good TV, baby!

John left us after that. He had enough footage and still had to do his nightly camera maintenance. That left us with just one more thing to do before we called it a night. I wanted a fake Rolex. For years I'd heard about pilots getting fake watches in Thailand and thought I'd get one for my brother as a gag Christmas present. They were not hard to find. It seemed every other vendor on night market street had a collection for sale.

Stu and I stopped at a booth and looked a few over. They were mostly crap. The bodies were cheap and light, the lenses thin and flat and the second hand ticked away like mad instead of moving smoothly, a sure sign of a fake. The vendor wanted thirty dollars each and I guessed they were worth at least half that. I decided not to waste my money and turned away. We didn't take two steps before a young man approached us and asked if we were looking for watches. I told him yes but weren't interested in the junk we'd seen. He agreed that the stuff on the street was crap. He said he had a store where we could get good quality watches.

He told us that it wasn't far, "Just around the corner, come see! Come see!"

We followed him, mostly out of curiosity. When he ducked into an alley with a sheet over it we began to get suspicious. Late night, back alley and Thailand were underlined danger words in the ferry pilot handbook. But the young man was so earnest and convincing I put my normal caution aside and followed him inside. Stu and I couldn't believe our eyes. Bright lights revealed a small room with literally hundreds of watches displayed side by side on the walls and counters. It was a watch collectors paradise, Breitling, TAG, Longines, and of course Rolex.

We got a quick lesson on fake watches. Our guide showed us a cheap fake Rolex like we'd seen on the street and one of what he called a replica. The difference was immediately apparent. The replica was heavy and solid, had ceramic bevels and high quality Seiko movements. He went on and on but he needn't have bothered. I was sold as soon as I held one in my hand. I picked a blue Rolex Submariner and Stu got an orange one. They were a lot more expensive than the cheap street ones but you get what you pay for. The next morning when I met Stu for breakfast I noticed he wasn't wearing his new watch. When I asked him about it he told me that he'd worn it in the shower that morning and it had immediately stopped working.

"It was supposed to be waterproof down to twelve thousand feet!"

"Maybe a real Rolex is waterproof but why would you test a fake one?"

Author's note: The blue fake Rolex is still keeping perfect time as of 2022!

The next day was another Pixcom field trip day. We were going to ride elephants! The only one really excited about it was John. When I heard the news, all I could picture was some agonizingly lame tourist trap filled with retired farmers from Iowa out for a big adventure riding sad, old beasts. Yes, I am an adventure snob. My motto is, if a grandmother can do it, I'm not interested. Now, before a bunch of gray hairs come after me with pitchforks, I do know some grandmothers that are badass skydivers, scuba divers and backcountry skiers, but they are the exception.

I tried to talk John out of it but he was committed. So off we went to go ride elephants. *Yay.* Soon after leaving the city my fears were confirmed. There, on the side of the road was a billboard saying that YOU TOO! Can, RIDE

AN ELEPHANT! And the picture was of a sad, old elephant with a big box on its back stuffed full with grandmothers. Not really, but close. I was even more depressed when I saw that.

Our driver took us out of the city and up into the hills as the green grassy plains gave way to thick jungle. We soon turned off the main highway onto a rutted dirt road that led up into the jungle. A faded and cracked sign read Bob and Vera's elephant rides. (Or the Thai equivalent.) This was looking promising.

After winding our way uphill we emerged from the jungle and found Bob and Vera's elephant sanctuary. It was perfect. The place was rundown but neat. There were two big elephants chained up on a hillside. And best of all there were no crowds of tourists around. Bob and Vera came out to meet us while two young men unchained the elephants and brought them up. Stu and I were each going to get our own elephant. That was more like it!

Without much delay we mounted up and took off down into the valley riding in small wooden boxes strapped to the backs of our elephants. It was nothing like I expected. It wasn't just a big slow pony ride along some well worn path. We immediately plunged into thick jungle and headed downhill at a frightening angle. I leaned back as far as I could to avoid falling over the front of the elephant. I'm not going to go so far as to say I was scared or terrified but I was concerned that the elephant might lose its footing and we'd all make it to the bottom of the hill faster than we'd planned. Can you jackknife an elephant?

We bottomed out in a narrow valley with a shallow, winding creek running peacefully through the middle.

Steep cliffs dripping with vines and overhanging trees completed the scene. My guide dismounted and led our elephant into the stream for a drink while Drifty tried to shoot video and take pictures of everything at once. When our elephant was done drinking our driver asked me if I wanted to drive! *Holy cow.*

"Yes, of course!"

I got out of the wooden seat and took position on the elephant's neck. It felt weird on my legs. I was wearing shorts and the elephant's skin had the texture of tree bark and had short stiff hairs that shot straight up and felt like wire bristles on my soft and delicate inner pilot thighs. The driver gave me the long metal hook that he used to suggest which way the elephant should go. It was simple, want to go left? Put the hook in the elephant's left ear and pull as hard as you can. It seemed cruel, but I suspect the elephant can hardly feel it through the tough skin. And I used the word "suggest" because even if you hook an ear and pull for all you're worth, if he doesn't want to go that way, he ain't going that way.

The driver pointed out the trail I should take to lead us out of the valley and I was on my own. Before I took off he offered me one last bit of advice.

"If you see a snake, hang on tight! They're afraid of snakes."

Great ... How am I supposed to see a snake from twenty feet in the air?

Then I was off. I have to say, that was pretty cool. The elephant was pretty responsive. Good thing, too, because I actually had to drive it. If I didn't tell it where to go it just stopped and stood there. It was amazing to be in control of that much power. It was like driving a massive tank that could smash through almost anything. I did get a little concerned at one point when the trail got very steep. I just couldn't see how those flat feet didn't slip and skid on the steep muddy trail. With nowhere else to go I urged Dumbo up the hill. When we got back to base camp Stu was already there waiting for me. He was pretty surprised when he saw me come riding in by myself. Later that night I logged thirty minutes of solo elephant time in my logbook.

"Myanmar Center, say again?"

The air traffic controller repeated himself in exactly the same, impossible-to-understand accent as his first transmission.

"Roger center, contact Bangladesh on one two six point three five."

I was mostly guessing on the frequency but I didn't receive a correction, so I must have guessed correctly. We'd left Chiang Mai that afternoon and were winging our way to Kolkata, India. The two days we'd spent in Thailand had seemed like a vacation. Now we were looking at eight hundred miles over Myanmar and Bangladesh before touching down in India. Drifty told us that we might have another field trip planned for Iceland but until then we'd actually be doing the job of ferry flying. We definitely had some work ahead of us. There were eighteen countries, four seas and a good chunk of the North Atlantic in between us and our next day off. In addition to an endless string of long flying days, we were entering a part of the world where the controllers can sometimes be difficult to understand. It's not a huge thing but it does add to the frustration level.

There are a lot of challenges a ferry pilot faces when flying small planes around the world. There are the obvious ones; bad weather, mechanical problems, fatigue, long legs and short fuel. Those are just the airborne challenges, the normal challenges. Then there are the things that you have to deal with on the ground that are unique to ferry flying. Navigating dozens of countries' customs, immigration, import and export tax plus the non-stop mountain of paperwork you get at each airport is exhausting.

One of the most difficult challenges can be trying to understand air traffic controllers with heavy accents. Probably the most common phrase I use when ferry flying is "Say again?" One thing that makes things harder sometimes is the practice of foreign controllers speaking to local pilots in their native language. It's not usually a big deal but it doesn't help my situational awareness. Like the time I was flying a Caravan across Bangladesh and into Myanmar and was handed off to a new controller on another frequency. When I made the switch I could hear the next controller speaking rapidly in his native tongue to a local pilot. When the pilot answered him in English I realized that the controller had been actually speaking English as well but I hadn't understood a single word he said. It was my turn to check in next and I was dreading the upcoming conversation.

It ended up being worse than I feared. I must have uttered the magic words "Say again" a dozen times. Confusion reigned, and in the end he gave me a turn to the south that made no sense at all. A few minutes later when a new controller came on the frequency he asked me where in the world I was going?

It was night by the time we made it into Kolkata. I'd been looking at the forecasts for the city for the last few days and each day they had called for low visibility due to haze and smoke. When we arrived over the city I understood why. Blanketing the city and the surrounding area was a thick layer of pollution mixed with humidity that reduced visibility to under two miles or less. It was depressing descending into the thick brown smog that night.

After landing we were met by our handler, who led us into the terminal and into the customs area. The air outside was so thick you could taste it and every street light had a yellow halo of smog glowing around it. Inside the building was just as bad. As we were sitting around waiting for our handler to get our customs papers and passports stamped, a man emerged from a back room with the biggest and longest mosquito fogger I'd ever seen. The thing must have been five feet long and had a burner chamber as big as a commercial chainsaw engine. I watched as the man walked out into the middle of the customs room, set the fogger down and fired it up. A gout of flame shot out of the end of the fogger before being replaced by a wisp of white smoke. As the man picked up the fogger and put the shoulder harness on Stu, John and I looked at each other, not believing what we were seeing.

"Is that guy going to turn that thing on inside?!" John asked.

Yes. Yes he was. The man adjusted the choke on the loud two stroke engine, gave the throttle a few test squeezes before going to full power and letting 'er rip! It was unbelievable. A thick cloud of noxious white smoke shot out of the end of the fogger that immediately filled the area we were in. We couldn't believe it. The fogger was obviously meant for use outside in a large area like a soccer field, or Kansas, not inside a closed building. The strangest thing was that nobody paid any attention to him at all. Everyone just went about their business like nothing was happening. The three of us pulled our shirts up over our noses and tried to breathe shallowly while the man walked around the room sweeping the fogger back and forth, making sure everyone got a good lung full. The only time I saw anybody even notice him was when he walked into the men's room with the fogger going full blast. He hadn't been in there long when two men burst through the door, choking and gasping for air. If this was the Indian's attitude about air quality inside it was no wonder why it was so bad outside.

The ride into town was worse. As soon as the taxi left the wide open spaces of the airport, buildings, traffic and people pressed in on the taxi from all sides. The absolute crush of humanity was both oppressive and amazing. There didn't seem to be one single square inch of space that wasn't occupied by a person, vehicle, building or pile of garbage. And the garbage was everywhere.

At one point we passed a mountain of garbage that was easily one hundred feet high. It looked to be as big as the Mandalay Bay hotel in Las Vegas and had dozens of children climbing all over it, picking through the trash, looking for something they could use. And if I thought the air at the airport was bad it was nothing compared to the air in the heart of the city. Millions of people, cars, trucks and cows all belching out noxious fumes made breathing a painful process. By the time we checked into the Hyatt, it felt like I'd just smoked a full pack of cigarettes. The air in the hotel must have been filtered somehow, so we hid out there until it was time to go back to the airport the next morning. No midnight stroll to check out the local flavor for us. The taxi ride had been enough.

When we got back to the Cirrus the next morning we found it coated with an oily film from the air pollution. It was also weirdly covered with hundreds of dead bugs that were stuck to the plane, trapped in the oily film. We hadn't been able to fuel the plane up the night before so we arranged for the fuel truck to come top us off before we left. OK, fuel truck might not accurately describe it. The first thing that showed up was an old car pulling a trailer with two fifty gallon drums of avgas.

Great, how in the heck are we going to get the fuel from the drums into the tanks? A bucket?

My question was answered when a tiny micro van pulled up with an air compressor in the back. Stu and I watched as the cluster of men attached an air line from the compressor to one of the fuel drums and a fuel line out and into the Cirrus. Then one of the men fired up the gas powered air compressor which smoked so badly you'd think it was coal powered. If you think using compressed air to force fuel out of a barrel and into the wing tanks is a fast process you'd be wrong, but eventually they managed to fill us up and cram the tangled mess of air hoses and assorted paraphernalia back into the van. The last thing one of the workers did was slam the rear hatch on the van which unfortunately hit one of the empty drums they'd stashed back there. The window shattered into a million pieces which were scattered all over the tarmac in front of the Cirrus. At least the clean up took forever. Not like we were in a hurry or anything.

Our goal for that day was Pakistan. We had only one fuel stop in central India planned and even with the late start we should be able to make Karachi easily. As we took off and climbed out of Kolkata I could almost feel the smog and pollution holding us back. The thick brown haze finally gave way to a clear blue sky as we headed west leaving the humid lowlands of eastern India behind.

The ramp in Nashik, India, was immense and modern looking. I assumed that being at such a large airport surely they'd have an avgas truck that could quickly fuel us and send us on our way. Wrong. If I thought the fueling in Kolkata was slow, I was about to see what slow really was, as a flatbed truck arrived with three fuel drums stacked precariously on the back.

Great, more fuel barrels. This ought to take forever.

At least they were following safety protocols: As the truck pulled up in front of the Cirrus I could see they had a skinny Indian kid in the back holding the barrels in place with his arms to keep them from tipping over.

As two men went about rolling one of the fuel barrels off the truck using an old wooden board as a ramp I looked around for the equipment they'd be using to pump the fuel into the plane. Did they have an air compressor? Electric fuel pump? Nope. As one of the men pried open the six inch opening in the top of the fuel barrel the other reached into the cab of the truck and emerged with a stainless steel bucket and funnel.

Are you shitting me?

Stu and I stared dumbfounded as the men carefully tipped the fuel drum over and began dribbling avgas into the three gallon bucket. Once it was full they poured the fuel into a funnel which they had stuck in the wing tank of the Cirrus. At least they had a bit of cheese cloth in the funnel to strain out any contaminants. I'd never seen such a Mickey Mouse operation before. I guess they didn't get a lot of small planes buzzing around in India.

While this long and painful process was going on I decided to try and get some footage of the process with a little hand held video camera. I say tried because for some reason the airport manager told John that we were forbidden from filming at this airport. Trying to be sneaky, I climbed into the cockpit and aimed the camera out the open door at the men pouring bucket after bucket of avgas into the wing tanks. As in Russia, I congratulated myself on being a master spy and getting the forbidden photos. Then I turned around and saw that I'd been caught red handed. One of the airport security guards who'd been monitoring the refueling process was standing on the other side of the plane watching me. *Busted.* He asked me to please come out of the plane and when I did he informed me that filming wasn't allowed and asked me to delete the footage. Of course being a master spy I cleverly deleted the clip from the internal storage that was showing on the screen but not the removable SD card. When I showed him that I'd deleted the clip he wasn't impressed.

"Thank you, now please delete it from the SD card as well."

Dang. Busted again.

I should have known better than to try and put one over on someone from India, the world's foremost provider of technical support.

The flight from Central India to Pakistan was a rough one, with massive thunderstorms bouncing us around like a ping pong ball. The monsoon season in India had been over for almost a month but I guess someone forgot to tell the thunder gods because giant mountains of white cumulus buildups popped up all along our route of flight. These storms were different than the ones we'd encountered in the Amazon. Down by the equator the storms were more embedded in a thick soup of humid gray haze that made it difficult to see exactly where they started and stopped. In India the area in between the storms was clear, giving each storm a unique and distinct boundary. They were easier to spot and avoid but I wouldn't want to try that at night. Luckily, by the time the sun went down we'd left the storms far behind.

When we finally made it to Pakistan, our handler took care of everything and got us out of the airport in record time. We were very happy about that because it had been a very long day and we were in a hurry to get to our hotel and relax. In retrospect, I think telling him that we were in a hurry might have been a mistake. Our handler escorted us out to the parking lot and introduced us to the driver who would take us to the hotel. The last thing he said to the driver was that we were in a hurry.

"No problem sir. I will get them to there quickly!" The driver answered with what I thought was a bit too much enthusiasm.

What followed was one of the most frightening car rides of my life. Our driver sped out of the parking lot and onto the main road like the devil himself was chasing us. If Karachi has any traffic laws, I'm sure our driver broke them all. He drove at breakneck speed, weaving in and out of traffic and pounding on his horn in the middle of each lane change. He basically drove like an expectant new father whose wife just went into labor for the first time. And every time he made what he thought was a particularly good dodge he would look back at us with a big toothy grin as if to say,

"What did you think of that move?"

While all this was going on he also managed to keep a running dialog of his entire life in Pakistan, how much he loved the US of A and a bunch of other stuff that I didn't hear because I was hanging on for dear life. Stu and I tried to get him to slow down a few times but every time we told him that he didn't have to drive that fast he told us,

"No problem sir, I am happy to get you to your hotel very quickly!"

He took the last turn into the hotel's driveway on two wheels and slid sideways to a stop at the front door. *Pretty close anyway.* We were all happy to make it there alive and I had to admit that he made good time!

It was late by the time Stu and I were all checked in so we just hit the buffet at the hotel restaurant and retired to our rooms to unwind with some crappy TV before bed.

The next morning it was more of the same. The same driver picked us up and raced us to the airport. I trusted him more this time because although he scared us, he got us there in one piece. He even managed to pick up his running monologue right where he'd left off the night before.

Once again the airport didn't have a fuel truck for anything but Jet A. This time they used a hand pump to refuel us from the now normal fifty-five gallon fuel drums. That method was a little faster than at the last two fuel stops we'd made but with a super dangerous twist. The fuel line running from the drum to the plane had a hole in the middle that leaked like crazy. This bothered the safety minded manager who wrapped a cloth rag around the leak that did absolutely nothing at all. Soon there was a good sized puddle of highly flammable avgas lying on the ground next to our plane. Did that bother the small crowd of men smoking cigarettes as they watched our plane get refueled? It did not. Stu and I took a few steps back, though.

Eventually everything was done and we were ready to go. Except for Stu, who was more than ready to go … Literally.

With a quick, "I'll be right back." Stu ran to find a restroom before we took off.

Which wasn't a bad idea because our flight to the United Arab Emirates was seven hundred miles and would take just under five hours. And it would also be a non-stop flight no matter what happened because it would be entirely over the Gulf of Oman in the Arabian Sea with nowhere to pull over if there was a problem. Okay, we would only be twenty to thirty miles off a coastline in case we had serious trouble. But it was the coastline we'd be paralleling belonged to The Islamic Republic of Iran, so the trouble would have to be quite serious before I diverted there. I mean, super bad, probably gonna die, holy cow we're on fire, serious.

Looking a little worse for wear, Stu finally made it back and we were off. This was our first long over water leg and I wasn't super happy about it because we didn't have any ocean survival gear onboard. No raft, no survival suits, not even any life jackets. Why? Because the FAA wanted to keep us safe that's why. Back when I started ferry flying I used to bring my own life raft and survival suit with me on the airlines when I went somewhere to pick up a plane. With that survival gear I could show up at a new plane and be ready to fly anywhere in the world. Then someone in the FAA's "Can't never be too safe" division decided that having life rafts in the baggage compartment was far too dangerous.

"My God! What if something happened and it inflated?!" Answer … Nothing. It's a six foot raft. It's not going to bring down a big jet.

Since then, the only way to have a raft with you on a ferry trip was to try to buy one at the location you picked up the plane. That option was usually not a good one because even if you could find a raft (not likely), it would be too expensive to buy just for one trip; because remember, once you get to your destination you will have to throw it away because you can't take it home on the airlines. I had looked for a raft while we were in Singapore but couldn't find anything suitable. Luckily there is one place you can rent a raft and survival suit for the North Atlantic crossing. Which meant if we survived the Gulf of Oman, the Persian Gulf, the Mediterranean Sea and the English Channel we'd get to a place where we could rent a raft for the final three ocean legs of the trip. Fingers crossed.

Flying a number of ocean legs without the proper, or any, survival gear is one of those situations where once you decide that you are going to do something dangerous it is best not to think about it anymore. Just pretend that you're on a normal flight over central United States and not over seven hundred miles of water where the only country in the vicinity wouldn't send out a rescue ship even if they could. That's not to say I don't do everything I can do to increase my odds of survival, it's just that it doesn't do you any good to sweat it.

And anyway, sweating it was Stu's job on this leg. About ten minutes after take off I noticed that Stu was fidgeting more than normal. He just couldn't seem to sit still.

"What's up with you today?"

"Nothing. I don't feel so hot. I went to the restroom just before we left and I'm still feeling like hell."

"Bummer."

Bummer indeed. I can't think of anything worse than being sick on an ocean leg of a ferry flight because there's nowhere to go … literally. We'd just started, maybe it would be best to abort.

"You want to turn back?"

"No, I can make it."

"You sure? We've got a long flight ahead of us."

"Keep going."

I didn't like his answer. If he was just being stubborn and the worst should happen, I'd be stuck six inches from him for hours. That would not be fun. As the hours went by Stu got worse and worse.

"Which end are you worried most about?"

"Both," Stu answered through gritted teeth.

"It's a good thing I got you that Buns of Steel workout video for Christmas, huh?"

"You asshole! Don't make me laugh!"

That seemed like good advice. I shut up.

Stu didn't say anything or even open his eyes the entire last hour of the flight. His concentration was that of a Buddhist Monk and for that I was forever grateful. When we got close to Fujairah I asked for no delay in landing and taxi to parking. I thought they might press me for details but I think they figured it out because they gave me what I asked for.

How fast can I land a Cirrus and get to the ramp? Pretty damn fast when my buddy's clench is starting to slip. I landed hot, got on the brakes and made the first turnoff. I didn't taxi quite fast enough to get airborne on the way in but it was close. I had the plane shut down and was stepping off the wing before the Cirrus came to a complete stop. I sprinted into the FBO building, located the nearest restroom then ran out to guide Stu in for his own landing. The noises that came out of there didn't sound human.

Citation:

"Stu Sprung is hereby awarded the Golden Clench Award with 'V' for Valor.

For conspicuous gallantry and intrepidity at risk of his colon above and beyond the call of duty on 11 November 2011 over the Gulf of Oman near the Iranian border. While on an international ferry flight Captain Sprung was struck down by a Pakistani biological weapon in the form of a dinner buffet rendering him nearly immobile and in great distress. In obvious pain and discomfort Captain Sprung elected to continue the flight and complete his mission. For 5.3 hours he battled pressure to surrender from both ends but remained closed and in control until being successfully relieved and evacuated upon landing in the United Arab Emirates. Captain Sprung's brilliant initiative, great personal valor and self-sacrificing efforts in the face of almost certain constipation reflect the highest credit upon himself and the United States Ferry Force."

After what seemed like an eternity Stu finally managed to drag himself out of the restroom; and boy did he look rough. It was like he'd been holding himself together in-flight as best he could and once we landed he let go and deflated like a balloon. John and I took him to the hotel and left him in his room to recuperate while we went out to shoot some video of Fujairah.

We spent two days waiting for Stu to feel better but the best he could manage was "less sick". I don't know what he ate that had such an effect on him but I know I dodged a bullet because we both ate at the same hotel buffet in Karachi.

Avoiding getting sick is an important skill for a ferry pilot. When I first started flying for Orient Air the owner Pete Demos, gave me the classic advice to not drink the water.

"Always drink bottled water McCauley! I can't afford to have you stuck in some hotel puking your guts out because you used a drinking fountain."

He told me about one of his pilots who got sick almost every time he went on a trip overseas. Pete told him to drink bottled water ... he got sick. Pete told him to stop using tap water to brush his teeth ... he got sick. Pete's final bit of advice was to stop getting ice in his drinks ... that seemed to do the trick. Or possibly the pilot finally built up an immunity to whatever was making him sick.

Being one hundred percent safe on the road is impossible. Sometimes you get sick because the only food available comes from questionable sources. Or you can get sick overseas even if you're careful and eat only at reputable establishments, like the hotel food that made Stu sick. Sometimes though, you're offered food or drink from a client that looks disgusting but you take it because it would be rude to refuse. Like the warm milk mixed with Sprite I was offered in Pakistan years ago. It sounded disgusting and I didn't want to drink it but it was offered to me by a wealthy businessman that I didn't want to offend so I accepted. It was actually delicious.

Stu claimed he was fit to fly by early afternoon the next day but I had my doubts. He still looked like hell and I hoped he wasn't just being a "man" and trying not to let the team down. Our first task was to fly over Dubai and get some footage. We flew past the Burj Khalifa tower which at 2,722 feet is the tallest building in the world, followed by the iconic palms formations. One thing that struck me was how dusty everything looked, even from the plane. I guess even one of the richest countries in the world couldn't keep the desert wind from blowing sand all over the place.

After Dubai we headed north into the Persian Gulf. It was fascinating flying over that famous part of the world. Look to your left and see Saudi Arabia, look right, Iran. As the sun went down over the desert the lights of the oil platforms and ships started popping up all along the narrow gulf and it was full dark when the lighted jewel of Kuwait City came into view. It's always amazing to fly into Kuwait City. Unlike most big cities, Kuwait City isn't surrounded by miles and miles of lighted suburbs. The city itself shines alone in the unlit desert like a candle in the darkness.

After landing we had a choice to make. Call it for the night or push on to our next stop in Jordan. Stopping for the night was tempting. It was already getting late and I wouldn't mind spending the night in an expensive Kuwait hotel. Let's face it, they're all expensive. John, on the other hand, was worried that Stu being sick had put us behind schedule and we needed to keep going if we were going to make some appointment he had for us in Iceland. That attitude and his push to keep going worried me. Deadlines on a ferry trip encourage pilots to make stupid decisions based on a time line.

A ferry pilot's job is to deliver the plane in the most cost effective way possible, i.e., cheapest. That means going in weather you'd rather not fly in and flying just one more leg when you'd rather call it a day. The pressure to save money and put miles behind you each day is significant enough. Add a deadline to your decision making process and you're just asking for trouble.

John telling us that we were behind schedule was exactly the kind of pressure to fly that I'm talking about.

"I know you're tired and Stu's sick but maybe we should fly all night? What do you say?"

Sure ... fine ... whatever. You're the boss.

At least we had two pilots, so if one of us got tired he could sleep while the other one flew. Plus, it would be nighttime over the desert. The weather's always good over the desert at night ... Right?

Looking at the forecast, I wasn't at all surprised that they were calling for thunderstorms all along the Saudi Arabian border. Because of course they were. And what was on the other side of that border? Iraq, that's what. So to recap: sick co-pilot, tired, night, thunderstorms, Iraq. Got it. Let's go flying.

The first hour of the flight to Jordan went smoothly. Stu and I watched movies and listened to music while Drifty waited in the back, fiddling with his camera like a big game hunter waiting patiently for something to walk down the trail. So far it was a peaceful night and the radios were quiet. It was literally the calm before the storm. That changed with a dim flash far out front of us. I looked up from the map on my iPad and frowned. There was nothing on the Cirrus's lightning strike finder yet but what are you going to believe, the screen in the instrument panel or your own lying eyes? A second flash removed all doubt ... then another … and another. I imagined it was what a nighttime artillery barrage might look like, the horizon lighting up as hundreds of cannons blazed away in the dark. Time to put our toys away and go to work. As we got closer we were able to pick out individual storms that marched across the desert like Chinese lanterns. It was intimidating and soon we could see lightning bolts arcing across the sky and down to the desert floor. Both Stu and I found it ironic that we would soon be battling thunderstorms in the desert.

The one thing we had going for us was the Cirrus's navigational display. It was a state of the art unit that among other things, displayed lightning strikes on the moving map. This made dodging individual storm cells much easier. It wasn't actual radar but it was the next best thing. When we hit the wall of storms I pointed Stu at the biggest gap in the line. The space between those first two cells was bigger than we thought. There seemed to be miles and miles of room and it was tempting to be lulled into a false sense of security. Just beyond there was another, bigger storm to dodge. This one took us miles off course and uncomfortably close to the Iraqi border. I was a little worried about our position. If for some reason we had to dodge north again we might be forced into potentially hostile airspace. One more storm, one more deviation north. *Getting awfully close to Iraq.* I had Stu hug the storm on our left but I still think our right wingtip scraped Iraqi airspace. No nasty call from the US Air Force though so they apparently didn't consider us much of a threat. Pushed up against the border we were unable to dodge the next cell and heavy rain pelted the Cirrus for what seemed like forever while the clouds around us flashed constantly.

It was a little rough but not bad enough to request an escape into Iraqi airspace.

Then, as suddenly as they appeared, the storms were gone and we flew into an unbelievably clear and starry sky. With the excitement for the night over, Stu went back to the movie he was watching. John turned the cameras off and I turned my music up. Still two hours to fly that night.

"November one five eight papa golf. Request denied. Please remain outside Israeli airspace."

"Roger, thank you. Well … crap … keep going south for now I guess."

Stu didn't answer, but the look of disgust on his face said it all. We'd left Jordan behind and were on our way to Crete with a fuel stop in Egypt but were being forced to take the scenic route. If you draw a straight line from Jordan to Crete you'll see it crosses a tiny little country called Israel. And seeing that we're in one of those airplane things, it only makes sense to travel in as straight a line as possible. It's faster that way you know. The only problem is that Israel is kind of picky about who they let fly over their little slice of heaven. And if you can't fly over their airspace the only other option you have is to fly around it. Definitely not how a crow would do it. Going around Israel isn't the end of the world but it is 250 miles farther and requires an additional fuel stop. All that means more time and money wasted. Two things that make my eye twitch.

I've tried to get overflight permission on past trips but was never able to pull it off. This time, however, I thought I had an ace in the hole.

When Stu and I had been getting the Cirrus ready back in Singapore we'd met two gentlemen who just happened to be from Israel. Not only that, they were from the Israeli version of the FAA. When I heard that I asked them if they could help us get permission to fly over their country.

"No problem. Just send me an email two days before you get there and I'll take care of it."

That sounded great and as instructed I sent them an email with our names, passport numbers and aircraft registration. What followed was two days of promises that turned into "Sorry, I tried." That meant instead of flying directly west from Jordan to Crete, we'd have to first fly south all the way to the southern tip of Israel, then turn around and fly back north. The detour turns an easy 660 mile direct flight into a two leg 900 mile, all-day slog.

After take off I asked ATC for permission to cross Israeli airspace but was denied. I asked again once we were south of Jerusalem where the countryside is nothing but empty hills and desert. Again … no. I asked one last time when the sliver of land we were flying around was only five miles wide. Nope. That was frustrating. The eastern and western borders of Israel meet at the Gulf of Aqaba at such an acute angle that I could literally look across our right wingtip and see our future selves flying back north once we'd flown around the tip. The closer we got to the turnaround point the more frustrated I became.

When the two borders were just one mile apart I was sorely tempted to just hang a sharp right and cut the corner. We'd be across and into Egyptian airspace in less than thirty seconds. There was no way the Israelis could stop us before we were safely across. Unless they had a hidden anti aircraft missile site down there I couldn't see. Which was probably more likely than not, now that I think about it. But even if they couldn't stop us they would know we did it. And they would know who did it too because we'd been asking for permission to cross their airspace for two days. Heck, they even had our passport numbers! So no, there was no reason to get on the Mossad's "Don't like, probably a terrorists" list. I would probably be back that way some day.

We made a quick fuel stop in Port Said, Egypt and were back in the air on our way to Crete in record time. I was thinking it would be an easy five hundred mile leg. We'd be chasing the setting sun across the sparkling waters of the Mediterranean and would arrive just before dark. I was looking forward to a nice peaceful flight followed by dinner in one of my favorite cities in the world. And no … we still didn't have a raft, life jackets, or common sense. We did have an ample supply of denial though.

Yep, it was going to be a nice flight, once we got that pesky MiG off our tail.

Another nice feature that came standard on the Cirrus was a traffic alert system that displayed nearby aircraft on the moving map display. Shortly after leaving Port Said I noticed an unidentified aircraft showing up on the screen. It was close behind us and closing. I pointed this out to Stu and John because it was much closer than another plane would normally be. MUCH closer. Also, we were on an IFR flight plan so there was no way ATC would have another aircraft that close to us. We watched as the target got closer and closer until it finally stopped so close to us that our symbols merged on the screen.

"It's an Egyptian fighter jet coming to check on us. It has to be," I said.

"You're probably right. What should we do?"

Well, if you're filming a TV show about ferry flying and you get intercepted by an Egyptian fighter you get footage of it, is what you do!

I told Drifty to get his video camera ready while I got my 35mm camera ready as well.

"OK Stu, he's on your side I think. Look back and see if you can spot him."

Stu turned in his seat and pressed the side of his head up against the window and tried to look behind us.

"Nope, can't see anything."

"OK. So Drifty, I want you to get the camera ready on the left side window. Then Stu, I want you to take the autopilot off and make a left turn. If he's back there we should take him by surprise and Drifty should be able to get a shot of him before he can react."

While John got ready in the back Stu looked doubtful.

"There's no way I'm going to do that."

"What! Why not?"

"We don't know what he'll do."

"Look, he's not going to shoot us down. We're a small single engine civilian aircraft on an IFR flight plan."

"Still not doing it."

I was beside myself. I tried every argument I could think of but Stu wouldn't budge. Pretty soon the blip on the screen moved off and I still couldn't get Stu to bank left and take a look at him. I guess I'll never know what it was so in my book that means it's classified as a UFO.

The westbound flight to Crete was one of those flights where nothing seemed to happen. We chased the setting sun across the sky and it hung there, balanced on the horizon, refusing to go down. There wasn't a cloud in the sky or a distant shoreline to mark our passing. Stu and John were silently sleeping and the radio was gratefully silent as if the controllers were embarrassed to disturb my state of suspended animation. Wearing my Bose A20 noise canceling headset makes flying a completely different experience. They filter out almost one hundred percent of the engine noise and when I Bluetooth in music the sound quality is unparalleled. Gone are the days when I used to cram hard plastic earbuds inside those clunky David Clark headsets. Having an unlimited supply of music was a game changer as well. I sure didn't miss having to listen to the same few tape cassettes I'd bring along on ferry trips in the 1990's. Not having to bring along a suitcase full of AA batteries was nice too.

It was such a beautiful evening that I was a little sad when the island of Crete finally rose out of the water and blocked the setting sun.

Stu was sick again. Or should I say still? The rest day in Fujairah had gotten him past the point of imminent eruption but he was still completely wiped out. He needed another day of rest.

Oh no! Please don't make me spend a day off in Crete! I'm not sure I can stand it!

Of course, ever the slave driver, John had to find something productive to do. We started out having him film me walking around the city's ancient waterfront looking at stuff. I enjoyed it because I love history and would happily spend all day looking at old buildings or museums. John wasn't happy, though. He put his camera down in frustration, knowing he was shooting boring footage that would probably never make it on the show. Then he had an idea.

"Can you ride a motorcycle?"

"Of course."

Sometimes Drifty has good ideas. We found a place to rent both a motorcycle and a car then spent the rest of the day racing around Crete with me on the bike and John following in the car. I have to say it was one of the more enjoyable days I'd had in a really long time. We went up into the hills and looked for interesting places to film, and there were plenty. Steep cliffs overlooking the Mediterranean and deep valleys with narrow switchback roads gave John lots of opportunities for filming. My favorite stop was when we found a tiny village nestled back in the hills. John and I stepped into the local tavern for … research, and met some truly wonderful people. Having a cameraman follow you around is an amazing ice breaker for meeting people. People who might have been standoffish to strangers would suddenly and open up the second they saw the camera. It was a great way to get to know the locals and be invited to all sorts of places and events that a normal tourist would never experience. Sometimes we would just point the camera at people without turning it on. It had the same effect. I hoped Stu continued to get sick in these wonderful locations.

Stu felt better the next day so it was back to the coal mines. The mission for the day was to try and make it to Cannes, France, with a fuel stop in Italy. I wanted to get an early start so we'd have time to grab some real Italian food for lunch.

The first leg was easy. Now that he was feeling better Stu was back to his happy old self. John and I were also very rested having had the last few days off had been a nice break. We were all rested, and full of energy. Let's go film a TV show! Oh, and continue to fly a small single engine plane over the Mediterranean without a raft, but we weren't talking about that.

We got good fuel in Italy but the food left a lot to be desired. I tried to talk John into having Pixcom spring for a ride into town for a gourmet meal but Dad said no.

"Get back in the plane dammit!"

While Stu took care of the fuel and landing bill I went and checked the weather, what I found wasn't good. The forecast was calling for thunderstorms and strong winds in the western Mediterranean for late afternoon and evening. What a perfect excuse to spend the night in Italy! No one could possibly question my decision if I thought that trying to battle our way through a line of thunderstorms at night was a bad idea. But I didn't want to do that. I mean, I did want to call it a day and go into town for a great Italian dinner and some sightseeing. But that wasn't me. I was a fighter. I saw those conditions and thought, "Bring it on!" I know, I know, there's definitely something wrong with me. I think we've already established that.

It wasn't my call though. I gave both Stu and John the facts and told them my thoughts. One last chance. I could tell them that I thought we'd probably die if we took off and that would be it for the day. If I did that we could be in town sipping a nice glass of wine within the hour. I didn't do that, though. I gave them the straight dope and told them we had a better than fifty-fifty chance of survival!

They both said, "Go for it."

The slow pace of the trip so far outweighed any sense of caution. They just wanted to go! Be careful what you wish for.

The clouds started soon after takeoff and they were magnificent. Towering cumulonimbus clouds formed on either side of us, glowing orange and gold in the afternoon sun. The massive walls that pressed in on both sides were intimidating but the way forward stayed open. We had to make a few moves to steer clear of the golden mountains and it seemed like we kept getting lucky again and again. But for how long? Was it a trap? As we flew on, the clouds continued to grow and I began to get concerned. We were heading northwest, fifty miles off the coast of Italy, heading for France, and most of the buildups were off to our right, cutting off any easy escape if we needed it. We did have Corsica off our left wing but I had no idea what kind of airports we might find shelter in.

Then three things happened in quick succession. The first was that it got very dark in the blink of an eye. One minute we were sailing between the golden ramparts and the next it was total darkness. Unable to see and avoid the clouds anymore Stu and I brought our heads inside the cockpit and went on instruments. Then we got a kick in the butt by a seventy knot tailwind! Now there's nothing I like better than a good strong tailwind. But seventy knots was the strongest wind I'd ever experienced. We were making good time but where did that power come from? Something was driving those winds, and I was afraid we were about to find out.

I stared intently at the nav screen, waiting for what I knew must come … there. A small x appeared on the screen. Then another … and another … lightning. I wasn't surprised. The forecast called for thunderstorms and they're rarely wrong when it comes to bad weather. As I watched more and more strikes started popping up ahead of us. Like the buildups we flew through earlier, the lightning seemed to be concentrated on either side of our course, leaving an open gap for us to sneak through … for now. It really was starting to look like a trap.

I zoomed the map out on my iPad and studied the situation. We were flying northwest in the open gap between the Italian coast and the islands of Corsica and Sardinia. As I looked at the map I noticed that the gap was shaped like a giant funnel, three hundred miles apart at its base narrowing to less than fifty at the other end. Now I knew where the wind was coming from and it explained the storm pattern as well. The storms were over and off the Italian coastline on our right and the islands on our left. And we were heading right for the narrow point of the funnel. Sure looked like a trap to me. Should we turn back before it is too late?

Then it got worse. The line of lightning strikes on both sides of our course suddenly exploded! Dozens upon dozens of strikes blossomed into a solid wall of x's on the Italian side. The Corsica side had fewer strikes but was anything but clear. Too many planes had been lost on a night like this. We were running out of room and I needed to make a decision now, not an hour from now.

In aviation, the future must be planned far in advance. The areas around the airports of the world were littered with the bones of aircraft and nine times out of ten it was the pilot who was at fault, not the elements. All too often the Captain had failed to plan ahead and found himself tired, low on fuel, surrounded by bad weather and running out of options. A major cell blocks the way to the airport, causing the pilot to divert. Then heavy rain and hail pound the aircraft as the pilot tries desperately to fight his way to his alternate airport only to find it socked in as well. Then, with the needles of the fuel gauges bouncing on empty he has no other choice but to attempt a landing in the middle of a thunderstorm which often results in a crumpled mass of aluminum and steel raining down on the dark countryside. Or a tired flight crew pushes a bad situation because they just want to get home. They risk a landing in conditions that they would never dream of attempting in normal circumstances but the lure of a warm bed tips the scales.

What to do? We couldn't go left or right. The storms on either side prevented that. We could turn around but I didn't think we had the fuel to fight the strong headwinds and make it back to the airport we took off from. Plus, I had no idea what the weather was doing two hundred miles behind us. The sky along our course was still tantalizingly clear of strikes but what if the French coastline was blocked by storms as well? We'd be in the bag for sure then. I had a brief thought of running out of fuel while we waited for storms to leave Cannes. No big deal, we could just pull the parachute. I'm sure floating down under the parachute in the middle of a thunderstorm, at night, over the Mediterranean would be a lot of fun. It would be good TV though.

The way ahead was still clear. *Go for it.* I hadn't included Stu in my decision making process. It wasn't that I didn't trust his input, it was just that I'd been in situations like this many times before and he hadn't. I was too busy thinking over the options to explain things to him and didn't need the distraction. I was too busy doing, no time for teaching. If I came to the decision to bail, and turn around I'd fill him in on my thought process at that point. For the time being my silence was my decision.

The blank area in between the two storm walls filled in with more lightning strikes than I'd ever seen before. As Stu and I stared at the screen little x's began popping up all around us at an alarming rate. The clouds on either side of us lit up and we started getting bounced around while moderate rain pelted the little Cirrus. Then we were through. We left the flashing storms behind and the rain slackened as we left the funnel and approached the French coastline. Once again we'd been lucky. The screen on the instrument panel showed more lightning strikes further inland but for now the airport looked clear.

There's one thing about a seventy knot tailwind, things happen in a hurry. It seemed like we'd just left the lightning storm before it was time to start the approach into Cannes. We were lucky in that the airport was right on the water and the wind, even though a strong crosswind, was favoring a landing from the beach side. The cloud base was reported to be at six hundred feet so it should be a piece of cake. Stu pulled up the approach on the Nav screen and the localizer course appeared. It should be an easy intercept. Our current heading was only forty-five degrees off the final approach course. Stu had the autopilot all set up to capture the localizer and bring us in but a forty-five degree intercept angle was far too much for the autopilot to handle. Especially with a smoking tailwind like we had. What you should normally do would be to revert to manual heading control and start making the turn early to make the autopilot's intercept easier. Except Stu wasn't doing that. I told him that he should start the turn early but he said that he'd let the autopilot capture the final approach course on its own before and it had worked just fine.

"With that intercept angle and tailwind you're going to blow right through the localizer like it wasn't even there."

"Nope, you watch. It will make the turn and bring us right in. This is what the autopilot was designed to do."

I knew he was wrong but we had lots of gas and there's only one way to learn this lesson. As we approached the localizer course Stu sat there with his hands on his lap and a smug look on his face that look got even bigger as the cirrus started to make the turn to intercept the localizer all on its own. The smug look quickly shifted from Stu's face to mine as we blew through the localizer course like a Greyhound on a linoleum floor and just kept going.

"Kick off the autopilot and make the turn yourself," I said as the wind pushed us further and further down wind and away from the final approach course.

"No, the autopilot will bring us back."

The autopilot struggled valiantly, but was unable to overcome the strong winds pushing us in the wrong direction. Then Cannes control called us and asked if we knew we were way off course and would we mind pointing our airplane, you know, in the direction of the airport? I told them we'd missed the turn and were on our way back to the final approach course. They seemed upset and impatient but allowed us to continue and report when we'd gotten ourselves re-established on course.

Stu finally agreed to turn the autopilot off and hand fly the plane. It was an ugly approach. Stu's instrument scan was rusty and it showed because he was all over the place and behind the airplane. In his defense the conditions were as bad as it gets, with strong turbulence and heavy winds pushing the little Cirrus all over the place. Then, just as we had intercepted the approach course and were breaking out of the clouds, the control tower told us to break off the approach and climb. They'd had enough. Our approach had been too unstable and they were going to take us out over the water and have us try it again. I didn't say anything as Stu followed their directions and made the turn outbound. Next would come a turn to a base leg, followed by a heading that would allow us to intercept the final approach course again.

Stu was still hand flying and had finally smoothed things out a bit.

"November one five eight papa golf, turn right, 240."

"Right 240, eight papa golf."

Stu took a moment to begin the turn, then banked us hard right. I watched as the artificial horizon showed our bank angle go past thirty degrees … forty-five degrees … sixty.

"Hey! Easy! You don't need to turn that steep!" … Seventy degrees.

A plane in a steep bank will not hold altitude unless the pilot pulls back on the yoke to compensate for the loss of lift or the airplane will descend. If the bank continues, the pilot must pull back harder and harder until he runs out of airspeed and the airplane stalls. A dangerous thing to do at a low altitude over the black Mediterranean ocean at night. Stu didn't pull back and the Cirrus went onto a steep descent.

"Level your wings! Pull up!"

Things were getting out of control quickly. *No more Mr. Nice Guy.*

I grabbed the side yoke and slammed it hard over to the left and leveled the wings while at the same time pulling back to arrest the descent.

"What the hell?"

"You were in a seventy degree bank and going down at over two thousand feet per minute!"

"No I wasn't! I had it under control!"

This wasn't the time or place for an argument, that would come later. For now we still had an approach to fly under difficult conditions. I turned the controls back over to Stu. He was hopping mad but got back to work and hand flew the approach until we were established on the localizer. We broke out of the clouds at five hundred feet and Stu made a good, although bouncy, landing despite the very strong crosswind.

The hardest part was yet to come. Stu and I couldn't talk about what had happened while we were flying because it would have been dangerous and distracting. That wouldn't stop us once we landed. And we couldn't ignore it even if we wanted to because John Driftmier was going to film our confrontation from six different angles and show it to millions of people. *Great.*

John told us not to say a word while Stu shut the plane down. He wanted to make sure he got every word of our upcoming argument. We all got out of the plane, John found a good spot and got ready to film. It was kind of like a duel.

"When I say go, take ten paces, turn and fire!"

At this point I still didn't know what I was going to say. I'd been thinking about that since the incident happened. My problem was that it wasn't just an argument between two pilots. It would be a who's right and who's wrong fight. And I didn't want to throw Stu under the bus and call out his mistakes in front of the whole world. On the other hand I didn't want to look like an over controlling asshole either. I somehow had to find a way to walk that fine line and make us both look … less bad. And that was going to be made harder by Stu because he didn't think he'd done anything wrong.

Stu was angry and told me that my grabbing the stick really scared him. I reminded him of the airplane's dangerous attitude and why I'd done what I did but he denied it was that bad. We argued back and forth about the situation but it boiled down to maybe he was on the verge of losing control of the airplane and maybe he wasn't.

Either way, my position was that I was scared and wasn't going to let us even get close to losing control.

Over the years I've had a number of friends die in plane crashes and it's almost always the case that if you could change just one thing about their flight you could prevent the crash. Like tell him to pull up just before he hits the ground in a storm, or bank left just before the mid-air collision, or pull up over those power lines you're about to hit. Or level the wings and pull up just before you enter a stall spin over the Mediterranean. There had been a number of times in my career that I had kept my mouth shut when an older, more experienced pilot had made what I knew to be a big mistake. Three of those times had almost cost me my life and I swore that I'd never stay quiet in that kind of situation again. That night over the Mediterranean Stu was the rookie and I was the old experienced pilot and I'd be damned if I was going to let Stu even get close to putting us in a spin fifteen hundred feet off the water at night. I didn't care if Stu's feelings got hurt or if I came off as an asshole on TV. I was going to make it home to my wife and kids.

While John had been filming us arguing, another storm had arrived in Cannes. We moved under an overhang of the main building and tried to keep filming in the downpour. Suddenly a security guard appeared and demanded to know what we thought we were doing. At least I assume that was what he was shouting about because I don't speak French. Drifty, on the other hand, has a passable command of the language and tried to answer the angry guard as best he could. It seemed the problem was that we didn't have permission to film on airport property and our doing so was a huge security violation. The guard told us to gather our things then marched us off to the security office.

And wow, what an office. It was more of a full blown police station than the usual tiny airport security office, which made sense because every year all the world's rich and famous descend on Cannes for the annual film festival. With all that wealth and power concentrated in one small airport it only makes sense to have a large security force to deal with potential terrorists, like us.

John and the guard went round and round. The head of security wanted to confiscate his big video camera and Drifty was hanging onto it like a lioness protecting her cub. In the end the guard agreed to let us go for the night as long as John surrendered the recording cards in the camera. John wasn't happy about that because they had all the days' footage on them but he had no choice. It was either that or spend the night sleeping with his camera in one of their comfy cells.

The ride to the hotel was a quiet one. Each of us sulking about the night's events and our part in them. But we all quickly got over it and bounced back. If there's one thing the three of us had learned over the last year of flying together it's that we can't dwell on any problems we might face. Especially any personal conflicts between us. If you're unable to let stuff like that go it will be a long and uncomfortable trip for everyone.

The next morning saw us winging our way across France headed to Scotland. Before leaving Cannes, John had managed to sweet talk the head of security into giving him back the camera cards with the promise to never film there again without permission. I definitely think John's ability to speak French had a lot to do with it.

Our fuel stop before crossing the North Sea was in Kortrijk, Belgium. I was in love with the airport as soon as we landed. It was a beautiful airport surrounded by trees and rolling hills just outside a picturesque old-world city. The airport was populated by a collection of old but well maintained hangars, perfectly groomed landscaping and neat brick main building topped with a short control tower. And of course like a lot of small European airports it had a small cafe and bar that doubled as the local flying club. This is something that I wish more small airports in the United States had because it seems to really bring a sense of community to the field.

As Stu was taking care of refueling the Cirrus I went up to the control tower to file the flight plan. Inside I met the typical friendly controller who took care of everything I needed, which is another thing I love about small airports in Europe. If you need to check the weather or file a flight plan you often take care of that up in the tower with the controller. I always love these visits. The controllers are always friendly and helpful, and if they're not busy (which is most of the time) they'll offer you coffee and conversion. I guess it gets lonely up in that control tower all day by yourself.

As we talked about the trip we were on, the controller told me that we should stay for a day or two in his fair city because the next day was the start of the local holiday celebrating the day the US liberated Belgium from the Germans in WWII. He told us that it was a wonderful two day party and if you were an American you were treated like a king! That sounded like my kind of party. After filing the flight plan I had John call Pixcom and see if they would let us stay and film the event. But Dad said no again. We had to get to Iceland.

I was very disappointed. The party sounded like a lot of fun! I spent a lot of time pre-flighting the Cirrus, looking for something, anything, that would give me an excuse to ground the plane for the day. But no luck, that damned plane was in good shape.

Ten years ... It had been ten years since I'd been in Wick, Scotland, and I'd thought I'd never see it again. As the "gateway to the Atlantic," Wick is the main jumping off point for pilots making the North Atlantic crossing from Europe to North America. When I retired from ferry flying all those years ago I'd done it for one main reason, I didn't want to die and leave my kids without a father. Because, let's face it, flying small planes across the planet is dangerous ... period. And if there's one spot on the planet that's a little more dangerous than all the rest it's the North Atlantic.

When I started ferry flying back in 1990, an average of three pilots a year lost their lives flying over the North Atlantic. Why is the North Atlantic so much more dangerous than other parts of the globe? There are a number of reasons, but chief among them is the weather, particularly the cold. Up north the cold affects every part of flying. If you run into a cold front anytime of year down close to the equator you get rained on. Off the coast of Greenland? Then you get ice. And if you can't get out of the icing conditions you've got a one way ticket to the drink. Which is, coincidentally, cold as ice.

Ditching in the North Atlantic has a unique set of challenges that need to be overcome in order to survive, the details of which most ferry pilots never really think through. First, you'll need to live through the ditching process itself which can be quite violent. The two main things to remember to survive impact with the water are land parallel to the swells and put on your shoulder harness. You don't want to hit the face of a thirty foot wave or eat the instrument panel, either of which will hurt … a lot. Then you need to get out of the sinking plane with your raft and as much of your survival gear as possible. Just getting out of the aircraft is a challenge all by itself. The plane is most likely sinking fast, being tossed around by the waves and probably upside down. Add in the fact that you're wearing a heavy neoprene survival suit, and it's probably at night, and you've got yourself a challenge. Then if you do make it out with your raft, you've then got to inflate it and climb inside without losing it. If you do somehow manage to beat the odds and make it out of the plane and into the raft, your troubles have just begun. First and foremost is that you're going to be cold, even if you're wearing a survival suit. And let's face it, if you're not wearing a survival suit your family will be telling people that you died doing what you loved.

The cold is going to be your main enemy. Once you're sitting in your raft shivering from your little swim there's no way to get warm again because everything around you is cold. The water's cold, the wind is cold and the floor of the raft you're going to be sitting on for the next twenty-four hours is cold. By the way, twenty-four hours is an optimistic number because the Atlantic ocean is BIG! Not as big as the Pacific, but still big. Once you're more than one hundred miles offshore, you're out of helicopter range and that means you'll be waiting for a boat to rescue you, and boats are slow.

Of course someone needs to know you're in trouble before they'll send that boat out to get you so first you'd better get out a mayday call before you go down. To help with the mayday call I always fly as high as I can when I'm making an ocean crossing. That usually means fifteen to eighteen thousand feet. Flying at high altitude has a few advantages. The aircraft usually has better range in the thinner air and you have more time to deal with any problems you might face, such as an engine out situation. If your engine quits at fifteen thousand feet you have up to thirty minutes or more to make your mayday call and prepare for ditching. If you're trolling around down at four thousand feet you've got less than ten minutes before you're in the water. Good luck with that.

Once you're in the raft, it's time to activate your rescue beacon. If all the rescue ship has to go on is the location of your mayday call, they'll have a search area of hundreds of square miles to cover. Having a working rescue beacon will cut that search area down considerably. Back in 1990 when I started ferrying we used emergency locator transmitters (ELT's) that were meant to be mounted in aircraft. They were big and cumbersome and didn't work very well when exposed to salt water but they were all we had. Nowadays I fly with a personal locator beacon that is truly amazing.

Small and waterproof, these beacons are tied into the GPS system and will hopefully lead rescuers to my exact location whether I go down on land or sea.

The last challenge is getting the rescue ship to actually see your raft when they get close. I used to carry a flare gun with me but the airlines started getting picky about having them in your checked bags so now I use a signal laser. I actually think this is an improvement over the flare gun. It's small enough that I carry the laser in a Ziploc bag with spare batteries inside my survival suit. At night the laser can be seen for miles. The laser isn't as effective in daylight but it's better than nothing.

Then there are the bonus items I try to bring with me. Handheld radio or even a satellite phone, a GPS, foil space blankets. All things that would come in really handy if you're sitting in a raft halfway between Greenland and Iceland.

Of course none of these things do you any good if they're at the bottom of the Atlantic. You need to bring them with you into the raft if you want them to do you any good. I used to keep all my survival gear in a ditch bag that I planned to grab after a ditching. That's right, my plan was after smashing a plane into the ocean I was going to undo my seat belt, lever my way out of the pilot's seat and somehow squeeze my way out of the door. I was going to do this while trying to hang on to both my raft and the ditch bag at the same time. What would happen if all I could manage to grab was the raft before the plane sank? I'd be out of luck as all my survival gear sank to the bottom of the ocean. Over the years, the more I thought about that plan the less I liked it. So now, instead of the "all or nothing" approach, I zip the gear I absolutely must have inside my survival suit. Rescue beacon, radio, signal laser, two space blankets, water bottle, and a candy bar will all fit inside my suit and still allow me to climb out of an upside down plane while it's sinking, I hope. I still have a ditch bag filled with goodies that would be nice to have if I get stuck in a raft but the essentials get out of the plane with me no matter what. Is the brandy flask part of my essential equipment? Take a guess.

Andrew Bruce, owner of Far North Aviation, has been the face of Wick, Scotland, for many years. In addition to providing fuel for the local commuter service and search and rescue helicopters, Andrew rents survival suits and life rafts to ferry pilots as they make their way back and forth across the North Atlantic. An iconic figure, Andrew dispenses advice, criticism, and condemnation along with fuel, rafts and survival suits. Like his counterparts in Reykjavik, Narsarsuaq and Goose Bay, Andrew has passed out flight plans and advice to thousands of pilots over the years. Some took his advice and lived and some ignored it and died.

A small, wiry and opinionated man, Andrew reminded me a lot of my first boss Pete Demos in that they both told you exactly what they thought, good or bad. Which is actually the perfect quality to have when dealing with the life or death issues of ferry flying.

It's also the perfect quality to have if you want to be on a reality TV show. John just ate Andrew up. He put a mic on Andrew and just followed him around for an hour, getting such memorable quotes as "Don't take a trip if you've got a deadline. That's the real killer!" or "We lose an average of three pilots a year in the North Atlantic. Most of them would still be alive if they'd just waited for good weather!" or "You tell that bastard that he'll get no more fuel from me until he pays his bill!". That last one was just an overheard phone call.

We rented three survival suits and a raft from Andrew which we'd leave in Goose Bay if we made it. Then I sat Stu and Drifty down and went over ditching procedures, how to exit the plane, what to bring and how to deploy the raft. We each had an additional bag of survival "luxuries" that we were responsible to grab if there was time.

One last thing we got from Andrew was a few gallons of TKS anti-icing fluid for the Cirrus. One of the innovations that they incorporated into the SR-22 was the "weeping wing" system that prevents ice from forming on the wings and tail. The system pumps anti-icing fluid (TKS) out of the leading edge of the wings and is a great system to have if you are forced to fly in icing conditions,- as long as you have enough TKS fluid in the reservoir, that is, which we didn't. Why? Because we'd picked up the plane in Singapore where there isn't much of an icing danger. Not having any TKS fluid didn't seem like a big deal at the time. We'd just pick up some on the way. Only problem was nobody had any TKS fluid at any of the stops we made on the way to Wick. Unfortunately Andrew only had two gallons of TKS fluid to sell us. I wasn't sure, but the book said that two gallons might only give us thirty minutes of protection before it ran out. That's not much seeing that we had to cross 2282 miles of North Atlantic ocean and 600 miles of northern Canadian wilderness. What do you think the odds are that we'd run into icing conditions that far north in November? One hundred percent was my guess. Two gallons of TKS fluid wasn't going to be nearly enough but it was better than nothing.

When we crossed the north coast of Scotland we ran into more autopilot problems. Stu had laid in the course to Reykjavik but the autopilot wasn't tracking it. We attempted to intercept the course from the east but when we approached the line the autopilot missed it and blew right on past. Stu gave it a few miles before setting it and giving it another try. When it missed again Stu started setting it up for a third try, I'd had enough.

"Hey Stu? Would you mind pointing the aircraft at Iceland? It's that way," I said, pointing north.

"Hang on, I'm trying to get the autopilot to track the course but there's something wrong."

"Yeah, I see that. But here's the deal. We don't waste fuel over the ocean. In fact we cut any corner and use any trick in the book to save as much fuel as we can. That means if the autopilot messes up even a little, we kill it and hand fly until we figure out what's wrong."

Stu disagreed. He said we had plenty of fuel for the seven hundred mile leg to Iceland and it would only cost us a few gallons of fuel to let the autopilot do its thing. I couldn't believe what I was hearing. I found myself having to explain that when you're over the ocean, fuel is king, and we don't waste it because you never know when you're going to need every last drop.

When we got to the halfway point I noted the time and checked the distance to the Faroe Islands. The Faroe Islands are conveniently located almost exactly halfway between Iceland and Scotland. They are a little east of the direct course so you never really see them but knowing that they are out there always made me feel better.

The coast of Iceland came into view without any fanfare or emotion. One minute losing the engine meant seeing how well the raft works, the next it was to pull the parachute and wait for a truck to come get us and take us to the hotel. In reality, we'd been in varying degrees of danger the entire leg from Scotland. The Scotland to Iceland leg is by far the least dangerous of the North Atlantic legs. Having the Faroe Islands and their rescue helicopters parked smack dab in the middle means that there are only a few gaps in helicopter rescue coverage along the entire route. In addition to helicopters, Scotland, Iceland and the Faro's all have modern and well equipped Coast Guard vessels they could send out at a moment's notice. If we went down on that leg it would be unlikely we'd have to wait long for rescue. We had another thing going for us on that trip. The parachute on the Cirrus meant we could land softly in the water instead of hitting it at seventy miles an hour. If the engine quit we would just float slowly down and land gently on the water like a leaf on a pond. OK, maybe not that soft, but still a lot better than the alternative. If we had to ride the parachute down the Cirrus would most likely remain upright and even float for a while, allowing us to inflate the raft on the wing and step into it without even getting wet. Drifty would probably love it because he'd be able to bring his big camera and film the entire event. Can you imagine the ratings that episode would get? Can you say "Grammy"?

The only issue I saw with using the parachute was that if the wind on the surface was very strong, the parachute would remain inflated and possibly drag the plane upside down over the waves, making it difficult or impossible to get out.

Once we hit the coast of Iceland we encountered broken and jumbled clouds that got steadily thicker as we went along. When we penetrated a few of the thicker clouds a thin layer of ice started to form on the windscreen and wings. Here it was, our first icing decision. Having only a limited supply of TKS fluid, we had to be careful how and when we used it. Seeing how much trouble we had getting just two gallons of the precious liquid we had to assume that's all we'd have for the rest of the trip. Once it was gone, it was gone.

So what to do? If we turned on the TKS system at the first sign of ice we might waste a few minutes of precious fluid on a non-event. On the other hand, if we gambled that the icing wouldn't be a problem and were wrong, we could be in serious trouble because the TKS system had one serious drawback. It was much better at preventing ice from building on the wings than getting rid of it once it forms.

I looked at how far Reykjavik was and decided that we could probably make it even if the ice continued. It was light rime ice and the plane could take a lot more of it before it became a problem. I thought so anyway. As we made our way across the barren volcanic lava fields and glaciers that make up most of Iceland's landscape the clouds and icing continued for a while then dissipated. Once we began our descent into Reykjavik the warmer air melted the ice off the wings quickly. Our first gamble in the game of ice roulette had paid off.

I love Iceland, but I'm not really sure why. The weather's usually gloomy, with clouds and wind being the norm. Reykjavik is nice but nothing extra special, the people are friendly but they all look, sound and dress the same as in Wisconsin, so nothing special there. Maybe it's the beautiful women, or the fact that if you're eastbound the most dangerous of the ocean legs are behind you. Or maybe it's because Iceland is just an easy place to stop. The hotel ferry pilots always use is right across the street from the airport, so no long taxi ride to suffer through after a long flight. Downtown is within easy walking distance and is filled with good bars and restaurants. Did I mention the beautiful Icelandic women? I did? Just making sure.

We got into Reykjavik early and because we had a Pixcom field trip scheduled for the next day we had the rest of the day off. John even put his camera away! The three of us spent the rest of the day just doing nothing. It was awesome. Drifty went out and did a load of laundry while I took Stu out to get one of Reykjavik's famous hot dogs followed by a beer at the Irish Pub.

That evening the three of us went downtown to check out what kind of nightlife Reykjavik had to offer and walked into a ghost town. It was Friday night at ten o'clock and there was literally no one on the streets. We walked into the first bar we came to and the bartender asked us why we were there so early? He then told us that nobody in Iceland went out until one or two o'clock in the morning because the government tax on alcohol makes drinking in the bars very expensive. The custom is for everyone to get together at someone's home for a few drinks before going out and having a few expensive bar drinks. But one o'clock in the morning is way past my bedtime so we went back to the hotel and called it a night.

The next morning we all headed down to the waterfront for our field trip. Today's experience, Arctic ocean survival. Pixcom had enrolled us in Iceland's maritime safety and cold water survival course. The institute's job is to travel around Iceland and teach cold water survival to the men and women who live and work on the ocean, primarily fishermen, sailors and offshore oil rig workers. These guys have a great gig. The government gave them a retired automobile ferry that they converted into a floating school. The ship is very impressive with living quarters for the staff plus classrooms, locker rooms and a massive hangar bay in the back of the boat. The enormous hangar bay is the most impressive part of the boat because the entire back end swings open allowing them to launch their inflatable boats and life rafts with a big crane that swings out over the water.

The first thing they did was run Stu and me through a long classroom session on ocean survival. Then it was time to get wet.

"What do you mean, we're going swimming? You mean out in the ocean?"

"If you're flying a small plane over the Arctic ocean in November you should practice getting into the raft in November," our no nonsense instructor told us.

I offered to leave the plane in Iceland for six months and then come back in the summer time but the instructor told us the water was essentially the same temperature all year long so it would be a waste of time.

They opened up the back of the ship and launched one of the big orange ten man life rafts and a safety boat. The three of us put on survival suits similar to the ones we'd rented from Andrew, piled into the rubber safety boat and went into the harbor towing the life raft behind us. The instructors brought us all the way outside the shelter of the harbor where the big waves lived.

"OK boys, get in the water!"

Stu looked at me. "Age before beauty!"

"Thanks," I said sarcastically before pulling my hood up and rolling over the side.

Yes, the water off the coast of Iceland in November is a bit chilly, in case you're wondering. I noticed three things right away. Number one, it's easy to float in the survival suit. Number two, the suits do a pretty good job keeping you warm in the cold water. And number three, the removable glove option of the suits we were wearing was stupid. The second I hit the ocean, ice cold water rushed into the gloves and my hands were instantly numb. I'm sure the ocean workers the institute usually train use these suits because they need their hands free to work but I was glad the suits we had in the plane didn't have the removable option.

Stu and I splashed around for a minute or two, riding the waves up and down. Then the instructors towed the raft to a point just a few feet down wind from us and yelled "Go get it!"

The second he let go of the rope the wind started pushing the raft away from us. I swam a few desperate strokes and made a lunge for the trailing rope but missed. Then both Stu and I took off after the wayward raft, swimming for all we were worth. We weren't even close. The raft drifted away from us at a slow but steady pace and it was immediately clear that we stood no chance of catching it.

"Even Michael Phelps couldn't catch a raft drifting in the wind!" The instructor shouted to us after we'd given up.

"That's your most important lesson. Never, ever, let go of the raft, even for an instant."

Then we practiced getting into the raft. It's a lot harder than it looks. Our first attempt was not what you would call graceful. More like a couple of walruses trying to flop onto the beach. We did manage to get in eventually. I sure wouldn't want to have to do that in thirty foot swells … at night.

As we sat inside the raft I imagined what it would be like to be stuck in that raft for real, hundreds of miles from the nearest point of land, waiting hours or days for rescue. I was reminded of a dream I had once about being in a raft at night. It was a very realistic and powerful dream and it played a big part in my decision to retire from ferry flying in 2001.

The next day was another day off. Freezing rain over Greenland made flying a bad idea. Scratch that, a REALLY bad idea. The weather was bad the next day too. And the day after that. Now, I know what you're thinking.

Kerry was just saying it's too bad to fly so he can spend more time in Iceland. He's already admitted that he likes flying in bad weather on more than one occasion.

I can see how you might come to that conclusion, but the Iceland to Greenland leg is not just another boring seven hundred mile flight. It's one of the most dangerous routes in the world and I've been scared on it enough times to treat it with respect. Aside from the unpredictable weather, the route itself is dangerous. You start off with a 660 mile leg over some of the coldest and most remote water in the world. Then you have to be able to climb up to ten thousand feet to clear one hundred miles of Greenland ice cap, finishing up with an approach into one of the most dangerous airports in the world, Narsarsuaq. Located deep inside a winding fjord, the instrument approach into Narsarsuaq airport is a scary one. You start out high above the airport then descend steeply on an outbound leg in between three mountains before turning back inbound and dropping into the fjord leading to the runway. A missed approach or go around is unlikely to be successful due to the rising terrain on all sides of the airport. If you do manage to find the runway you'd better not overshoot, because the sloped runway points right at the base of the ice cap and you'll be unlikely to pull off a go-around. To make matters worse, strong winds coming off the ice cap cause crazy crosswinds and violent turbulence.

The most dangerous aspect of flying into the southern coast of Greenland is the unpredictable weather. Weather systems coming out of Northwest Canada and off the Labrador Sea are difficult to forecast. Without warning a cold front can sweep in from the west and wipe out both Nuk and Narsarsuaq with low clouds and rain. If that happens when you're on the way to Narsarsuaq and past the point of no return ... you're screwed! So yes, I was waiting for good weather.

"November one five eight papa golf, airborne time zero eight two three Zulu. Climb and maintain one two thousand. Contact Reykjavik on one two seven eight five. Have a nice flight."

Iceland receded behind us as we climbed into the bright morning sun. We'd waited three days in Reykjavik for a good weather window. The cold front that had been dropping freezing rain over southern Greenland had finally moved off and the forecast called for clear skies over the ocean and broken clouds over Narsarsuaq.

As we leveled off at our cruising altitude of twelve thousand feet Stu set the power at seventy-five percent. Full throttle, full RPM. As fast as she would go.

"We should probably set the power at forty percent. That's the max range setting and will give us the biggest fuel reserve," I said, looking at the performance charts in the Cirrus's operating manual.

"Naw, we don't need to do that. The weather is supposed to be good and with these winds we'll have almost an hour reserve when we get there."

"That's not good enough. You should always try for the biggest reserve you can get when doing an ocean crossing. Especially this leg."

"I'm leaving the power up. I want to get there fast. We still have to fly to Goose Bay after we get fuel in Narsarsuaq."

Stu's cavalier attitude didn't sit well with me. He seemed to be thinking that these ocean crossings were no big deal. I can see why he thought that. He hadn't had the training I'd been lucky enough to receive at the school of Pete Demos and Orient Air. He didn't get to hear all the stories about how many men had gone out over the ocean and not made it across. About all the crazy unexpected things that can happen when you fly away from the safety net that is dry land. He's never heard the panic in a young pilot's voice, lost over the Atlantic, pleading for help. But I had, and this leg scared the crap out of me. Maybe I should have shown that more. Maybe Stu would have believed me if I didn't put up such a brave front.

"Iceberg! Dead ahead!" That's supposedly what the lookout on the Titanic supposedly shouted just before impact. For us, seeing the little white dots on the horizon meant we were getting close to Greenland. Greenland is my favorite place in the world to fly. Yes, I love flying in the Caribbean. Italy and Greece, but I love flying in those places because of what's on the ground after I land. Tropical beaches, stunning architecture and good food, oh so much good food! Greenland, on the other hand, is amazing to fly over. The first thing you see are the mountains that ring the southern coastline. A band of darkness separating the water from the sky. As you get closer, you realize it isn't the sky you're seeing but the massive ice cap. Rising up ten thousand feet, the huge dome of perfectly smooth snow and ice covers everything, oozing down into hundreds of glaciers that break up into the thousands of icebergs that ring the island nation.

The sharp mountain peaks that dominate the southern tip of Greenland are some of the most spectacular in the world. Rising out of the ice like church spires, the jagged peaks claw at the sky while glaciers flow like rivers in between them. The sheer magnitude of the scenery is difficult to comprehend. You don't know where to look first. The mountains? The glaciers? Or the thousands of icebergs surrounding the island like a string of pearls.

We crossed the coast and headed up over the ice cap. All three of us were shooting videos and taking pictures of everything. The conditions were perfect as they usually are over the ice cap. Known as the Greenland anticyclone or "Greenland high" this phenomenon produces an almost constant area of high pressure over the ice cap. This means smooth air and sunny skies no matter what the conditions on the coastline might be. It was a beautiful day for flying.

"November one five eight papa golf, United 443 on guard."

The radio crackled with static as I heard a United flight call us on the emergency frequency.

"Go ahead United. This is eight papa golf," I replied, grabbing my notebook. Getting a relay from another aircraft usually means ATC has lost contact with you and needs you to switch frequencies.

"Yes sir, Narsarsuaq has been trying to contact you. They're reporting that the airport is currently closed at this time due to low ceilings and visibility."

"Crap! Throttle back! Throttle back right now!" I yelled at Stu as I threw my notebook on the instrument panel.

"That's why you don't waste gas on ocean legs!"

I was pissed. I thanked the United flight for the relay, then angrily switched frequencies while checking the distance to the next closest airport. We were just ninety miles from Narsarsuaq when we got the call. Way past the point of return for Iceland. I put the Nuuk airport into the GPS and stared at the result. Three hundred and ten miles. If we changed course immediately we would just barely make it on the fuel we had left. The problem was that no matter what frequency we tried we'd been unable to contact anyone on the radio so we had no idea what the weather was like in Nuuk. I pulled up the phone number for the airport and told John to try and call them on the Sat phone.

Then Stu and I went over our situation and our options. The bad weather that closed Narsarsuaq could just as easily closed Nuuk as well. If we diverted to Nuuk we'd have almost no fuel reserve when we got there. If the weather was bad we'd have to shoot the approach to a closed airport and hope for the best or pull the parachute when we ran out of fuel. If we continued on to Narsarsuaq we'd have an hour's worth of fuel to play with. It might just delay the inevitable but at least we'd have time to explore other options.

So what were our options if both airports were closed? Option one: Shoot the instrument approach even if the cloud base was below legal minimums and hope for the best like Marcio and I did in Russia. Except the approach into Anadyr hadn't been into a deep fjord with mountains on all sides. Option two: Fly back up to the top of the ice cap and find a nice smooth place to set down like the lost squadron of P-38 Lightnings did back in WWII. That option would be easier in the Cirrus because we could just pull the parachute and float down to a soft landing on the ice cap. Someone would come get us eventually and I did have some beer onboard so John could still do end of the day interviews. Then there was the final option or the "last ditch" option that I'd always wanted to try. Back before there was a GPS approach into Narsarsuaq, the cavemen used to have to fly a non-precision approach into the airport if you were unlucky enough to arrive in bad weather. It was a scary procedure that had you find the airport's NDB beacon, then fly a descending outbound leg for a few minutes before turning around and flying back inbound and hope you found the runway before you found a cliff. Like I said it was a scary approach that was to be used only as a last resort.

The other last ditch option was probably more fun and harkened back to the days of the early ferry pilots in WWII. If the weather was bad at the airport the pilots would fly back west out over the ocean, then let down slowly until they got under the clouds. Then they would head back toward Greenland and try to find the fjord that led to the airport. If they found the correct one they could follow it all the way to the runway, even if the clouds were as low as fifty feet. The trick was to find and identify the correct fjord because there were three of them and they all look pretty much the same. One led to the airport and the other two …

"Hello? Hello? Can you hear me? Yes, this is Cirrus one eight five papa golf, is this the Narsarsuaq control tower? … Hang on one second."

John had apparently gotten through on the Sat phone and handed it to Stu. Stu put the phone to one ear and covered the other with the palm of his hand. It was nearly impossible to hear anything above the engine noise. I throttled back to idle to help him hear better.

"What are the current conditions at your location? ... I understand ... is it supposed to get better? ... How about Nuuk? ... OK, thank you."

Stu punched the phone off and turned to give me the news.

"Narsarsuaq is still closed and they have no idea if it will get better."

"How about Nuuk?"

"Nuuk is still open but they don't know for how long."

That didn't sound like a ringing endorsement for Nuuk. At least it was open ... for now.

"What do you think?"

"Not much choice. Nuuk's open, Narsarsuaq is closed. Let's head to Nuuk and hope it stays open."

With that we altered course for Nuuk.

Fifteen minutes later everything changed again. Narsarsuaq got in touch with us on the radio and told us that the clouds had lifted and the airport was once again open but they didn't know for how long. The controller also told us that while Nuuk was still open, their cloud base was dropping fast.

I quickly recalculated the time and distance to both airports against our remaining fuel. We had enough fuel to reach either airport but if we turned back to Narsarsuaq we'd be committed. If it closed again before we got there we couldn't change our mind and head back to Nuuk. One or the other, flip a coin and take your chances.

Screw it.

We were only forty minutes from Narsarsuaq. We decided to head back and hope we got in before the weather changed again. We hadn't gone very far before we saw what was causing the weather problems at Narsarsuaq and Nuuk. A massive cloud bank that stretched out across the western horizon as far as we could see. Like waves on the ocean the clouds covered the ocean and coastline and half way up the ice cap. Only a few of the tallest mountaintops poked through the thick overcast.

Then it was time to enter the clouds and start the approach. A light coating of rime ice started building on the wings immediately. It wasn't building very fast but we decided to risk some of our precious TKS fluid to keep it from becoming a problem. Stu flipped on the TKS switch, turned it to the low setting and waited for the thin layer of ice to slide off. And waited … and waited. It looked like the fluid was seeping out from beneath the layer of ice and flowing back across the wing. Stu turned up the flow rate but the ice remained stubbornly fixed in place. Oh well, too late to worry about that now. We had an approach to shoot.

Stu followed the GPS line to five thousand feet over the airport and turned to the outbound leg while dropping us down to three thousand feet. Suddenly we flew through a freak break in the clouds and I saw the fjord that led to the airport. Stu saw it too.

"What do you think? Should we go for it?"

The break in the clouds looked tempting and I was very familiar with the fjord.

"Go for it!"

Stu kicked off the autopilot and dove for the water. In only a few seconds we were below the clouds and could see the runway. The landing was a tricky one with a thin layer of ice covering the uphill slope, making the crosswind even more treacherous. Stu handled it masterfully and before long we were slipping and sliding our way across the big ramp to the base of the tower.

When we got out we could hardly walk, the ramp was so slippery. The first thing I did was peel the layer of ice off the leading edge of the wing. It looked like the TKS system didn't do a very good job of shedding ice once it was formed. We should turn on the TKS system sooner next time.

How scary were the events of the last hour or so and how did we feel about it? Shut up and get back to work! Amateurs and Sunday pilots sit around and rehash close calls and things that make them go EEK! Professional ferry pilots file that conversation for later and continue working.

We told the fuel guy to fill her up while we went inside to check weather and file our next flight plan to Goose Bay. As we walked through the double glass doors leading in from the ramp my eyes went to the familiar round sticker pasted to the lower panel of the right hand door. Both doors were covered with stickers from military and civilian aircrews that had passed through doors over the years. There were so many you could hardly see through the glass. The sticker I was looking at was an old Orient Air sticker and I had put it there twenty-five years and a lifetime ago. *Was I ever really that young?*

The entire world had changed since I put that sticker there. The Berlin wall had come down and now I flew across Russia like I owned the place. Fifteen of my friends had died and my children had been born. I used a compass to find Greenland the day I put that sticker there and now a GPS will hold your hand all the way from takeoff to your hotel room. But I only paused at that door for a few seconds. I could sit around and dream about the good old days some other time. I have miles to go before I sleep.

Stu and I went upstairs to the control tower and met Hans, a skinny middle aged Danish man with wispy blond hair and matching mustache. Hans welcomed us into his control tower and told us that he was glad we'd made it in. He told us that he knew we were in trouble when he was forced to close the airport due to the low clouds. He'd been watching us on radar and knew we were probably low on fuel and had limited options. While he was telling us the story from his point of view it sounded like he was almost as glad that we made it as we were.

He then showed us around his little kingdom. I have to admit, if you're going to be stuck in a control tower all day, the one in Narsarsuaq isn't too bad. Overlooking the massive ramp, the tower's view extended up the valley to the ice cap, down the runway to the fjord and across the water to the steep mountains beyond. It was a fantastic view. Suddenly we saw a wall of low clouds roll over the hills on the other side of the fjord and sweep in towards the runway. In no time the ceiling dropped, visibility went way down and it started sleeting.

"That is what happened three hours ago when I closed the airport on you. This is common this time of year. It comes suddenly and leaves just as fast."

Then he excused himself as he checked the instruments that measure cloud height and visibility. Stu and I looked at each other, both knowing that if we'd been just a few minutes later we'd have been stuck trying to land in that crap.

Stu, John and I cooled our heels in the airport offices and waited for the weather to clear. I didn't care much one way or the other if we spent the night or pushed on, because Narsarsuaq has a nice hotel with a decent restaurant in it. Plus the scenery is magnificent. On the other hand we'd all been on the road for a long time and we were ready to go home.

The weather made the call for us. About an hour after the low clouds and sleet moved in, the clouds lifted just as quickly as they came. The forecast for Goose was acceptable, so with no other excuses we piled back into the Cirrus and took off for Canada.

I always love the takeoff and departure from Narsarsuaq. The steep downhill gradient of the runway allows the plane to accelerate quickly and it ends right at the shoreline so you shoot out over the water and into the bay. Once airborne the route that leads to the Atlantic is hemmed in on both sides by steep rock walls as you wind your way through the forty mile iceberg-filled fjord. I typically don't climb above five hundred feet until I'm clear of the fjord and out over open ocean. It might not be the safest way to depart Greenland but there's no way I'd forgo some of the most enjoyable flying on the planet just to be a tiny bit safer. Not my style.

The flight to Goose Bay was a quiet one. The crew was tired and beat down from the road and our energy reserves were running low. John was asleep in the back and Stu watched a movie on his iPad before dozing off as well. The music in my headset blocked out the drone of the engine and put me in my normal long cross country trance as I watched the sun win the race and beat us to the horizon.

Our dark and cozy little cocoon was starting to show the effects of our long trip. Food wrappers, customs forms and empty water bottles littered the floor, and John's once neatly organized back cabin was now a jumble of bags, camera equipment and dirty clothes, piled around his seat. It was surprising how the three of us had gotten along so well being crammed together in that tiny airplane filled with cameras, cables and all our crap for so long. We'd spent nearly every waking moment together for two weeks and somehow managed to still be on speaking terms. It was nothing short of a miracle.

Goose Bay, Labrador, garden spot of Northern Canada. Also known as "Happy Valley", Goose was the home of the largest airbase and town in northeast Canada. Back when I started ferry flying the airbase hosted fighter squadrons from all over the world who came to take advantage of its remote location in order to fly low and make noise without any pesky neighbors to complain about TOPGUN wannabes thundering over their heads at ridiculously low altitudes. It wasn't unusual for me to be sitting in some tiny plane waiting for my turn at the runway alongside a dozen British Tornadoes or Canadian F-18s. With the cold war over, the military base is deserted now, but that doesn't take away Goose Bay's romance and history as bush and ferry pilots still depend on Happy Valley as a base of operations.

It was a bittersweet evening. We were all ready to be home again but reluctant for the adventure to end. We still had air-to-airs to do in Montreal but Canada is practically civilization. The hair raising, probably-going-to-die, portion of our journey was over … mostly.

The forecast for most of the routes to Montreal was filled with all kinds of good news. Low clouds and icing would make the first half of the trip tricky. Icing conditions over Northern Canada in November wasn't much of a surprise. It also wouldn't be much fun with the TKS tank running on empty. The weather guessers thought it should only last for an hour or so but seeing that we only had twenty minutes of de-ice fluid left in the tank flying in the clouds didn't seem like the best idea in the world. So what do you do if you can't fly in or over the clouds but still want to go home? Why, you fly under them of course.

The ceilings were predicted to be around six to eight hundred feet with scattered snow showers which wasn't great but the visibility was supposed to be about four miles which wasn't too bad. I've done worse.

I love scud running. To me there's nothing more fun than ripping along at five hundred feet (or lower) under a solid overcast, dodging power lines and radio towers. If there are a few heavy snow showers to dodge around so much the better. Remember, you can only tie the low altitude record, you can't break it. And as long as you're in a plane that has the ability to pop up into the clouds and go on instruments if things get dicey, it's not the craziest thing in the world. It also helps if you've had a lot of experience and you're good at it. Which I am.

The overcast layer started at eight hundred feet and the visibility was around four miles so I wasn't overly concerned about running into any of the low hills that are on the route to Montreal, so long as we didn't do anything stupid … stupider. Cruising along down low is also a great way to see the countryside. At five hundred feet you see details that you'd totally miss if you were up at altitude. It's also great TV and John was digging it. There were a few snow showers along the route that we had to deviate around but nothing too scary. I was actually disappointed that the conditions weren't worse. Unfortunately after an hour of good low level flying over remote Canada the clouds lifted forcing us to fly at a higher and safer altitude the rest of the way.

We finished up most of the filming in Montreal. The air-to-air day was fun as usual but with a twist. We needed to get some shots at night so we could recreate the stormy night over the Mediterranean. Pixcom thought the controversy of me grabbing the controls from Stu would make a riveting segment and when they reminded viewers of what I'd done in Brazil with Cory I'd be forever branded as the control grabber.

Great.

SUPER GIRL

"Do you want to do the takeoff?"

"Sure Dad."

Why was a nineteen-year-old girl my co-pilot for this ferry flight? Because she was my daughter, and six months ago I'd had an idea.

Season one of the show had been a big success. It was being shown in dozens of countries on the Discovery Channel. Unfortunately the Discovery Channel decided not pick it up in the US and it ended up on the Smithsonian Channel instead. The show also finally had an official name. They called it *Dangerous Flights*. I wasn't crazy about the name at first, but it grew on me. At least it was an accurate description of what we were doing. After only a few weeks on the air the ratings were good enough that Discovery green-lit season two.

While season one of *Dangerous Flights* had turned out to be a good show and very popular, everyone involved wanted season two to be even better, but how? The producers and directors at Pixcom scratched their collective heads and tried to come up with new ideas that would make the show more exciting and interesting. They even went so far as to ask us lowly pilots if we had any ideas. I had one right off the bat.

"How about we make my nineteen-year-old daughter my co-pilot on one of the trips?"

To my surprise they said yes! It was the best idea they had for season two! Alright, it was the only idea they had, but it was still the best!

I shouldn't have been surprised. Claire was a perfect fit for the part. She is young, beautiful, in shape and had a background in acting. Growing up she had been in a dozen plays and singing competitions so hopefully she would be great on camera. Claire is also a very athletic and adventurous young woman. She is an expert skier, had gotten her scuba card at age twelve and started skydiving at sixteen. She was also a student pilot and was on the verge of getting her private pilot's license.

Pixcom loved Claire from the moment they met her and immediately hired her to be my co-pilot on my next trip ferrying a Bonanza from Montevideo, Uruguay to South Carolina.

We flew down to Montevideo in mid-December and I started teaching Claire how to be a reality TV star. I needn't have bothered. Claire was a natural on camera. She was funny, easy going and full of energy. The director for this trip was Tyson Hepburn. Tyson and John Driftmier had been best friends since college and were partners in the video production company they started after graduation. Tyson was a tousle-haired Canadian in his late twenties with a good eye for the camera and a very loud laugh.

The pre-flight filming days in Uruguay went well. I'd never been there before and found the people very friendly, especially the guys at the small airport the Bonanza was based at. It was one of those close-knit community airports that are so enjoyable to be at. All the pilots and mechanics on the field know each other and each afternoon the hangar doors open up and clusters of pilot-filled lawn chairs would pop up everywhere. I really enjoyed chatting with these guys every evening after we were done filming for the day. When the day finally came to leave, the airport gang threw us a going away party complete with a band comprising entirely local pilots. Of course everyone at the airport liked Claire, especially one particular pilot who offered to take her flying in his Cessna 172. I gave that idea a big thumbs down. I wasn't about to let some kid take my daughter for a ride and try and impress her with some fancy flying. That's a Dad's job. Plus, I don't trust pilots I don't know.

Our first fuel stop was Salto, Uruguay. Here Claire immediately proved her worth when we tried to pay the landing fees and get fuel for the plane. I like stopping at small airports whether I'm ferrying a jet around the world or just out for a Sunday joyride. The atmosphere at a small airport is more laid back and friendly. The shop is often an unintentional museum of old aircraft in various stages of repair, and it's not uncommon to snag a free cup of coffee and stale doughnut or two while you check the bulletin board to see whose wife is forcing them to sell that damn airplane they never fly. In this sense most small airports around the world are the same. What's not the same everywhere is the language that they speak.

Followed by Tyson and his ever present camera, Claire and I walked into the fuel shack, fired off our standard questions at the two gentlemen behind the counter and got back blank stares in return. I'd seen that stare before. It said, *"No, I don't speak English. You're in Uruguay not*

Iowa, you idiot." They then answered me in Spanish which prompted me to make the same face back at them.

I was about to bust into some international charades when Claire stepped up and took over. Claire had taken four years of Spanish in school and here was her chance to have all that studying pay off. When she translated my request the head man's face lit up with a big grin. The two of them talked back and forth while I stood there with a stupid grin on my face, completely lost. I caught a few words like "avgas" and "aeropuerto" but other than that I was lost. It appeared like they had come to some sort of understanding with the head man saying "Si, si" and sending his helper off to hopefully get the fuel truck. Claire said one last sentence with the word "padre" in it while pointing to me and they both laughed hysterically. I knew that "padre" meant father and assumed that Claire had said something like, "Can you believe I have to fly this plane all the way to the United States with my dad yelling at me the entire way? It's going to be awful! Meanwhile, Tyson was circling us with the camera on his shoulder, getting the encounter from different angles.. I could tell he was loving it.

"Next, on *Dangerous Flights* ... Kerry McCauley, world famous ferry pilot is unable to communicate with the locals until his beautiful young daughter swoops in and saves the day!"

Claire finished talking to the airport worker. "Everything's all set. He's going to get us the bill for the landing fee and the other guy will go get the fuel truck."

"Perfect! Way to go Claire! I had no idea you could speak Spanish so well!"

The humble smile on Claire's face quickly disappeared as Tyson suddenly started swearing and carrying on as he looked at his camera.

"Crap! The white balance was WAY off! It looks like hell. We'll have to do that again."

Unbelievable. That whole scene had been pure gold! Doing it again would take a lot of work and would probably come off scripted and stiff. It took me almost a week to learn how to re-do conversations convincingly on my first trip for Pixcom. Oh well, Claire had to learn sometime. First she had to explain to the two men that we had to have that exact same conversation all over again. That took a while, but she finally got the confused airport workers on board with what we wanted them to do.

Then Claire knocked it out of the park. She was smooth and convincing and took control of the scene, leading the men back through the conversation. I played the part of "Man who doesn't speak Spanish " perfectly. When she was done I was convinced that Take Two was even better than the first time. I should have known that the actress in Claire would come in handy. In no time at all we were back in the air and on our way to Foz do Iguacu.

Our first stop had been a sleepy little airport and Claire had come through like a champ. Time to step it up a notch. The city of Foz do Iguacu had a large international airport and like most big airports, the official airport offices a pilot needed to visit before leaving were spread out all over the place. That sounded like an opportunity for good TV.

When we'd arrived the night before all we'd done was go through customs before leaving the airport and heading to the hotel. Now we were back in the main terminal and needed to pay landing fees, check weather, file a flight plan and arrange for fuel. It was time to give Claire a challenge.

"I'm going to go and get the fuel coming. Claire, I want you to see if you can find out where to pay the landing fees. Also, find out where the weather office is and where to file a flight plan."

There was a moment's hesitation in her eyes. I could tell she wanted to ask if she had to go alone, but to her credit she just looked around and asked,

"Where do I go?"

"No idea. Here's some money. Make sure you get a receipt."

With that, Claire grabbed the small stack of cash I handed her, turned on her heels and marched off with Tyson in her wake. I was immensely proud of her as I watched her march down the terminal, looking for the airport offices. I had every confidence in her because I'd been preparing her and her brother Connor for this their whole lives.

I have, what most people would consider, a crazy philosophy on raising children. Well, my children at least. From day one I had put them in as many risky and difficult situations as I could. My theory is that dealing with difficult situations is a skill like anything else, and the younger you learn that skill the better you are at it. I had both Claire and Connor downhill skiing by the age of three and pushed them down the expert runs by seven. They got their Scuba diving licenses when Connor was ten and Claire was twelve. I took them camping, hunting, and fishing in as remote and uncomfortable locations as I could find; and they both started flying and skydiving before they were eighteen. I tried my best to put them in harm's way whenever I could and the more I pushed the better and more skilled they became. Some people might call it child abuse and endangerment but I think failing to prepare your children for the real world is neglect. And anyway, they came out of it with no stitches or broken bones so I must not have been too crazy. Can't blame a dad for trying.

When I returned from paying the fuel bill Claire and Tyson were waiting for me.

"How'd it go?"

"Pretty good," she said as she handed me a receipt. "I had to use a little international charades because they speak Portuguese here."

It was like watching Connor score a touchdown. I wanted to jump up and down yelling my head off but I had to play it cool. Act like I'd expected nothing less. Because I hadn't.

"Cool. Let's go."

Our mission for the day was to fly around Iguazu falls a few times and shoot some footage then head north and see how far we could get that day. We took off, made our laps around the most amazing set of waterfalls I'd ever seen, then headed north like it was no big deal. Our plan was an ambitious one. The date was December 21st. Our goal was to try and get to the Caribbean by Christmas. That gave us four days to fly almost the entire length of South America, a distance of over two thousand miles that also included that little area known as the Amazon Jungle. Still, two thousand miles in four days shouldn't be difficult. Barring any problems with the usual afternoon thunderstorms we should be able to make it in two days, easy. That's two days without trying to shoot a TV show. I'd learned that filming made trips take two or three times longer than they normally would. With that in mind we'd be pushing hard whenever we could.

The next leg to Campo Grande was an easy one. Puffy white clouds steadily built all morning into tall cumulus towers. Towers that were just right for a little training … and a little fun.

One of the things that a lot of new pilots don't do these days is learn how to fly. OK, sure, they can get their aircraft off the ground, follow the magenta line of their GPS from point A to point B. Enter the pattern and land. Rarely do they go out and really FLY! They never exceed a thirty degree bank or a five hundred foot per minute limb or descent. They don't do these things because they perceive them as being "dangerous". To which I say nonsense! They're so obsessed with safety they don't realize they're training for the wrong thing. The pilot in question has forgotten or never knew why they are there in the first place. You're sitting in the left seat "in case something goes wrong!" That's why you're there. Because, let's face it, almost anyone can fly a perfectly good airplane on a nice, sunny day. There are many stories of non-pilots flying and landing planes after the pilot dies. Heck, an old lady even landed a King Air all by herself. It's not that hard. You want to know when you need a good pilot? When the shit hits the fan, that's when. That's why we practice stalls, spins, steep turns and emergency descents. Because someday you might need those skills. Like everything else, I like to push those skills to the limit.

The bright white clouds shining in the Brazilian sunshine were perfectly spaced along our route to practice some advanced stick and rudder skills by doing a little cloud surfing. Cloud surfing can be defined many ways, but the simplest is the action of taking a very expensive airplane and using it for a purpose that the owner, your mother and the FAA would never approve of … if they only knew. And for which, if you got caught, you could easily find yourself seeking new employment or explaining to an FAA judge why it was that you busted the cloud clearance limits one hundred times in a five minute span. The act usually involves clouds of various shapes and sizes, high and low angles of attack and non-approved aerobatic maneuvers. See also: Barnstorming, Screwing Around, Having a Blast.

One of the things that bite general aviation pilots from time to time is getting caught deep inside a mountain range without enough smash, speed or energy to extricate yourself from whatever stupid predicament you managed to get yourself into. For example, sometimes pilots get themselves in trouble by inadvertently flying into box canyons. Sometimes they "turn the corner" and rather than see a path ahead leading ever onward to blue sky, they see a sheer rock wall or large hill staring them in the face. In far too many cases, it will be the last thing they will ever see. They don't have the speed or power to climb over the rapidly rising terrain, and usually don't have the skill or turn radius to go back the way they came. Running out of altitude, airspeed and ideas, the hapless pilots of these planes will often try to convert their pitiful supply of excess airspeed into altitude. But since they are usually in a climb already it's mostly not enough and they end up hitting the canyon wall right at, or even just past, stall speed. Which is just barely fast enough to kill you.

Now I think you'll have to agree that getting yourself into such a predicament is generally something to be avoided. I think you'll also agree that if you did find yourself in said predicament (through no fault of your own I'm sure) you would be ever grateful that you had practiced various escape maneuvers and strategies that could be employed in just such a situation. But when should one practice such things? Surely not in actual mountains filled with rocks and other unyielding surfaces. That wouldn't do at all. No, you need something that looks like tall mountains and box canyons but won't scratch the paint if at first you don't succeed, i.e., clouds.

I'd been watching the Bonanza's transponder and hadn't seen the return light go off for quite some time. That usually indicates that we were out of radar coverage, and seeing we were flying out over the middle of nowhere South America it was reasonable to assume Claire and I had the sky to ourselves. I had Claire kick off the autopilot and told her to have some fun! The main value of cloud surfing is to just get a better feel for your aircraft. It's simple. Just point the plane at a cloud face, then see how close you can get before turning away. Points off for hitting the "mountain". As you get better try some more advanced maneuvers. Pick a cloud top and practice climbing up and clearing it just above stall speed. Then nose over and regain speed as you fly down the other side. Lastly you can practice your hammerhead stalls. Pick a tall and vertical cliff face, fly directly at it, then pull straight up, flying up the cliff wall until you're almost out of airspeed. Then stomp on a rudder pedal to pivot the aircraft in place before diving back down the way you came. That last ditch maneuver is probably impractical to use in the real world but it sure is fun!

I let Claire go through a good series of cloud surfing maneuvers and she did pretty well, though it wasn't her first time. I'd let both Claire and Connor practice cloud surfing maneuvers many times growing up. The Bonanza was heavier than the little Cessna Claire was used to flying and she often had to use both hands on the yoke to pull out of a steep dive. We'd have to work on that.

"November one five eight papa golf, I realize you're attempting to stay clear of the weather, but could you please attempt to maintain eleven thousand feet?"

The ATC call made both of us pause. Busted! Apparently they could see us on radar after all. We shared a good father daughter laugh, stopped screwing around and got back on course.

Early afternoon, Alta Floresta, Brazil. Claire and I walk into the big open room that is the airport office, Met office and welcome wagon all rolled into one. Inside, two middle aged women manage a collection of desks, computers and radar screens.

I walk up and hit them with some good old American English in a foreign country, loud and slow.

"HELLO … WE … WOULD … LIKE … TO … FILE … A … FLIGHT … PLAN!"

Both ladies are all smiles and attention but shake their collective heads in frustration. Claire tries Spanish. Nope. Our choices are Portuguese or international sign language. International sign language it is.

With a bunch of pointing, saying the same words louder and slower and holding up old flight plans and weather reports, thing one finally understands and pulls up the weather forecast on her computer while thing two fires up the radar. From what I gather they are calling for isolated thunderstorms and rain showers in the area for the rest of the afternoon and into the evening. Welcome back to the International Tropical Convergence Zone. The radar has limited range but shows a scattered collection of red and orange cells one hundred miles north of Alta Floresta. Beyond that? … Dragons. I have to assume.

As I'm staring at the radar screen and listening to a steady stream of Portuguese in stereo from the twins, a short pudgy pilot walks in from the Cessna 182 I'd just seen taxi in and park. We exchange greetings and he tells me that he's a local ferry pilot who's just come in from Manaus.

"Where you guys going from here? Manaus?"

"Yep."

"It's terrible that way. I was jumping around like a kangaroo."

He went on to describe the storms and heavy rain that he'd battled on his way south from Manaus. He then talked to the twins and after a few minutes they all seemed to come to a conclusion.

"Not such a good idea this afternoon. Better you should go in the morning."

That sounded like a good idea to me. The storms on the radar looked challenging and it sounded like the forecast for that evening wasn't any better. And if a local ferry pilot suggested we call it a day it's probably a good idea. Plus, we'd made two legs that day so even though there was still a few hours of daylight left, the professional ferry pilot in me was satisfied.

"Sounds good. We'll wait until tomorrow then."

I started looking at filling out the flight plan for the morning when Claire spoke up.

"So we're not going?"

"No. We'll probably call it a day. Sounds kind of bumpy."

"I don't know. If we have enough fuel I say we try it."

That threw me for a loop. Having Claire aboard was the main reason I was calling it a day. If I'd been by myself I'd probably keep going and work my way through the storms. But now here was Claire, looking at me with that look that she used when she wanted to get her way.

"I don't know, it's up to you," she said.

"I know it is."

That look again.

"I mean, we can stay here if you don't think you can handle it?"

Oh hell no. She didn't just say that!

I couldn't believe it. Claire was calling me out! This was something completely new to me. Usually someone's telling me **not** to risk flying in bad weather conditions, not the other way around. And if someone did try to talk me into flying when it was clearly not advisable, I'd explain to them the risks we'd be taking and the reasons it would be better to be drinking beer in some rundown hotel instead of sweating it out over the Amazon in the middle of a thunderstorm. But this wasn't a normal situation. My little girl had called my … *Scary Kerryness*, into question. I couldn't let that go.

"All right, I'll go for it. Crazy girl!"

I turned back to thing one and told her I was ready to file my flight plan. The local ferry pilot translated.

"For tomorrow morning or afternoon?"

"Today."

Three sets of eyebrows shot up, they looked at Claire then back at me. I could tell what they were thinking.

"Daddy's girl."

Shaking their heads, the twins filed my flight plan and we walked out to the plane.

Author's note: Ten years later I ran into that ferry pilot in Ft Lauderdale. He was on his way to Brazil again and I was on my way to Thailand. He told me that he always wondered if we made it or not.

"So what's the hurry Claire?"

"No hurry. I just don't want to sit here all day. Plus, I've grown up hearing all your great stories about flying in all kinds of bad weather and wanted to experience some for myself. So far this trip has been too easy."

"OK, but remember that you asked for it."

I may have created a monster.

An hour later we saw another monster. Multiple monsters actually. Medium and large thunderstorms were marching across the Amazon Jungle making things interesting. Just like Claire wanted.

"Each one of those little x's is a lightning strike," I said, pointing at the small stormscope mounted in the instrument panel.

"Where you see them clustered together … like that … that's a thunderstorm." Two clusters of x's soon crowded the screen with a third just creeping into range. We'd been watching the clouds build in front of us for some time and the clear, clean air turned murky as the humidity increased. The reduced visibility was going to make dodging the storms even more difficult. Going by what the stormscope revealed I adjusted course and showed Claire how to weave in between the storms like a skier dodging moguls. So far, so good but with the point of no return fast approaching it was time to make the decision whether to turn back or press on. Our options were to admit defeat and head back to Alta Floresta or take the chance and push on to Manaus. If we turned back we'd have to face the twins and admit we were wrong. (Not something I'm good at.) If we went for Manaus we'd be committed to landing there or the jungle because there wasn't another airport anywhere within range.

"What do you think Claire? Go for it or … ?"

"Go for it," she said, interrupting me.

Where in the world did she get this full speed ahead, damn the torpedoes attitude? Where indeed?

Claire got out her phone and started taking pictures with one hundred percent confidence that her dad could handle whatever we ran into. I on the other hand was only in the seventy-thirty range. No one asked Tyson.

As we got closer to Manaus and the Amazon River the sky took on a darker and more foreboding appearance. Somewhere behind the clouds the sun was setting and the change in temperature was causing tendrils of mist to snake their way up from the jungle. We were now flying in a triple layered sky. Patchy ground fog on the bottom, a scattered layer of clouds not far above the treetops and a thick overcast layer above. Throw in a few heavy downpours and you've got yourself some fun now! Even with the reduced visibility I wasn't having too much trouble avoiding the storms. They seemed to lose their intensity and peter out as we got closer to the river. About the only thing I was really worried about was a big storm planting itself on top of the runway and refusing to move. If that happened we'd be forced to go to max endurance power setting, orbit at a safe distance and hope our fuel lasted longer than the storm. I tried not to think about what would happen if we ran low on fuel and the storm was still there. Shoot the approach I guess. Nowhere else to go except the river or the jungle and neither of those options sounded like fun once it got really dark. Probably not much fun in daylight either.

Heavy rain. That's the main takeaway I got from the control tower's report of conditions at the field. No mention of micro bursts or wind shear but this little airport in the middle of the Amazon Jungle probably didn't have the instruments to detect them anyway. The only other way to detect a microburst or wind shear was to fly through it.

The stormscope looked clear, so I briefed Claire on the approach and what I expected from her. I wanted her to keep her head outside the cockpit and let me know when we saw the runway lights while I concentrated on the flight instruments. Then I told her that if she saw the runway environment to tell me then transition her attention back inside and focus on the instruments while I transitioned to looking outside. This was her first real exposure to good crew resource management. I didn't anticipate a difficult approach but I thought I might as well get her in the groove in case we ran into real trouble later on in the trip.

"November three one six papa established on the localizer."

Localizer and glide-slope needles centered. Gear down and locked. Already getting some breaks in the clouds. Much to my disappointment, the approach looked like it would be an easy one. Claire called out the runway and I looked up to see the runway lights laid out in front of us with only light rain to contend with. My disappointment stemmed from wanting at least something on this leg to be a little scary. Claire had made the call to take off and continue in questionable conditions. I didn't want her to think that it would turn out like that every time. Fear is an excellent teacher. Also, easy flying is boring TV.

After landing and shutdown I put Claire in charge of fueling the Bonanza while I got my pre-interview beer on. I knew the fuel guys here would only take cash (only new American hundred dollar bills please) so I gave Claire the money pouch. There's always a big money bag or pouch on any ferry trip. Some places only take credit cards and some only cash. There have been many times when the ten or twelve thousand dollars I started out with wasn't nearly enough to get me to the finish line.

Manaus is the last big city on the Amazon River, or the first, depending on which way you're headed. The city itself is fairly modern with a lot of amenities you might expect from a big city. But the Amazon Jungle lay just beyond the city borders. You didn't have to go far to walk back into the stone age. It's not hard to believe that just one hundred years ago the area was almost entirely unexplored except by the natives who'd lived there with no contact with the outside world.

A lot of ferry pilots focus solely on ocean survival and completely ignore the rest of the world. That can be a mistake because there are still dragons out there and one of them lives in the Amazon Jungle. So of course we had to have a field trip into the jungle to see if we could get some survival training.

The next morning we hired a car to take us to the jungle survival school where we met our instructor for the day. I was immediately impressed. He was a young native man in his mid-twenties with classic high cheekbones and long dark hair. His penetrating eyes and air of easy confidence commanded instant respect. He, on the other hand, took one look at the father and daughter TV stars from Wisconsin and was less than impressed.

"You are wearing shorts and sandals in the jungle?" A frown replacing his initial smile.

"That's not smart. There are all kinds of dangerous insects and snakes that live in the jungle. Especially snakes. You would do best to stay on the trail."

I looked at what he was wearing and slapped my head. *Kerry you idiot!*

Our guide was wearing a short sleeved shirt, long Army BDU pants with cargo pockets and high top leather boots. Claire and I? Shorts and sandals which seemed appropriate seeing it was incredibly hot and humid. Didn't the natives wear loincloths and go barefoot for thousands of years? Of course they only lived until thirty. *Oh well, too late now.*

The survival school hired a man with a nice speedboat to take us up the Amazon River about ten miles where he ran the boat up on a remote stretch of beach and let us out. Sporting a small backpack and a machete, our guide led us into the jungle. I was excited. Honing my survival skills in different environments had been my hobby for years. I've been building my own survival kits and testing them out in the woods since I was a teenager. I couldn't wait to see what ancient knowledge our native guide could pass on to me.

I couldn't have been more disappointed. It wasn't that our guide was a bad instructor. It was just that the course was super basic and more geared towards tourists. I got the first hint of this when he showed us how to make fire without matches. Did he use a bow drill? Flint and steel? Some other secret method the natives use? Nope, he pulled out the old battery and steel wool trick. It's a technique where you use steel wool to short out the positive and negative ends of a 9 volt battery which makes the steel wool overheat and burn. It's a neat trick but absolutely useless in the woods. I can't remember the last time I saw a steel wool tree. He followed that little bit of useless information with more of the same. How to bang on tree roots with a stick to signal others, how to wrap vines around your feet to help you climb trees and how to make a platform in a tree to help hunt wild game. All of the things he showed us were interesting but of little practical value.

It was a fun day anyway. Tyson got a lot of great footage of us climbing trees and putting palm fronds on a makeshift shelter. Our instructor did give us one useful bit of information. If you want to survive in the Amazon Jungle you better bring your own food. He told us that a few years ago a native hunter got lost and starved to death in that very area. He'd been armed with a shotgun and intimate knowledge of where to find food and game and was still dead when searchers found him months later. I think instead of bringing steel wool into the woods I'll bring a sandwich.

We were all done by late afternoon and made our way back to the beach. Once there, Tyson wanted to get some footage of Claire walking along the water's edge. The two of them were just out of sight when we heard a call. I looked back and saw the boat owner running down the beach waving his arms and yelling for us to get back to the boat in a hurry.

I ran to get Claire and Tyson and when we got back the owner told us to hurry and push the boat back into the water because a storm was coming. Sure enough when I looked back up river there was a massive thunderhead bearing down on us and by the looks of things it would be on us any minute! We all heaved the big boat back into the water and jumped in. The second we were in, the owner hit the gas so abruptly that Tyson was thrown into the back of the boat but like a good cameraman he made sure his body took the brunt of the fall instead of the video camera. As we entered the main channel I looked back and saw the dark storm clouds were gaining on us. The race was on!

As the boat picked up speed the owner told us that the afternoon storms could be very dangerous and violent. He told us that only one week before a family had been caught on the river by a storm and had all been killed by a lightning strike. It was then that I realized that the storm that was chasing us was the same type of storm that I see popping up every afternoon along the equator. It had never occurred to me that the people who lived under these storms might be in as much danger as those of us in the air.

The boat was fast. The storm was faster. A wall of wind and rain swept down the river and hit us hard. The visibility dropped immediately and the once calm river was transformed into a windswept sea of whitecaps. The boat driver didn't back off the throttle an inch and the ride became extremely rough as we hit the waves at full speed. Tyson caught the worst of it. Before the storm caught us he'd moved into the front of the boat so he could film the storm approaching us from behind. When the wind hit, the front of the boat started smashing into the waves tossing Tyson violently up and down in the bow. He suddenly had the impossible job of trying to hang onto the big video camera and steady himself at the same time. He began begging the driver to slow down just for a second so he could get under the cover and into one of the seats. The driver was having none of that. He had the look of pure terror in his eyes and wouldn't slow down even for a second, it was crazy. Claire and I started laughing hysterically at the absurdity of the situation until the waves got even bigger and the boat started smashing into them so hard I was convinced that something would give way and break. I yelled over the storm to the driver that he needed to slow down. He refused at first but when I told him that he was damaging his boat and if something important broke we might be stranded in the storm he finally relented. Then suddenly the river turned to the left and out of the path of the storm. In just a few minutes we shot back out into bright sunshine and calm water. Tyson was pretty upset. He not only got his camera wet but he didn't get much useful footage of our race with the storm.

"Dad, I **really** want to make it into the Caribbean by Christmas."

Two thoughts popped into my head when Claire blurted out that statement at dinner after our rough river run as we called it. The first was that of course, I want to make it to the Caribbean by Christmas, too. Who wouldn't? And if my baby girl wants a tropical island for Christmas I'll move heaven and earth to get her one. The second was that as a professional ferry pilot this kind of statement annoys me. I fly as hard and fast and far as I can every day. That's my job, and deadlines, whether artificial or not, shouldn't have any effect on my go or no go decision making process. I push as hard as I can every day no matter what. But it was Christmas Eve in Brazil and if my daughter wants to make it to the Caribbean by Christmas then I'll just have to push a little harder.

That night at midnight the people of Manaus shot off fireworks over the city to celebrate Christmas. I went outside on my balcony to watch and looked over to see Claire on the balcony next to mine doing the same thing.

"Pretty cool huh?"

"Pretty cool. Thanks for bringing me on this trip Dad."

I told her that I was glad she was with me on this adventure and that I was proud of her. Then I went back to watching the fireworks.

I think I got something in my eye.

Christmas morning over the Amazon Jungle. I'd talked Claire and Tyson into getting an early start on the day and we managed to get airborne just after the sun rose. I told them that the sooner we got going the sooner we could hit the beach in Grenada. It was only a thousand miles away and if we were lucky we could be sipping rum punch in seven or eight hours. Our last stop in South America before heading out over the water was Boa Vista, Brazil, where we'd get some fuel and clear outbound customs before the last leg of the day. The winds aloft and weather were cooperating and our final push into the Caribbean would be easy. I let Claire do the landing into Boa Vista unassisted and she nailed it. It was looking like it was going to be a perfect Christmas day of flying. Just a quick gas and go and we'd be on our way to the Caribbean.

We grabbed our passports, hopped out of the Bonanza and were greeted by two policemen armed with sub-machine guns walking our way. The machine guns didn't bother me, a lot of policemen in South America are armed that way. The look on their faces bothered me though. No smiles, no greetings, just a curt "follow us" before they turned on their heels and marched back into the airport building.

Claire gave me a "What the hell?" look. I just shrugged and followed the officers into the airport building. They ushered us into the immigration office where a handsome young man sat scowling behind a big metal desk. Without so much as a hello he thrust out his hand and in his best Nazi impersonation said, "Papers please." At least he said please.

"Sure thing grouchy, here you go," I said. Maybe I just said "Yes sir," I forget.

He took his time looking over our passports while the three of us stood in awkward silence. After what seemed like an eternity he looked up and informed us that someone was missing their inbound paperwork for Brazil. I immediately looked at Claire. When we first arrived in Uruguay and had gone through immigration I'd cautioned her to hang onto all the papers she'd received because they were important. She promised she would but it seemed that my words of caution had fallen on deaf ears. Damn kids.

"I'm sorry sir, my daughter will go out to the plane and look for it."

"No. I have one for Claire McCauley and one for Tyson Hepburn, I'm missing … Kerry McCauley."

That brought a snort from my so-called devoted daughter.

"I'm sorry sir. It must be here somewhere," I said as I dug through my folder of paperwork. But it wasn't there. When I asked if it was really necessary all I got in response was a cold stare. We then went back to the plane and tore it apart looking for that stupid entry form. Unfortunately I was pretty sure I'd thrown it away two nights prior when I was cleaning out my folder. A lot of junk accumulates on these trips and you need to clean house once in a while. At least Claire had her slip. A fact that she reminded me of every thirty seconds or so.

We finally gave up looking and slunk back into the immigration office to face the wrath of Grumpy, the immigration agent. On the way up we finally figured out why the agent was in such a bad mood. It was Christmas and we were probably the only reason he had to come in to work. Well, if he wanted us gone all he had to do was say goodbye and we'd be a speck on the horizon before he made it out of the parking lot. But no, Grouchy told me that losing that form was a serious offense. He even looked it up in the official big book of serious offenses and showed it to me. "Punishable by fines and or imprisonment."

Imprisonment?!

He told me to sit down at his desk while he typed up my official offense paperwork.

Crap, this is getting serious!

I gave it one more attempt at getting on the agent's good side. On his desk was a small figure of a downhill skier. I was a skier! Maybe I could get him talking about skiing and he'd cut me a break.

"You a skier?" I asked, pointing at the little figurine on his desktop.

He paused in his typing and looked at the little skier.

"No."

Then he went back to typing. Claire and I shared a look and almost lost it. Why would someone have something like that on his desk if he wasn't a skier?

Soon after, Grouchy pulled the violation form from the printer and handed it to me. He explained that it was a $50 fine and that I would have to pay that fine if I ever came back to Brazil.

Wait a second. Are you telling me that you went through all this hassle and kept us here for two hours for this? A fifty dollar fine? That I didn't even have to pay unless I ever came back? Are you kidding me?

I took my violation sheet, thanked Grouchy and walked out of his office. But not before getting him to sign the Pixcom release. Because even though he was super grouchy, he still let Tyson film the entire process! I still can't believe he said yes when Tyson asked him. Normally government officials say no to that request. Especially grouchy ones. But the agent didn't seem to care at all. Tyson was all over the office, filming my ordeal from ten different angles. I just don't understand people sometimes.

Last stop before leaving for Grenada was customs. We walked up to the customs office and tried the door. Locked. I called the number posted on the window and got in touch with a customs officer who told me that we'd just missed him and no, we couldn't talk him into coming back. Didn't I realize it was Christmas? I tried begging, pleading and bribery but nothing worked. It looked like we were going to spend Christmas in Boa Vista instead of Grenada.

Dang it.

Both Claire and Tyson were pretty disappointed. Hell, I was disappointed too! But what are you going to do? I briefly thought about just getting in the plane and blasting off for Grenada but the little angel on my shoulder talked me out of it. The airport guards had machine guns, remember?

Resigned to our fate, we grabbed a cab, found a hotel in town and tried to make the best of it. Boa Vista wasn't the worst place in the world to spend Christmas. There were palm trees, nice weather and rum. (No Eggnog though!) All it was missing was the ocean. That night we went out and met some locals at dinner who gave us a tour of the city's finer establishments. Once again the city erupted with fireworks at midnight. Claire and I both agreed that if we couldn't be back home in Wisconsin or the Caribbean, Boa Vista wasn't the worst place in the world to spend Christmas.

The next day it was back to work. The customs guy didn't show up until late morning so we didn't get an early start. I let Claire do the take off and after skirting Venezuela and leaving South America we reached Grenada by late afternoon and called it a day. That night at dinner Tyson mentioned the fact that there hadn't been near enough near-death emergencies on this trip and he was worried that this episode might not be as exciting as some others.

Sorry for not almost killing us multiple times a day but sometimes reality can be boring.

I knew what he was getting at though. For a TV show to be successful there needs to be some drama but I couldn't quite bring myself to hope for engine trouble over the jungle or ocean just to get good ratings. Then I was reminded of a conversation I had with one of Pixcom's producers when I first got on the show.

"There's one thing you need to remember Kerry. Make sure the audience either loves you or hates you. Just don't be boring."

After hearing that I'd decided that being a hated jerk was a lot easier than trying to always be a lovable guy. It was more fun too. Unfortunately there was only one person to be mean to on this trip.

It was an absolutely beautiful morning to go flying. Bright sunshine, light winds and the vivid colors that can only be found in the Caribbean. Whitewashed buildings dotted the lush green hills that rose out of the picture perfect turquoise water. The airport in Grenada was a gem. Neat as a pin, it seemed designed to give visitors a first impression worthy of a tropical paradise. Once again I was disappointed that the pre-flight inspection didn't reveal a defect that would ground the Bonanza. And trust me, I looked hard.

Claire would be doing the takeoff again and my briefing was short. Takeoff, gear up, turn northeast, contact ATC. She taxied to the end of the runway, applied full power and soon we were lifting off into another perfect Caribbean morning. Claire brought the gear up and turned left over the medical school where the American students had been rescued during the 1983 invasion.

The scenery was so stunning that I grabbed my camera and took a few pictures out the left window. As I looked to see if there was anything worth taking a picture of on the right side I noticed that Claire was taking pictures with her phone. She was holding the phone with her right hand and flying with her left. At first I was proud of her. Her speed was good, climb rate right where it should be and she was right on course.

Good multi-tasking Claire!

Then I remembered, *oh yeah, we're filming a TV show here!*

"I have the controls!" I yelled as I grabbed the yoke away from Claire.

She looked at me in surprise.

"Don't ever let me catch you taking pictures while you're supposed to be flying again!"

"But you do that all the time!"

"Well, when you have eight thousand hours of flight time then you can do that too! Now put your phone away, take the controls, and pay attention to what you're doing!"

Claire put her phone in her tiny purse and reached for the yoke once again. We were both silent for a minute.

"Aaaaaand scene. Good job Claire. You played the part of 'immature teenage daughter pilot' to a T."

"Gee thanks, Dad."

Was there a hint of sarcasm there?

"OK Claire, are you ready for your Christmas present?"

"Are you getting me a pony?"

"No, even better. I'm giving you a Caribbean island for Christmas!"

"What?"

"I'm giving you your choice of any island we're going to fly over. You pick and we'll land there and give you a day off to spend on the beach."

Claire was overwhelmed. It's not every young girl who gets a beach day on the island of her choosing.

"So which island do you want?"

"I don't know. All I know is that it has to have white sand beaches and turquoise water."

We spent the day looking for an island that fit Claire's specifications. We flew low over three different islands and she said no to all of them. Maybe I should've gotten her a pony. It was late afternoon before Claire found an island she liked. Claire picked the island of Nevis. As we rounded the island and set up for landing I noticed clouds moving in from the west. I didn't think much of it. Clouds and rain showers were common in the late afternoon in the Caribbean and usually didn't last long.

After we landed we were met by an impossibly cheerful and bubbly woman named Amel. Amel was the head of tourism for Nevis and was beside herself to have a TV show film crew drop in on her little paradise. She took care of transportation and accommodations and promised she'd do something about the dark clouds that threatened rain. Amel came through in two out of three.

It started raining as soon as we checked into our beachfront cottages. The rain continued through the afternoon and into the evening. Claire was understandably disappointed. Out of all the islands in the entire Caribbean chain, she picked the only one where it rained that day. Tyson was happy though. He got to get footage of a sad Claire standing under the eves of her cottage watching it rain. Claire didn't have to try very hard to look sad.

We burned through the rest of the Caribbean pretty quickly and made it into Ft. Lauderdale just in time to sit in a three-hour traffic jam before reaching our hotel. Welcome back to civilization.

Suddenly it was the last day of the trip. Claire flew us up the coast to Columbia, South Carolina, where we'd do the final interviews. Claire was extremely happy. I'd had her on many adventures over the years but this trip was one she would never forget. We only had two things left to do. Get through the final interviews and shoot the air-to-airs. The interviews were painful as usual, but they were even more difficult than usual because the Columbia airport had a lot of military traffic. Monstrous twin rotor Ospreys, Black Hawk helicopters, and Marine Harrier jump jets used the airport frequently. Ever try to film an interview with an Osprey hovering overhead?

The air-to-air's were a blast as usual but even more so because we were working with my old friend David Gibbs. This session was even more fun than usual because David was flying a twin engine airplane called a Partenavia. This particular plane had a camera that could be lowered from the belly of the aircraft and was mostly used to get the aerial shots for Monday night football. Its ability to fly faster than a helicopter made it the perfect airplane to fly air-to-airs with. During the planning session we decided to use Cape Fear as our filming location due to its proximity to the ocean and a large area of forest that could pass for the Amazon Jungle.

After we were done for the day we flew back to Columbia. On the way I suggested to David that we fly in formation and when we got to Columbia we requested an overhead break.

An overhead break is how most military aircraft enter an airport's landing pattern by flying up the runway in the direction they intend to land, then at the mid-field point, break off one by one, pulling hard into the downwind leg of the landing pattern. It looks as cool as it sounds; Which was why I wanted to do it.

David and I were grinning ear to ear as we flew up the runway at one hundred eighty knots. I was tucked in close to David's left wing and as we hit the midfield point he looked over, gave me the "kiss off" signal, put his plane into a hard right bank and peeled off. I counted to five and followed him. It was awesome! I pulled at least three G's and Claire was suitably impressed. We both landed, taxied in and shut down side by side. A fuel boy came up to us as we were high fiving each other and said that our display looked cooler than when the Marine Harriers did it. I thought so too.

David packed up the rest of his gear, gave Claire a big bear hug, then flew away. That was the last time I saw David. Three weeks later David was killed while filming another reality show. He was flying a helicopter at night and had been asked to drop a rucksack to someone on the ground. The report was sketchy but it sounded like when he came in for a low pass someone on the ground or in the helicopter turned on a bright camera light. Blinded, he pulled up too late and flew right into the ground, killing himself and a cameraman. But that tragedy was still in the future.

With all the filming and interviews complete our Pixcom mission was done. All that was left to do was to complete that actual ferry flying part of our mission and deliver the Bonanza to its new owner in North Carolina. The three of us packed up one last time, hopped into the plane for a quick night flight to Greensboro. Claire would fly the last leg and it would be her first night takeoff. Night takeoffs are always special. Moving into position on the runway, in between the double rows of lights laid out in front of you just looks … futuristic. Claire thought so too and we shared an eager smile as she pushed the throttle forward. Rolling down the runway the lights flew past faster and faster as we accelerated. Claire pulled back on the yoke and we lifted off into the night sky. Three seconds later the door next to Claire popped open and the quiet and serene cockpit suddenly became a maelstrom of wind and noise. Nosier than it should be but that didn't matter at that point. What mattered was flying the airplane. I quickly looked over at Claire and saw that she was unfazed by the door coming open and was continuing to fly the plane, just like I'd taught her.

A door popping open on takeoff is an emergency that every pilot should train for but few ever give much thought to. Getting distracted by having a door come open in flight has killed more than its share of pilots. Which is a shame because, in my opinion, it's not an emergency but a minor situation because the plane flies just fine with the door ajar. Which is all that really happens because the wind only allows it to open a few inches. It does, on the other hand, make a terrible racket. So what do you do if the door comes open on takeoff? Nothing! Keep flying the plane! Don't try to close it. Don't slip the plane … don't … do … anything. Just keep climbing to a safe altitude then figure out your next course of action. Usually it's best to turn around and land because they are very difficult to close in-flight. I'd covered this with Claire before we left Uruguay because the door on the Bonanza is notorious for popping open.

When the door popped open I instantly knew what happened but my hands never even flinched towards the controls. I wanted to see what Claire would do. Still looking straight ahead I spared a sideways glance at Claire and saw that she was ignoring the door and flying the plane. I kept my mouth shut as she grabbed the handle and brought the landing gear up. Neither of us said a word as she made the left turn on course. It was then we figured out where the extra noise was coming from. It was Tyson screaming in the back of the plane. He wasn't just screaming, he was also frantically reaching past Claire's seat and trying to grab a seat belt that was flapping in the breeze. I told him to sit back and calm down. Passing through eight hundred feet I told Claire I'd take the controls while she closed the door.

Then it was over. Claire flew the last two hour leg to Greensboro and brought the Bonanza in like a pro. It had been one hell of a father-daughter adventure and we were both a little sad when we handed the keys to the Bonanza's new owner. That was until the owner gave me a jar of locally made strawberry jam. I was pretty happy about that until Claire grabbed it for herself. Damn kids.

THE BIG GUY

Ever try to stuff ten pounds of something into a five pound bag? Well, that's Marcio in a Cirrus. Pixcom's latest ferry flight was a doozy if only from the standpoint of talking the big Brazilian into ferrying an SR-22 Turbo from Augsburg, Germany to Las Vegas, Nevada. The crazy part wasn't just that at six foot three, Marcio was going to be a tight squeeze in the little four seater. No, the crazy part was that Marcio hadn't flown an aircraft with a propeller since he'd been in flight school. Had he ever flown a single engine airplane over the North Atlantic? Also no. The pull to be a TV star must be very strong to talk someone like him into doing something like that.

And just to make things really interesting they wanted us to ferry this little single engine plane over the North Atlantic and Northern Canada in January. Hmmm, maybe wanting to be a TV star was affecting me as well because I probably wouldn't have agreed to the trip otherwise. But the shining lights of showbiz drew us like moths to a flame.

Marcio and I met up in Germany and were introduced to our new home for the next two weeks, the mighty SR22T. The SR22T is the new and improved version of the original SR22. The improvement? The "T" stands for turbo charged! I was looking forward to flying this version because the turbocharger would allow the plane to fly higher and faster than the other SR22 I ferried. Two of my favorite things.

The first thing we did was give the plane a good once over. Check the log books, do a thorough pre-flight and look for any red flags. Because the plane was being taken care of by what appeared to be a highly professional aviation shop I wasn't anticipating any problems. If there's one you can count on it's the German's attention to detail. We were also getting a feel for our new roles. On this trip I would be Captain and Marcio would be my first officer. This arrangement made the most sense because I was the expert on single engine ocean crossings as Marcio had been the expert at jet trips. I also had more flight hours than he did but who's counting?

I didn't find anything that the Germans had missed (shocking) so it was time to see how it flew. When we climbed into the Cirrus one problem popped up almost immediately. Marcio's head stuck out of the top of the aircraft almost four inches when he sat down in the right seat. It was hilarious. It looked like someone was going to be doing a little slouching on this trip.

We took off and did a quick test of all the systems and found everything in good working order. Until we came in for landing. As I reduced power to begin our descent the engine started running a little rough. Not alarmingly so, but enough to get my attention. I tried to think about what might be the problem. Usually if a power change results in a rough running engine the problem is in the fuel air mixture. Either it's too lean or too rich.

I pulled the mixture lever back to lean it out. No change. Richer? Better … then worse. Boost pump on? No … worse. Nothing seemed to work. The roughness changed intensity and frequency with power changes and mixture manipulations but with no discernible pattern. After messing with it for a while I finally got the engine running somewhat smoothly. I stayed higher than normal as I came in for landing. Test flight complete. Result? Meh, I liked the plane but the rough running engine bugged me. I'd figure it out. Let's go to Las Vegas.

Tyson Hepburn would be the guy in the back again on this flight. I'd lobbied for Drifty but Cory and Pete Zaccagnino snagged him for a trip to Kenya first. Cory and Pete would be leaving the US about the same time as us and our two flights would cross paths somewhere in the vicinity of Reykjavik. Tyson and an audio tech from Pixcom got the plane all set up with cameras while Marcio and I got our pre-flight interviews done.

"I'm getting some kind of background noise on the audio channel," Tyson said as he rummaged around in the back of the Cirrus.

We were flying on instruments two hundred miles northwest of Augsburg, heading for England and making good time. No ice, good winds and the plane was running well. I wanted to just pretend I didn't hear him and enjoy our progress.

"Guys, I've been listening to some of the playback from the in-flight video and I'm getting this weird feedback."

Not sure what you want us to do about it.

Marcio and I turned around in our seats to look back at Tyson. Well, I turned around in my seat. Marcio's big frame only allowed him to turn his shoulders and head slightly.

"Are you guys running any extra radios or electronic gear of any kind?"

Marcio and I confirmed that we didn't have anything out of the ordinary running. Tyson swore and went back to messing with his video gear. I understood his concern. One of the first trips Pixcom filmed was a ferry flight from the US to Moscow. The cameraman on the trip had done a great job of filming what turned out to be an epic adventure across Russia. Unfortunately when he brought his tapes back to Montreal for editing they found that there was no audio at all. The cameraman had some switches on the video camera set incorrectly. He could hear what he was filming in his headphones but nothing was being recorded. The entire trip was a bust. No one knew for sure, but Drifty told me once that he guessed Pixcom lost close to half a million dollars on that little oopsie.

Ever since then the cameramen double check the footage at the end of each day and back it up on their computers. So I completely understood the swearing and carrying on I heard from the back of the Cirrus. Soon after we heard Tyson talking to someone on his sat phone. Presumably he'd contacted someone at Pixcom who was hopefully giving him some guidance. It wasn't long before he had his answer.

"Guys, we need to land."

"Where?"

"I don't care. I need to get at the camera's power supply and find a way to shield it somehow."

Great. That should be super easy.

If there's one thing European controllers hate, it's alternating an IFR flight plan.

Especially an international one. They would have to shift slot times around, and call British Customs and Immigration to tell them we weren't coming.

Somehow we made it happen with a minimal amount of pain and landed at Cologne, Germany. As soon as we shut down Tyson was busy tearing down the power supply they'd hardwired into the plane. He had the audio tech on speakerphone so I was optimistic he'd solve the problem. Two hours later he declared victory over the issue and we once again left Germany for England.

And once again diverted. Same problem, same story. This time we landed at Annecy, France. Pixcom's latest solution would be to fly in the audio expert that installed the system in the first place. Luckily he hadn't left Germany yet and he could get to us the next day.

In the meantime Marcio and I would get to enjoy Annecy. In my thirty years as a ferry pilot I've been stuck in places all over the world. Some nice, some not so nice. I'll have to say Annecy is definitely in the top ten places I'd like to be stuck. A medieval alpine town, Annecy is a picturesque little gem with cobblestone streets, winding canals and a large lake framed by a magnificent view of the Alps. The city is also filled with excellent little bars and upscale restaurants. Somehow Marcio and I managed to survive the full day it took to get the audio tech to us. We're team players after all.

Meanwhile, Cory and Pete were battling storms, icing and bitter below-zero temperatures as they made their way across Northern Canada and Greenland. Seeing that we might both arrive in Wick, Scotland around the same time, I proposed we make a little wager on who would get there first. Cory instantly agreed and a bottle of Glenlivet scotch whiskey was on the line. The race to Scotland was on.

The audio tech finally showed up and got right to work while Tyson filmed Marcio and me playing tourist. We saw some sights, had some great food. Saw some more sights, had some more great food. Skipped seeing any more sights and went right back to the food.

The audio tech pronounced the camera system fixed early the next day and we were finally back in the air and on the way to England ... and back to Annecy. Still not fixed! Now don't get me wrong. I loved hanging around France on Pixcom's dime, but I was chomping at the bit to get going. Topping off our frustration was the fact that Cory and Pete had made it to Wick ahead of us. So we'd also lost the race and the scotch.

The delays were also making another problem worse. Marcio's wife was pregnant. Super pregnant. Like any day pregnant. And like any good husband Marcio promised his wife that under no circumstances would he miss the birth of his daughter. Why was he on this trip in the first place? Because Pixcom wanted him on it. And as long as we didn't run into any problems he should make it back with time to spare. A single engine ferry flight ... over the North Atlantic ... in February ... where nothing went wrong ... Right.

We'd already burned up two full days sitting on the ground in France. If we didn't get moving pretty soon Marcio might have to fly home before we finished the trip. Then what? Have someone come replace him? We already did that with Stu. If we had to do it again the audience wouldn't buy it. We **had** to get moving!

Two possible solutions were proposed. Fly another unit in from Canada. But that would be very expensive and worst of all, take way too long. Or something else.

Now that they'd won the race to Wick, Cory and Pete were going to fly to Annecy so Pete could get checked out at Courchevel. Courchevel airport is a tiny little strip tucked way back in the Alps and is considered one of the most dangerous airports in the world. Seeing that their aircraft would just be sitting for a day or so, our idea was that we'd take/steal their audio gear so we could get moving and they could wait for a new one to be shipped in from Canada. I was positive they would hate that idea, but it might keep Marcio from having to leave the flight and ruining the episode.

Cory and Pete would first have to get to Annecy before we could have that argument and that was proving to be difficult. When they got to Wick, Cory and Pete quickly fueled up, filed a flight plan and took off. All except for that last part. Flying in the crowded airspace of Europe wasn't like flying anywhere in the world. To fly from Scotland to France you not only needed a flight plan but also a slot time so ATC would be able to fit you into their busy airspace. When the boys filed their flight plan they were shocked to see that their slot time was six hours away! That didn't sit well with them but try as they might they were unable to change it.

So our little welcoming party at the Annecy airport hung out and waited for the boys from Wick. And waited, and waited, and waited. The sun went down and we began to get worried. The Annecy airport closed for the day at 9pm and after hours landings were not permitted. We finally got a call from Cory telling us that they had landed at an airport in Northern France and would be leaving soon. When I told him about the deadline Cory thought that they might be just a little bit late getting into Annecy before it closed for the night. I told him that I'd see what I could do but that they should hurry.

As closing time approached, I went up to the control tower to see if the controller had any leeway. The tower was dark and the middle aged Frenchman reclining in his office chair was bathed in the glow of his computer screens. He was happy to have a visitor and when I told him about our situation he called up Cory and Pete's location on his radar screen.

"It looks like they will arrive fifteen minutes after the airport is closed for the evening."

I bent over and looked at the little green dot on the screen that was Cory's Caravan.

"I don't know, it looks like they will just make it in time. Perhaps after they land you would like to join us for dinner?"

The controller looked at me and didn't say anything for a minute.

"I am expected home after I am done working for the night. My wife would not like it if I went out without her."

"Well, I hope you can join us anyway. If you arrive before us please have the first drink on us."

After I said this I slid a fifty Euro bill across his desk. He didn't say anything but the money soon disappeared. At nine o'clock with Cory and Pete's plane still not in sight the controller told me that he was going to leave the control tower and go have a cigarette. He also told me with a wink

that he hoped no one landed while he was away. I quickly
went down to the ramp and climbed into the Cirrus and
turned on the master switch. I then put on my headset and
turned the radio to the control tower's frequency and made
a call in the blind.

"Hey Cory, do you read Kerry?"

"Kerry! What's up buddy?! What's the scoop? Can we
land?"

"It's all taken care of. Just bring it in and park next to
the Cirrus. Don't make any more radio calls. The wind is
calm."

I left the radio on and continued to monitor the
frequency in case they needed anything. I could see the
control tower operator smoking at the base of the tower,
watching things. A minute later a flashing red light
appeared out of the night and I watched it arc around for
landing. After they landed and taxied in I got on the radio
one last time,

"Welcome to Annecy,"

I then looked over at the tower and watched as the
controller went back inside and shut the lights off. A
minute later I saw the controller give me a wave and walk
to the parking lot.

With the gang back together we went to the hotel to
discuss what to do about our situation. It was good catching
up with those guys on the ride to the hotel but the mood
was tainted by what we all knew was an upcoming
argument.

And it was ugly ... sort of. The argument was simple.
Marcio and I wanted Cory and Pete's audio gear and they
wanted to keep it. They didn't care that Marcio had a

deadline. We pointed out that it wasn't their equipment but Pixcom's, and handing it over would be the best thing for the team and Pixcom. Things got a little heated and would have been a lot worse if not for the fact that we were all friends and professionals. Marcio was the most upset because he had the most to lose. In the end Cory and Pete wouldn't give up their gear unless ordered to by Pixcom. We decided to table the argument for the time being and go out to dinner.

Before we left I brought up one last topic, air-to-airs. Specifically the camera ship pilots. I pointed out that David Gibbs was one of the best pilots I'd ever worked with and he still managed to get killed doing the non-standard flying required to film a TV show. It's in a cameraman's nature to always get the shot they think will look best and ask the pilot to do it, that's their job. They always want to go lower and slower which are the two most dangerous things to do in aviation. The problem is that the pilots are so excited to be a part of "show business" that they will agree to things that they would never consider doing in the real world in order to please everyone and show just how good they are. I wasn't so worried about the pilots on the show because we'd been doing it for a while and were immune to John and Tyson's crazy requests ... mostly. It was the random pilots that Pixcom hired to film us during air-to-airs that worried me. During the air-to-airs with Stu in the Cirrus the year before I'd seen the pilot of the helicopter fly backwards and sideways five feet off the ground at eighty knots in order to get a cool shot of our take off. And just who was vetting these pilots? We didn't know that pilot from Adam. We just assumed that if Pixcom hired him he must be good. I tried to hammer this point to John and Tyson because in the end they were the ones flying with these guys.

The night out in Annecy was fantastic. We found the best restaurant in town and had an unbelievable meal. Then we found a charming little bar and met some young locals who hung out with us until the wee hours. I had a great time and it was really good to see Drifty again. We'd become good friends during our around the world adventures shooting season one.

The next day the Pixcom audio tech had some good news for us. He'd looked at Pete and Cory's plane and figured out what the problem with ours was. He said we should be good to go by early afternoon.

Early afternoon stretched into late afternoon before the tech finally declared us fit to fly and we finally took off for what we hoped was a flight to England. Imagine our relief when Tyson told us that the audio was crisp and clear. The flight from France would only take three hours and even though we'd gotten a late start we should make landfall before it got too late. As we approached the English Channel Marcio brought up the airport information page on his iPad and made an unfortunate discovery. The airport we were landing at would be closing soon and we might not make it in time. Rather than risk it we looked at the map and decided to land at Southampton instead. It was actually pretty easy to change destinations but they didn't seem to buy our story when we told them the reason for the change. I tried to explain that we'd made a mistake in our ETA and the controller eventually let it go but it put a bad taste in my mouth.

It was a beautiful night for flying. The dark void of the channel ended abruptly at a shoreline that was littered with lights. As we made our way inland and began our descent into Southampton I could see the light dome of London clearly in the distance. Before long we'd landed and began taxiing in. Surprisingly, the ground controller told us to taxi in and shut down directly in front of the executive operations center and lounge. Finally someone was giving us the respect and preferential treatment we deserved. We're famous TV stars for cripes sake!

The second the propeller stopped moving, four armed men burst through the terminal doors and surrounded the Cirrus. Two of them had hand guns and two had sub-machine guns and all of them were pointed at us!

"OUT OF THE PLANE! WITH YOUR HANDS IN THE AIR!" One of them screamed at us.

At least that's what I assumed he was screaming. None of us could hear him because we were all still wearing our noise canceling headsets. We got the message though and our hands shot into the air. Or as far as they could inside the tiny cockpit. So there we were, three men in a small plane surrounded by screaming men with guns, completely shocked and confused. We still had our headsets on so all we heard was yelling. We had no idea what they were saying. To top it off I still had music playing in my headset so the whole scene was like something out of a movie with a classic rock soundtrack. One of the men awkwardly climbed up onto the wing and tried to open Marcio's door but couldn't figure out the latch. Afraid to move, Marcio yelled through the closed door and asked if we could get out. They agreed but told us to do so slowly. Have you ever tried to get out of a small plane without looking like you're reaching for a gun? It's not easy, you should try it sometime.

We finally managed to extricate ourselves from the Cirrus without drawing a hail of bullets. My obvious first question was, "Excuse me sir … but … What the hell?!"

"British Secret Service! Don't move!"

This order seemed rather silly. After all, they had allowed us to take our headsets and seat belts off and climb out of the plane onto the ground. Once again we raised our hands with kind of an "Okay" shrug. Then while three of the agents kept us covered the third stuck his head inside the plane. After his brief search failed to turn up a squad of suicide bombers he reappeared.

"Awful lot of camera equipment in there. Care to explain yourself?"

Apparently they didn't watch the Discovery Channel.

"We're filming a TV show."

That response seemed to take some wind out of their sails. Two of the agents put their heads together and conferred for a few moments then told us we could put our hands down as they lowered their weapons. Then two of the agents escorted us inside while the other two remained to search the plane. Ever the professional, Tyson immediately asked if he could film the process. The stunned agents angrily refused permission but Tyson's request seemed to convince them further that we were what we said we were. Unlikely a terrorist would want to video his capture for a Facebook post. As we walked into the executive lounge I asked our captors what this was all about but they remained stubbornly silent.

A few minutes later the two agents that were searching the Cirrus came back inside and joined us.

"Right, now suppose you tell us why you changed your destination tonight?"

"What? That's what this is all about? We changed airports because we couldn't make it to the original one before it closed for the night."

"Then why did you file flight plans to England and then cancel them three times in the last few days?"

Marcio and I looked at each other confused. Then it made sense. We had done that hadn't we? I gestured to Marcio that he could go ahead and he began to tell our tale. Not only why we had changed our flight plans but everything! Marcio told them about the rough running engine, the audio problems, his wife being pregnant, the argument with Cory and Pete, everything! Oh he wove a fascinating tale! The big Brazilian was walking around waving his arms as told the story while the Secret Service agents hung on every word. When he finally ended his story I half expected one of the agents to ask,

"And then what happened Marcio?"

By the time he was done Marcio had convinced them that we weren't terrorists, but they still wouldn't let Tyson film them. That drove him crazy.

When we got to the airport the next morning Marcio and I got our first taste of stardom since starting on *Dangerous Flights* when we were mobbed by fan. That's right, fan, singular. A line boy came up to us as we were getting the Cirrus ready and yelled,

"Hey! It's Marcio and Kerry!"

I immediately corrected him.

"That's Kerry and Marcio, thank you very much!"

The young man was star struck. He told us that *Dangerous Flights* was his favorite TV show and we were his favorite pilots.

We hadn't had much of this back in the states because the show was on the Smithsonian Channel, which wasn't quite as popular as the Discovery Channel. I could count the number of times I'd been recognized on one hand.

For some reason I usually get lucky flying over Great Britain. Commonly known for its gloomy weather, I almost always get to fly in clear skies whenever I fly over the British Isles. Our trip from Southampton to Wick was no exception. Literally flying from the southernmost point of England to the northernmost tip of Scotland, we planned on traversing Great Britain in one big leap. In order to do this I planned on using the Cirrus' great performance enhancer, the turbocharger. There were favorable winds aloft I wanted to take advantage of and the SR22T's ability to cruise along at over two hundred knots at altitudes of up to twenty-five thousand feet. And with a range of just over one thousand miles we could make Wick non-stop. Perfect.

One thing though. Bopping along at twenty-five thousand feet in an unpressurized airplane wasn't exactly Marcio's cup of tea. He would prefer to stay lower if at all possible. A lot lower. Unfortunately, that wouldn't be possible, because plodding along in the thick lower air would eat up too much fuel, speed and time. Which would in turn necessitate a fuel stop, costing us both time and money. As professional ferry pilots, that is just the sort of thing we're hired to avoid. Our job is to push the aircraft and weather to the limits in order to get the job done as quickly and cheaply as possible. Plus, Tyson wanted to film us flying at high altitude with oxygen tubes shoved up our noses. Good TV and all that.

Full disclosure, I like getting high. Tooling along in the flight levels (that's anything above 18,000 feet) is almost as much fun to me as scraping the treetops with my landing gear … almost. If you're going to fly way up there you're going to need supplemental oxygen or you're going to, you know, pass out and die. Before that happens though you'll be feeling fine because one of the first symptoms of hypoxia is a feeling of euphoria. Which isn't all that bad … I've … been told.

Now, different people can have very different levels of high altitude tolerance based on age, physical fitness, smoking habits and acclimation. Old fat guys who smoke and rarely leave sea level can have problems starting as low as eight thousand feet. Mountain climbers who spend a month on Mt. Everest can climb to the top without using any bottled oxygen at all. I've got a pretty good high altitude tolerance. I'm young (at heart) and I spend a lot of time doing hard physical labor at high altitude. As a professional skydiver I climb up to fourteen thousand feet ten to fifteen times a day, strap two hundred fifty pound students to my chest and drag them out of the plane. Do that for thirty years and you'll have a good high altitude tolerance too. When I'm flying I can function at eighteen thousand feet without oxygen as long as I don't have to move around much. The ability to do this has come in handy as a ferry pilot. It allows me to take advantage of favorable winds aloft and increased aircraft performance even if I'm delivering an aircraft that isn't equipped with onboard oxygen. Back in the 1990's I used to bring along a portable oxygen bottle but the airlines have since made it impossible to bring them home with me so the plane doesn't have any, I'm out of luck.

Luckily the Cirrus was so equipped, so when we passed twelve thousand feet the three of us stuck the little rubber cannulas up our noses and went on the juice. The nose tubes blow one hundred percent oxygen but don't seal around your face like an oxygen mask so they lose effectiveness the higher you climb.

We stopped our climb at twenty-two thousand feet and I was quite pleased with our ground speed and low fuel flow. If the upper winds stayed favorable we'd be in Wick by early afternoon.

An hour after reaching cruising altitude I looked over at Marcio and noticed he wasn't looking so good.

"How do you feel Marcio?"

"I feel just OK. Not great."

No kidding. His eyes were glazed, his face flushed and his head had been bobbing for the last few minutes. I didn't bother checking to see if his fingernails or lips were turning blue. I could tell Marcio was suffering from hypoxia. Time to get him more O2.

"I think you should switch from the nose cannula to an oxygen mask."

"I think you're right." A little slur in his speech was evident.

I handed Marcio a blue rubber oxygen mask and watched as he unplugged his nose cannula line from the O2 line and attempted to plug the oxygen mask line into it. He had a little trouble untangling the two lines and couldn't figure out how to get the mask hooked up properly. Marcio had been off oxygen for only a minute or two but his mental capacity had fallen off dramatically. Faced with an unfathomable mess of tangled lines he just stopped functioning.

"I don't know what's going on."

"Here, let me do that for you," I said as I reached for the O2 lines. "Just put the mask on and I'll hook it up."

"I'm starting to really feel it."

Marcio looked at me blankly for a second then let the tangled lines fall to his lap and reached for the mask. I made quick work of the hoses and soon had life giving O2 flowing to Marcio's mask. The result was almost instantaneous. His head perked up and his eyes focused as he looked around as if waking from a dream.

"Feeling better?"

"Yes … thank you … Whew! That was scary! I thought I was about to pass out!"

With each passing second Marcio's slurred and halting speech got better.

"I was getting a little panicky. It was like … you get the air but there's no oxygen!."

Looking back I was kicking myself for not seeing that coming. Even though I could function just fine at twenty-three thousand feet with just the nose cannula Marcio was a different story. Yes, he was younger than I was but I was in much better physical shape. I also spent a considerable amount of time working at high altitude each year. As an airline pilot, Marcio works in a pressurized aircraft each day and thus is never exposed to the thinner air found at higher altitudes. I should have had him put his oxygen mask on right away. Once we figured out how to keep Marcio from passing out we pressed on and made our way to Wick.

It was good to see Andrew again. He took care of getting us and the Cirrus all ready for the ocean crossing. He topped off our fuel, oxygen and thankfully our TKS anti-icing fluid. I was happy to be going into battle with the North Atlantic with a full complement of weapons. One of the funnier things was the survival suit Andrew had for Marcio to use. The normal suits came in an orange rubber bag labeled, small, medium or large. Marcio's survival suit bag was green and was labeled "Jumbo". I died laughing when I saw that.

The next morning we were all ready to go, but had one small problem. Marcio couldn't get the upper half of his survival suit on very easily while sitting in the plane with the doors closed. Normally what I do when ferrying a single engine plane over the ocean is wear the suit only up to my waist, leaving the upper half of my body and my arms out. That way I can be somewhat comfortable and also use my hands because the built in gloves are far too thick and cumbersome to fly in. If I was ever faced with a ditching scenario I could just put my arms in the sleeves and zip it up. I know that sounds easy but try it in a small plane some time. It takes a lot of manual dexterity to twist and turn your body and arms enough to get them inside the neoprene suit. Now try that in a plane who's engine has just died and is heading for the cold dark waters of the North Atlantic. With me so far? Good. Now try doing all that as a six foot four inch, not so flexible, slightly overweight

Brazilian airline pilot. You see the problem? I had Marcio sit in the Cirrus with the doors open to see if he could get his suit on and zipped up while inside the plane. He couldn't. He could barely get it on while standing on the ramp. *Well ... shit.* If he couldn't get the suit on he might as well not bring the damned thing. Either that, or wear it the entire time. Then I had an idea. The biggest problem he had was getting the first arm in and up over his shoulder. What if he flew with that arm and shoulder already in? That way he could already be mostly in the suit but would be sort of comfortable. He sat in the plane and gave my method a try. It was ugly but it worked.

I hurried us up and got in the air before we found some other reason not to go. I purposefully avoided asking Marcio how he felt about flying a single engine plane over the North Atlantic. I figured if I could get him in the plane and keep him distracted, he might not notice when the Scottish shoreline disappeared behind us. I didn't care how the baggage (Tyson) felt.

It was a beautiful morning to make the Scotland to Iceland trip. Marcio looked a little nervous when we took off and headed north out over the water but after we got up to cruising altitude he seemed fine. As usual there were unusual scary sounds and vibrations coming from the plane as we headed out over the ocean. It's the same every time. Did the engine always sound like that? I can't tell if the vibration is worse than normal. Always a little extra fear associated with over-water operations. Today's was a slight high pitched squealing sound coming from the engine. I speculated that it might be the alternator going out, but only for the cameras. I was pretty sure it was nothing.

After an hour I looked over at Marcio and felt it was time for a little surprise he probably wouldn't appreciate.

"Tyson, turn the cameras on."

"Rolling."

"Hey Marcio."

"Yeah?"

"I need to use the restroom."

"OK, but we're halfway to Iceland. We can't just pull over."

"That's okay. I came prepared," I said as I held up my trusty Ziploc bags.

"No."

"Yes. I'm sorry but I have to go and as nice and warm as it would feel, I'm not going in my survival suit."

"I told you not to have that second cup of coffee."

I set the bags on the instrument panel (Bags, always use two bags! Going to have to trust me on this one!) and pulled my survival suit down to my knees and got to work. I didn't really really have to go but we're filming a TV and … well … good content is good content.

"Don't watch me!"

"I'm not watching you!"

Sitting shoulder to shoulder with someone who's filling a Ziploc baggie is uncomfortable and awkward to say the least. Even if it is for a TV show. It's also one of the reasons I'd rather fly solo over the Atlantic. I can't imagine having to do something worse in that closed cockpit. Cory and Pete told us over drinks in Annecy that Drifty had to do just that in the Caravan on the way to Greenland. Apparently he had a bad reaction to some Canadian Mexican food and things just couldn't wait. They both laughed themselves silly as they remembered how bad it smelled even though John went all the way in the back of the plane to do his business.

With my gear stowed away we continued on to Iceland. I was relieved, Marcio was traumatized.

Reykjavik was Reykjavik. We had hot dogs at the famous outdoor hot dog stand. Paid a visit to the Blue Lagoon hot springs (too expensive, not hot enough for me) and did the cold water survival course that Stu and I had gone through the year before. Watching Marcio get into the raft unassisted was … amusing.

That night we went out on the town and somehow ended up at a nightclub that catered to a much younger and better looking crowd than Marcio and I. But oh my God was it worth it! I would call it a supermodel bar but your average supermodel wouldn't be allowed inside. Wow, the women were beautiful! Then there was us. Two middle aged married guys standing against the wall trying to look hip and failing miserably. At least the drinks were outrageously expensive. Now we know why no one goes out to the bars until late at night. Then it happened. A stunningly beautiful woman made eye contact with me and slowly walked up to me in a most provocative manner. I didn't know what to do so I just stood there, frozen like a deer in the headlights. The enchantress stopped uncomfortably close to me and paused, looking me square in the eye. Then, she bent down toward my waist, put her lips around the straw in my mixed drink and took a very long and hard pull before standing back up. Smiling at me, she slowly walked away. Marcio and I watched her walk away then looked at each other, totally blown away and dumbfounded.

"What the hell?"

Then I looked down at my ten dollar drink and realized that she'd taken about a six dollar swallow! I felt pretty dumb but we both laughed pretty hard. About ten minutes later the same thing happened again when a different girl walked up to me.

But this time when she started to bend down I pulled my drink back and said, "Oh no!" *Not this time! Keep walking sister!"*

The next day we were halfway to Greenland and things were going well. We'd had to dodge a little icing getting out of Reykjavik but the majority of the route looked beautiful. When we arrived over the ice cap it was one of the nicest days I'd ever seen there. We were fat on gas so I flew us over a few glaciers and mountain peaks before dropping down into the iceberg filled fjord that led to Narsarsuaq. I turned the controls over to Marcio to allow him the pleasure of flying up the winding trench that ended at the airport. To my utter shock and revulsion Marcio immediately engaged the autopilot and started flying using the heading bug.

"Are you kidding me? Every pilot in the world would give his right arm to be flying here right now and you're letting the autopilot do it?"

Marcio didn't care. He was comfortable with the autopilot and I wasn't going to change that. I half jokingly threatened to take the controls back from him so as not to waste the opportunity but let him continue with a look of disgust on my face. Dammed airline pilots.

After landing I went up to the control tower to say hi to my friend Hans whom I met on my last trip into Narsarsuaq with Stu. It was always fun making these connections around the world. I missed the days when I was a full time ferry pilot and knew airport managers and weather briefers in a dozen airports around the world.

When I got back to the plane instead of finding a smiling co-pilot ready to make our final North Atlantic leg of the trip I was greeted by a scowling one with a cell phone in his hand.

"There is a problem. Apparently someone forgot to file some paperwork to export the Cirrus before we left Germany and it can only leave Europe after it's completed. The plane has to remain in Iceland for two more days or it's a one hundred twenty thousand dollar fine. We are in Greenland. We might have to fly back to Iceland"

I was shocked. I've been on the receiving end of export paperwork snafus before, but never one as catastrophic as this.

"I told them that I'd charge sixty thousand to go back."

The gravity of the situation hit me like a ton of bricks. Here we were in Greenland with just one more ocean leg ahead of us before we'd be safe and dry. Now we were looking at three.

"This is the worst place for this to happen. Cannot leave the plane here, cannot go to Canada, don't want to go back to Iceland."

It wasn't only the stupidity of tempting fate by flying back and forth across the cold Atlantic ocean but Marcio's looming deadline that worried us. There was nothing we could do about it that afternoon so I went up to see Hans and told him we were spending the night. Hans was so sympathetic he invited us to his home for dinner that night.

"We have dried whale meat, whale blubber and fermented seal meat that has been buried in the ground for over a month. We also call it seal juice."

The three of us were in Hans' quaint, little house just off the end of the runway. Our hostess was Hans' Inuit wife who'd prepared a table full of native delicacies for us to try. I dove right in and found it all delicious, mostly. Marcio ... not so much. Tyson seemed to enjoy the food, but he loved filming Marcio's face as he gnawed on a piece of fresh whale blubber.

The next morning there was no news. I made plans to go back to Iceland while Marcio looked into commercial flights home in case that was needed. It was not one of our more pleasant mornings. Then Marcio got a text.

"Interesting. It says you can continue to the United states. Five words. Let's go."

And just like that, the emergency was over. We didn't ask how they fixed it because we didn't care. We jumped in the plane and blasted off for Goose Bay before someone changed their mind.

The Narsarsuaq to Goose Bay leg is six hundred seventy-five miles of open ocean. Challenging enough all on its own. But just to make things "safer" the Canadian government has imposed a rule that if your aircraft isn't equipped with an HF radio you have to make the crossing at an altitude of no less than twenty-five thousand feet. Not a big deal for most turboprops or jets but it would be really pushing the little Cirrus to its limits. We had another problem facing us as well. We'd been unable to get our oxygen bottle filled at either Reykjavik or Narsarsuaq and it was less than one third full when we took off for Canada. With three of us sucking on it at high altitude there was no way it would last. That is if we all used it the entire time we were supposed to. It looked like I was going to have to prove just how good my high altitude tolerance really was.

When we reached twelve thousand feet Marcio and Tyson put their oxygen masks on. I waited … and waited … and waited. Once we arrived at twenty-five thousand feet I grabbed my mask but held off putting it on right away. The longer I waited the longer our meager supply of O2 would last. Plus, I wanted to see how well I could perform at that altitude. I don't know what I was worried about. My head was clear, my thinking unaffected and I was feeling fine. Really fine! In my opinion I could fly all day like that. Marcio and the camera told an entirely different story. I was indeed fine, for about ten minutes. Then I grabbed Hula Girl and started singing to her the song I was hearing in my headset. I was clearly suffering from hypoxia. At first Marcio found my antics amusing. Then he began to worry about what he would do if I passed out so he suggested I put my mask on. I agreed but first I put the pulse oximeter on my finger to see what my blood oxygen level was at this altitude. Seventy-seven percent! That was pretty low. OK fine, I'll go on oxygen. The effect was immediate. My head cleared and the world went from black and white to color. OK, experiment complete. Now I know that my personal limit is somewhere below twenty-five thousand feet. The O2 gauge on the instrument panel read under one quarter of a tank left. We'd have to keep a sharp eye on it and make sure we descended to a lower altitude before it ran out completely.

The weather in Goose Bay was typical for Northern Canada in February. Bitter cold, strong winds, low clouds and icy runways. Luckily, with the air temperature thirty-three degrees below zero Fahrenheit it was far too cold for in-flight icing to be a concern. If you want to call that lucky. The oxygen gauge was bouncing on the empty mark when we were finally allowed to let down from our high altitude perch. We got topped off with fuel and oxygen and were soon back in the air and on the downhill run to civilization.

Air-to-airs and an expensive dinner with the Pixcom producers made Montreal an enjoyable stop, but the highlight of the trip was stopping in my hometown of Menomonie, Wisconsin, to get a little footage of Kerry's home life. Tyson filmed the usual stuff. He followed me to my home, got footage of my dog and even talked my wife Cathy into being interviewed, which she hated. Then we went out to my hunting cabin and had dinner with a few of my Army buddies. Of course Tyson filmed the manly men talking about manly things in a manly setting.

The next day it was "kiss the wife and go flying" time. One last day in the air before we reached Las Vegas and put another trip in the books. The mood in the cockpit was good, as it usually is on the way to the finish line. Marcio was especially happy because Las Vegas was only a short hop from his home in San Diego. Even if his wife went into labor sometime that day we could still get him home in time for the birth.

Tyson was also happy the trip had been a successful one from a filmmaker's perspective. He'd overcome the initial audio problems and managed to put together what we thought was a pretty good episode.

And me? I was just happy to have another North Atlantic crossing under my belt. The trip had been a stressful one and doing the crossing in February certainly hadn't helped in that regard.

We stopped in Rapid City, South Dakota. Told the line boy to top off the Cirrus then borrowed the crew car and made a short drive into town to grab some fast food to eat in the plane on our last leg to Sin City.

On the way back to the airport my cell phone rang. It was Nicola Merola, the president of Pixcom. He wanted to speak with Tyson. As I handed the phone back to Tyson Marcio and I exchanged glances. That couldn't be good. For the president of the company to call one of us in the middle of a trip probably meant bad news of some kind. I steeled myself for what was about to come.

"WHAT? NO! ARE YOU SURE? NO! NO! NO! OH NO!"

Someone is dead. A close family member probably. Father?

"John's dead!" Tyson shouted from the backseat. Marcio continued driving ... I stared straight ahead, not moving, letting the news wash over me.

"How? ... Where? ... Okay ... I'm sorry. Yes I'll call her ... No, wait, I can't." Still on the phone, Tyson was on the verge of breaking down. I'd seen it before, it wouldn't be long.

"He died in a plane crash!" he said to us before listening to the phone again.

A plane crash? What about Pete and Cory? If John died in a plane crash they most likely had been in the plane as well. I wanted to scream that question but Tyson was still listening to Nicola on my cell phone. All Marcio and I could do was wait to find out how many of our friends were dead. Finally Tyson hung up and handed the phone back to me. Between sobs he told us that John had been flying in a small plane with a doctor who had also been killed. He didn't know why John was flying with that doctor but didn't think Pete and Cory were even there. Then Tyson lost it. He was inconsolable.

"How can you guys keep going up there? First David, now John!"

Marcio pulled into the airport and parked the crew car next to a row of empty hangars. Tyson threw open the door and burst out.

"And you Kerry! You've lost even more friends! How do you do it? Why do you do it?"

Tyson went on and on while Marcio and I tried to console him. Finally he told us that he was done. And by done he meant he would never get in another small plane again, including the Cirrus. We would have to finish the trip without him because he was going home. Then Tyson stormed into the terminal to check on flights home while Marcio and I called our wives. Finally able to stop focusing on Tyson I broke down telling Cathy about John. I hadn't counted up all the friends I'd lost to plane crashes and skydiving over the years but the number was approaching twenty. That was way too high a price to pay.

Marcio came over and told me that his wife was still OK and wasn't due for another day or two so we didn't need to keep flying that day. I was relieved. I really didn't feel like getting back into the Cirrus and pretending like nothing had happened. Tyson came back and told us that the next flight out was the following day. So we tied down the Cirrus, found a hotel, then proceeded to get stinking drunk. I could tell you about it but that night was just for us.

The next day Marcio and I said goodbye to Tyson because he hadn't changed his mind about getting back into the Cirrus. He spent an hour teaching us how to turn on the cockpit cameras so we could finish filming the final leg of the trip. We would also film each other with a small handheld video camera. He didn't let us have the big one because it was too complicated. Plus he didn't trust us with such an expensive piece of equipment.

The two of us finished the trip alone. The air temperature got increasingly warmer as we flew farther south toward Vegas. We turned the cameras on, said clever and interesting pilot things and laughed like nothing had happened. When we finally got into Las Vegas we had a line boy film our final goodbye scene. Then I dropped Marcio off at the main terminal where he caught a flight home. His timing couldn't have been better because the next day he was there to witness his daughter being born.

That week the world gained one beautiful life and lost another. You may be tempted to call it a wash or the circle of life but in my opinion the books didn't balance.

After leaving us in Annecy the gang in the Caravan made their way through Europe, across the Mediterranean and down to Kenya. They were delivering the Caravan to a safari outfitter located at the base of Mt. Kenya. When they arrived they flew over the wreckage of an old airplane they'd been told about. The wreck was located up on the mountain at eleven thousand feet in an area called "Deadman's corner," known for its strong downdrafts and swirling winds.

Never one to miss an opportunity for a good shot John had Pete fly over the crash site so he could get some video. Pete obliged but didn't fly low enough or slow enough for John's liking. John urged Pete to make another, lower pass but Pete refused. The wreck was located in a deep bowl subject to strong downdrafts. Flying low and slow in there would be foolish.

"There's a reason it's called Deadman's corner," he said.

After having to scare a few zebras and wildebeests off the runway with a low pass they landed and finished filming the episode. John again pressed Pete and Cory to fly up the mountain to get better footage of the crash site. Once again they refused. When Pete and Cory left Africa after filming was complete John stayed behind to take advantage of the fact that he was in Africa. He planned on going on safari and possibly climbing Mt. Kilimanjaro. John's grandfather had spent time in Africa and he wanted to recreate the experience. But not getting an acceptable shot of the wreckage on Mt. Kenya continued to gnaw at John. Being nothing if not a perfectionist, John hunted around, looking for a way to get the shot. Then he met Dr. Anthony King. Dr. King was a renowned conservationist and pilot who has access to an ultralight aircraft. John somehow talked Dr. King into flying him up to the crash site so he could get the shot he'd been looking for. John spent the better part of an afternoon begging Pixcom to approve the expense and getting the insurance company to allow and cover it. When he finally received permission for the flight the two men plus John's big video camera climbed into Dr. King's tiny, underpowered AN-22 Foxbat and took off for the mountain.

Exactly what happened is pure speculation but it is generally believed that a strong downdraft forced the ultralight aircraft down, killing both John and Dr. King.

When I finally heard the details of the incident I was pissed. That was exactly what I had been talking about that night in Annecy! John had gone up with an inexperienced pilot (Dr. King had only 200 hours) and had gotten himself killed.

A number of things had contributed to the accident. First was the aircraft itself. I was shocked when I heard that they had been flying in an ultralight up at fourteen thousand feet. It must have taken forever to coax that little aircraft up that high. Then there are the winds. I'm sure that little ultralight was barely able to hold altitude up in the thin mountain air. It wouldn't take much of a downdraft to claw the underpowered and overloaded ultralight from the sky. The final and in my opinion the most critical link in the fatal chain of events was the combination of Dr. King's inexperience and John's desire for the perfect shot. I'm sure John asked for exactly what he wanted, a low and slow pass over the aircraft wreckage. Unfortunately his trust in the skills of his pilot were misplaced.

In the end it didn't matter. John was gone and my prediction from the year before had come true. But fate had one more cruel blow to land on the *Dangerous Flights* team.

The last flight of season two was with Brad White and Stu Sprung. They were hired to ferry a Beech 1900 from South Africa to Vancouver, Canada. It was a difficult flight with all the usual challenges. Poorly maintained aircraft, foreign governments and airport hassles, bad weather and terrible food. A typical ferry flight that made for great TV.

After they finished filming the end of trip interviews Brad immediately went to see a doctor. He'd been feeling poorly during the trip and wanted to find out what was wrong. An extremely fit and healthy young man, Brad was shocked when he was diagnosed with liver cancer. It was shocking to see how fast the cancer devoured Brad. In less than a year he was gone and the *Dangerous Flights* gang was now short two of our brothers.

With season two all wrapped up it was time for all of us to take stock. Did we want to continue being on the show or go back to our normal lives? So far none of us had really made much money being on the show. We'd been paid a daily rate for shooting but nothing in the way of royalties. I'd been told that the average reality show loses money the first season, breaks even on the second and really starts making money if they can get a third season. We all talked it over and agreed that we'd stick around for a third season and see what happened. We thought we had a great show that had the potential to give *Deadliest Catch* a run for its money. That was an appealing prospect. The agent Marcio and I had met in Las Vegas told us that if *Dangerous Flights* took off we could be looking at some real money!

Would it be worth it? Did I really want to be famous? Did I want strangers coming up to me on the street and bugging me for my autograph? I had to admit that the answer was yes, as long as a big check came along with it. My biggest fear was being famous without the money to make up for all the hassles. The experience of being on a major TV show had been an interesting one. There were times when it was amazing, having make-up artists, producers, and camera crews all there to film you can be a big ego boost. Then there were times when it wasn't so amazing, like when you realize you just did something really stupid that will be watched by millions of people for eternity. One thing that I didn't anticipate was becoming a public figure, albeit a minor one. Immediately after *Dangerous Flights* aired, dozens of online pilot chat forums started commentating on the show and the pilots. Most liked the show but there were a lot of pilots who were turned off by what they called the "over-dramatization" of the situations we faced. And that was a fair point, but what these pilots failed to grasp was that they weren't the target audience, non-pilots were. There just aren't enough pilots in the world to make a TV show just for them so the producers at Pixcom had to make the show interesting and entertaining for the average viewer. If that means making a big deal out of going on instruments of landing at night, so be it.

One thing that took getting used to were the personal comments directed at the individual pilots. Some people thought we were great guys and skilled pilots and some thought we were jerks with big egos who took unnecessary risks. What they failed to understand was that these were real ferry flights and unlike recreational pilots, a ferry pilot has to push the limits to get the job done. We can't wait for the perfect weather day to go flying if we want to accomplish the mission in a timely and cost effective manner.

We also had a story to tell which we still had a story to tell which didn't always paint us in the best light. Cory seemed to take the brunt of the negative comments. The online commandos thought he was a pushy jerk that put money ahead of his pilots' safety when nothing could be further from the truth. Cory was a great guy to work for and even though he was concerned with money (What good businessman isn't?), he always put our safety first. My favorite comment about Cory was when someone from the UK called him a "Perm-headed Porn star!"

How did they like me? Well I was the second favorite pilot to post negative comments about. It seems that I can come off as a self centered jerk on TV. Which means that I did my job well. One of the first things the producer at Pixcom told us when we started filming was that the audience had to either love you or hate you. Just don't be boring. When I heard that I yelled, "Dibs on being the asshole of the show!" I figured it was easier to make the audience hate you all the time than love you.

Season two of *Dangerous Flights* was a success. Its ratings were much better than season one and everyone was confident that we would get picked up for another season.

We made plans to secure an agent to represent us and had high hopes for season three! Unfortunately the Discovery Channel had other ideas. John's accident spooked the senior executives at the network. I wasn't privy to their decision making process but it sounded like they were uncomfortable with how dangerous the flying was. Didn't they ever look at the title of the show? The entire concept was that what we were doing was dangerous. Nevertheless the Discovery Channel was scared and decided to cancel their commitment to purchase and fund season three with Pixcom. Without Discovery Channel's support, Pixcom couldn't justify producing the series anymore. *Dangerous Flights* was no more.

The crew was both devastated and relieved. We were pretty bummed out that the show wasn't going to make us all rich and famous. On the other hand, some of us were happy to not have to risk our lives flying small airplanes over big oceans again.

Marcio retired from ferry flying and went back to being a full time airline pilot and father once again. Pete dove headlong into the Reno air racing scene, taking gold in the open jet class in 2015 and miraculously surviving a crash in a Vampire jet the next year. Taking a page from my book, Stu got a job flying skydivers in California to build up flight time before being hired by a small commuter company and starting his airline career. Tyson went back to filming reality TV shows. He was the director of "Cold water cowboys" and "Rust valley restoration." His days of filming aviation shows were over. Claire put her flying career on hold and moved to Oceanside, California to become an indoor skydiving instructor in a wind tunnel.

Flying in the wind tunnel came naturally to Claire and she soon began to compete nationally in the freestyle category.

Me? I was extremely disappointed. I'd loved being on camera and filming the show. It was both fun and challenging. I was also looking forward to possibly making some real money. As disappointed as I was about the show being canceled I was still happy about being a ferry pilot again. I hadn't realized just how much I'd missed it until I started doing it again. And just because the show was over that didn't mean that CB Aviation was out of the ferry business. It wasn't long before I got another call from Cory to fly another sketchy airplane to the other side of the planet.

THE BANGKOK EXPRESS

"Both engines leak a little oil, but that's to be expected on a plane that hasn't flown for three years."

Three years? Looks more like five.

The plane I was looking at was a 1976 Piper Navajo Chieftain and it had seen better days. Its all-white paint scheme wasn't too faded and dull and there was a new THAI REGIONAL sticker on the tail. But that couldn't hide the general feel of too many miles in the air and too many years on the ramp. I assumed that was why the new owner hired me to ferry this latest addition to his growing airline. Why risk losing one of your expensively trained charter pilots when you can find an experienced ferry pilot to fly it from Florida to Bangkok? Plus, he probably couldn't talk one of them into doing it, anyway.

Standing next to me, also listening to the aircraft broker tell his tale of lies was my best friend, Lee Wolfgram. Like most of my pilot buddies, Lee had been bugging me for years to take him on a ferry trip. But unlike those other guys, he'd somehow managed to come up with the time off and the balls to accept when I asked him to join me on this trip.

And what a trip it was going to be! We'd be taking the Navajo from Southern Florida up to Northern Canada, across the North Atlantic via Greenland, Iceland and Scotland. Then down through Europe, the Middle East and across India before reaching Bangkok, Thailand. It was a distance of over twelve thousand miles or roughly half the circumference of planet Earth. Should probably pack an extra pair of underwear.

Step one: Get out of Ft. Lauderdale. We'd flight tested the Navajo and confirmed that it did indeed leak oil. Although a thin layer of oil over everything was great at preventing airframe corrosion, it wasn't conducive to long range flying. We had a mechanic see what he could do about keeping most of the oil inside the engine case. Once the mechanic said the plane was fit to fly, Lee and I loaded it up with all our junk and took off for Maine. I wasn't thrilled that the mechanic who fixed the leaks had been the one who had performed the annual inspection but was in no position to argue with the choice.

Northbound out of Bangor, Maine.

It was a beautiful day for flying, I had my best friend in the co-pilot seat and the oil leak had finally stopped. Nothing could damage my good mood. Except …

"CRAP! I forgot to call CANPASS!"

The only two countries in the world that require pilots to call a phone number before entering their airspace are the United States and Canada. I'd remembered to call US customs telling them we were leaving but had been distracted by something and forgotten to call the Canadians. It was a pretty boneheaded move but we hadn't actually landed in Canada yet so I still had the option of going back to Bangor and starting over. Which would cost us time and money. Two things I hate to waste.

Instead, I gave Canadian ATC a call and asked if they would do me a huge favor and please call CANPASS for me? Please? Pretty please? The controller was actually pretty cool about it and after a few minutes claimed success. Sort of. When we got to Goose Bay, customs made us wait another hour and a half before showing up and then bitched us out for not calling sooner. I guess a three hour heads up wasn't good enough.

After checking into the hotel Lee and I grabbed a cab to head into town and eat. When the woman cab driver looked in her rearview mirror she freaked out.

"Holy moly! You're Kerry McCauley!"

"I am."

"I can't believe I have you in my cab! Wait until I tell my husband about this! *Dangerous Flights* is my favorite show!"

I thanked her for watching the show and signed an autograph as she let us out at Jungle Jim's bar and restaurant. Inside, the Kerry Show was just beginning. It seemed that everyone in Goose Bay was a fan of *Dangerous Flights*. Not surprising, for it it was, in my opinion, a great show. We also featured Goose Bay on a lot of the episodes so it wasn't surprising that the residents of this small town in the middle of nowhere were fans of the show. We'd put Goose Bay on the map. I was signing autographs and taking pictures with the locals all evening. I have to admit being famous was kind of intoxicating. Even if it was only in one small corner of the world.

"Hey boss, you got some oil here."
Great. The oil leak is back.

Lee and I were in Narsarsuaq for a quick fuel stop before heading on to Reykjavik and the last thing we needed was a delay. I walked around to the right engine that the fuel boy had pointed to and surveyed the damage. Sure enough, the entire right side of the engine was covered with a thin coating of oil. This was a lot more oil than we'd seen before and definitely not a good sign.

Sigh.

I busted out my trusty screwdriver and got to work taking the cowling off the right engine. When I was done I found the entire row of cylinders on the right side of the engine were shiny with oil. Looking closer the oil seemed to start at the front cylinder.

Just then two men walked up and asked if we needed any help. They were from a Douglas DC-3 that had landed just after we did. The plane was painted desert camo brown and had black and white D-Day invasion stripes painted on the wings. We found out later the plane was on its way back to the US from a Normandy D-Day anniversary celebration. The men were both aircraft mechanics and after looking the engine over determined that the oil was coming from the front cylinder's valve cover. The cover was easy to remove and when we got it off we found that the gasket was broken in two places.

"That's your problem right there."

"I don't suppose you guys have a spare one in your plane do you?"

"Sorry, we have a ton of spare parts for the DC-3 but nothing that will fit this."

I thanked the men and went inside to see if my friend Hans could be of any help. Hans was glad to see me but was unable to magically produce a valve cover gasket for a 1976 Piper Navajo. Oh well, never hurts to ask. I got on the phone to a parts supply company and was lucky enough to find one that could be shipped out to us that afternoon! Unfortunately when I checked on how long it would take for that little gasket to make it all the way to Greenland I found that Lee and I could expect to be enjoying the fine accommodations of the Narsarsuaq hotel for over a week. Because this trip had been set up by CB Aviation I called Cory with the news and he said he'd see if he could do anything better from his end.

That night Lee and I got a taste of local life in Narsarsuaq. After dinner Hans came over with a few of his friends and we all just hung out in front of the hotel drinking beer and talking. And drinking beer. It turns out that there's not a whole lot to do at night in Greenland except watch satellite TV and drink beer. Apparently there was nothing good on TV that night.

The next morning I got an email from Cory with the message I expected. Eight to ten days to get a gasket to Greenland. And that was it. Stuck. But I'd been in this situation before and knew there was more than one way to skin a cat. If you can't get a new part, fix the old one. There were cars in Narsarsuaq so there must be a repair shop. I asked around and found that there wasn't an official garage but one of the locals did a lot of repairs and maybe he could help us out. Lee and I walked down the dusty gravel road to a small house at the end of the runway and met the wrinkled old native man who was the community handyman. After I explained that we were looking for some gasket material to fix our airplane he dove into the junk pile in his garage and in a few minutes came up with exactly what we needed. A small square of dark blue gasket material. Unbelievable! I paid him double what he asked for, which wasn't much, and headed back to the airport to use those art skills I learned in third grade.

First I retrieved the metal valve cover from the right engine and carefully removed the broken pieces of gasket. Then I reassembled them on top of the sheet of gasket material and traced the outline onto the sheet. Then I got out my Gerber multi-tool and using its knife and scissors cut out what I hoped was an exact copy of the original valve cover gasket. I then reassembled the engine with the new homemade gasket and threw the cowling back on. Fixed? Only one way to find out and that's to fly it and see if it leaks. Just heading off to Iceland would be crazy so Lee and I used this opportunity to show Lee the ice cap. We spent the better part of an hour buzzing up and down the fjords, up over the glaciers and back again. It was exactly the kind of flying I wanted to show Lee when I asked him on this trip.

Reykjavik, Wick, Rotterdam, Augsburg. The cities and countries fell like dominoes. Lee and I were having a blast together. It was the adventure we'd been dreaming of since we were young. World travelers.

My homemade valve cover gasket hadn't leaked a drop and the Navajo was running way better than expected. Especially since when I saw Andrew in Wick and he told me that this was the third Navajo the owner of Thai Regional had tried to buy and ferry back to Thailand. Apparently the other two had been in such bad shape that both ferry pilots had abandoned them before reaching their destination.

We did have one tiny problem looming, though. The international handling company that we were using on the trip was having issues getting landing permission from Pakistan. As soon as I heard this I started looking for alternate routes. At first glance not being able to land in Pakistan looked like a non-issue. We could go down to Muscat in Oman and jump directly over the Arabian Sea to India. It was only six hundred miles coast to coast. I looked on my iPad and saw that there were two Indian airports not too far inland that we could reach with the fuel the Navajo carried. Remembering the avgas situation I'd encountered in India while filming *Dangerous Flights* I checked to see if either of those airports had fuel. The results were discouraging. One airport only carried jet fuel and the other did have avgas but it was only for use in the aero club aircraft that were based there. Hoping to get an exception I called the aero club to plead my case. No go. The man who answered the phone made it clear that we could land but there would be no fuel available for us. After hanging up I thought about what I'd heard and had an idea. If worse came to worst I might have a way to keep going.

Leaving central Europe we headed down to one of my favorite stops, Corfu, Greece. Corfu is a beautiful Mediterranean island with just the right mix of warm weather, great food, local flavor and stunning views. It was also our last stop before hitting the Middle East and India, so if we needed anything for the plane this would be our last chance.

I checked my email as soon as we got to the hotel, hoping to see good news from the handling company. No such luck. They were still having trouble getting us permission to fly into Pakistan. Okay, plan B it is.

Ferry tanks are a useful tool when ferrying small aircraft around the world. Sometimes even with ferry tanks long distances or adverse winds can make some legs problematic. Over the years I've had to resort to a somewhat desperate measure. Bringing extra fuel along in whatever containers I could find. I developed the technique while ferrying a beat up Cessna 207 from Austria to Seattle back in 1992. On that trip I did have a ferry tank installed in the plane but when I got to Santa Maria in the Azores, strong headwinds prevented me from making the 1,700 mile crossing back to St. John's Canada with the fuel I had onboard. Santa Maria is the easternmost island in the Azores chain. The island of Flores is the westernmost island and is 350 miles closer to Canada and it had an airport I could land at. Unfortunately, even though it had an airport, it didn't have any fuel available. That was when I came up with the idea of hauling extra fuel in the cabin and self fuel along the way.

I looked around the airport at Santa Maria and found a thirty gallon plastic container that had been used to deliver battery acid to the island. I cleaned out the container with a combination of baking soda and water and filled it with avgas. Then I just put it in the back of the plane, intending to fly to the island closer to Canada, stop and put the thirty gallons of fuel into the wing tanks. That was the plan anyway. But when I shoved the container into the back of the 207 the plane's tail dropped down and hit the ground. *Hmmm, maybe a little aft center of gravity there.* Luckily the 207 had a nose compartment that the container fit into perfectly. Then I took off and flew to Flores and refueled there. Sort of. When I got to Flores I found that the airport was nothing but a runway. No terminal, no services and more importantly, no ladder. Ever try getting a thirty gallon container of fuel up onto the high wing of a Cessna without a ladder? Not easy. I somehow managed to get the container up onto the wing and spill over half of the fuel into the small opening in the wing tank. At least I was able to entertain the large gathering of locals who came to watch the stupid ferry pilot put on a show. Apparently none of them spoke any English or were inclined to help me. But it worked. I got enough fuel into the tank to make St. John's and complete the mission. Since then I've used that somewhat risky trick two other times. Time for number three.

Before heading to the airport the next morning I stopped and bought twelve five gallon plastic gas cans. There were larger containers available but I'd learned my lesson with that 207 all those years ago. We didn't fill the gas cans up right away because we didn't need to fuel just yet. Plus I was pretty sure the strict EU rules at Corfu prohibited us from filling plastic gas cans inside the airplane. Strict rules wouldn't be a problem once we reached the Middle East.

Aqaba, Jordan. Our visit strangely enough started out with a job offer and a terrorist attack. I got the job offer when I was talking to a pilot at the airport after we'd landed. When he found out that I was a skydiving instructor who owned a dropzone in the US he wanted to hire me to help get his own school off the ground. I passed on the offer. Skydiving in the middle of the desert didn't sound like a whole lot of fun. And the terrorist attack? Well, it sure sounded like one. Lee and I were having dinner on the roof of our hotel when we heard a huge explosion nearby. There were a few people running around in the street and a single emergency vehicle sped past with its siren wailing. But that was it. After a few minutes everyone around us went back to eating like nothing happened. Weird.

The next day it was time to put the first phase of my plan into action. When we fueled up the Navajo we also laid out all the gas cans we'd bought in Greece and filled them almost full. It wasn't too hot for an early afternoon in the desert so I left some room for expansion in case it got hotter. In case it got hotter? Who was I kidding? We were headed for the Arabian Peninsula. Of course it was going to get hotter!

Lee loaded up our twelve red juice boxes of avgas while I peeled off two thousand dollars worth of hundreds before we mounted up and dragged the overloaded Navajo into the steadily warming desert sky.

"November six four sierra sierra, climb and maintain ten thousand on heading zero two zero."

The heading Jordanian ATC gave us right after take off was exactly one hundred eighty degrees off from the heading we needed to go.

"What the hell?"

I looked at the map and then the high ridgeline off our right side and told Lee my deduction.

"I'm sure they just want to make sure we're high enough to clear the ridge before turning us south."

"Well we're high enough already. I can see over the top for crying out loud!"

I agreed with Lee and asked ATC for a turn south … denied. We flew farther north as the sun got higher and our fuel got lower. Another request to turn … another refusal. Lee and I ranted and raved the entire one hundred miles ATC had us pointed in the wrong direction before they finally turned us around like nothing had happened. That little detour added two hundred miles to our nine hundred seventy mile leg to Bahrain and put us dangerously close to the limit of our max range. They did not do us a favor. It didn't help that the Navajo was performing and handling like a dog in hot desert air. Being overloaded with a cabin full of gas cans didn't help either.

Night fell over the desert and once again I was lucky enough to have to fight thunderstorms over the Arabian Peninsula. Lee was flying and had to divert around a few flashing cells, further depleting our meager fuel reserves. If we hadn't been re-routed we would have had a comfortable one hour and a half margin to work with. Now? Not so much. I put off the reality of the situation for as long as I could but with every passing minute it became more and more obvious that we wouldn't make Bahrain. Which was very disappointing for two big reasons. One: I'd never been to Bahrain and I always love seeing new places, meeting new people and experiencing new cultures. And two: Bahrain is the culture we wanted to experience that night. Because they allow alcohol in Bahrain and our alternate …

"Control, Navajo six four sierra sierra. We need to divert to Riyadh."

Saudi Arabia, garden spot of the Middle East. I'd stopped there once before, and even though they had good services at the airport I wasn't at all excited about staying the night. Unfortunately, it was too late to press on, so Lee and I grabbed our bags and headed into the terminal to clear customs and find a hotel. Inside, airport security had us put our bags through an x-ray machine before we continued on to the customs desk. When Lee put his bag through the machine, the guard manning the laptop it was hooked up to stopped the conveyor, stared closely, then quickly slammed the laptop closed.

"Please, come here!"

Lee looked confused as he walked over the guard as he took Lee's bag out of the machine and set it on the ground.

"Please open."

Lee unzipped the bag and stepped back as the guard rummaged around for a second before exposing a one liter bottle of Captain Morgan's Spiced Rum. He looked back up at Lee before quickly closing the bag. The guard was clearly upset as he quickly zipped Lee's bag closed.

"Alcohol is strictly forbidden in the Kingdom," the guard whispered to Lee. "You must put it back in your plane. Do not show it to anyone or let anyone see you put it back. It is forbidden to even have it in your aircraft."

Lee is nothing if not a cool customer. As casually as he could he hoisted the bag up onto his shoulder.

"I forgot something in the plane. Can I get back out on the ramp please?"

Playing along, the guard raised his voice.

"Yes, sir. Right this way."

I joined Lee on his walk across the dark ramp back to the Navajo.

"That was a close one. I thought you knew you can't bring alcohol into Saudi Arabia."

"I did. I just forgot the rum was in there."

"Well you got lucky. The other guy said that if a different guard had been on duty you would have been in big trouble."

We walked up to the Navajo and I opened the door while Lee opened his bag to take the bottle of rum out.

"Damn it!"

"What?"

"The cap wasn't on tight and the rum leaked out! All my clothes are soaked!"

I looked over and chuckled as Lee pulled handful after handful of clothes out of his bag all dripping with spiced rum. I was laughing but Lee was pissed. All his clean clothes he'd been carefully rationing to last the rest of the trip were completely unwearable. I couldn't think of anything worse to spill over all your clothes than spiced rum. The only clothes he had left were the ones on his back which consisted of a pair of khaki cargo shorts, sandals and a white, short sleeve crew shirt complete with first officer epaulets. I was wearing the same uniform only with Captain's stripes because in the Middle East as with most of the rest of the third world, airport personnel treat you with a lot more respect if you're wearing crew uniforms. OK, most professional crews wore dark slacks and dress shoes as well but it was like one million degrees out and I felt that matching shorts and sandals were called for. It looked like Lee was going to be in uniform until he could find a way to get some clothes washed. I felt bad for Lee but also found it completely hilarious.

"It doesn't look like it's getting better."

"No, not really. I talked to a pilot in the briefing room and he said that the dust can last for days or weeks sometimes."

"Great. What do you think? Should we go for it?"

The conditions we were talking about was a thick shroud of dust that had been hanging over the airport all afternoon. The thick tan cloud wasn't the only reason we were still in Riyadh late in the afternoon instead of halfway to Oman. The other reasons were just too numerous to mention. That morning it seemed like everything and everyone was conspiring to slow us down and hold us back like a thousand tiny fingers clutching at our clothes. Every … single … thing took three times as long as it normally did. And now the weather looked … well, shitty. The sky was the color of something you'd find in a baby's diaper. And I had no idea what it would do to the plane, or more specifically its instruments. Would all that dust in the air foul up any of the delicate mechanisms inside the flight instruments? I knew the vacuum pumps had filters on them but were they good enough? As if in answer to my questions another plane in the continuous stream of aircraft that were operating out of Riyadh took off. Planes had been taking off and landing the entire time we'd been at the airport that day. Apparently they weren't worrying too much about the dust. Fine, then neither would I.

We went back inside, filed our flight plan to Oman and headed out. On our way out of the building Lee and I met an airline Captain walking in from outside. He looked down at the shorts and sandals we were wearing along with our crew shirts.

"How come you get to wear shorts? You guys hiring?"

I felt for him, it was well over one hundred degrees out on the ramp.

Packed up, started up, flew up. I immediately had to go on instruments as the brown fog soon obscured the outside world. It didn't matter, I like flying on instruments and one way or another we were getting out of Saudi Arabia. We hadn't been in the air more than ten or fifteen minutes when suddenly an RBL (Really Bad Light) illuminated on the left side of the instrument panel. I looked down.

"LEFT PNEU. SOURCE MALFUNCTION." Pneumatic source ... the vacuum pump.

I looked at the gyro pressure gauge and it was still showing in the green. It looked like we'd lost the left vacuum pump but the right one was still producing enough pressure to run the flight instruments. *You gotta love the redundancy of a multi-engine aircraft!*

With a vacuum pump out there was a decision to make. Turn around and head back to Riyadh? Or continue on to Oman? Losing one of our vacuum pumps wasn't a big emergency at that point. The dust was supposed to continue for a few hundred miles but halfway to Oman it was forecast to be gone. And it wasn't like Riyadh had a great maintenance facility on the field either. Then there was the fact that neither Lee or I wanted to go back to Saudi Arabia. On to Oman it is!

Leveling off at twelve thousand feet I noted that we were still in the brown soup and it was starting to get dark. The setting sun cast a weird light inside the dusty snow globe. The indistinct sky made it look like we were on some kind of sound stage as the fading light turned the brown to gray.

Why are we turning?

I looked at my GPS mounted on the yoke and saw that our once straight as an arrow track line now had a left hand curve to it. I glanced at the artificial horizon to see if I'd gotten sloppy and put us in a left bank. Nope, wings level. Directional gyro? That's odd, it showed us heading right of course when the GPS showed left. What the hell?? … CRAP! LOST THE OTHER VACUUM PUMP!

Too late, I saw the second bright red RBL shining next to the first one.

"RIGHT PNEU. SOURCE MALFUNCTION."

Quick … partial panel drill. Needle, ball, airspeed.

I looked down at the turn and bank indicator and saw that it showed the plane in a steep left turn. Or is it a right turn? I looked closer at the turn and bank indicator and saw that it was a style I hadn't seen in a long time. In a normal instrument when you turn the aircraft left the little plastic plane in the window of the instrument banks left. The old turn and bank instrument in the Navajo was almost exactly the opposite in that the little airplane is fixed in the window and the card behind it turns left or right. So when you bank the aircraft left, the card in the instrument turns right making it look like the little plane is banking left. It was very confusing and I had to figure it out immediately because without the artificial horizon the turn and bank became my primary instrument to keep the Navajo under control.

It was a tense few minutes. My instrument scan became critical using a method I hadn't practiced since … well, I had no idea how long it had been since I'd done it but I was in it now. *Airspeed climbing means I'm descending, pull back on the yoke a little. Level the wings … remember, turn left to make the card go right. Check the GPS, get back on course. Airspeed dropping … lower the nose a tad.* And on and on. *Keep the scan going … don't concentrate on one instrument for too long.*

Lee tried to help with a few words of warning when my airspeed started getting slow or my heading was turning but I cut him off with a curt, "Don't help me." His comments were more distracting than helpful.

After a few minutes I had the Navajo more or less under control and headed in the right direction. Or was it? Did we still want to be heading to Oman or should we turn back to Riyadh? You could definitely say we had a real emergency now but what should we do about it? I glanced at the map in between instrument scans. Al Kwifrich, Al Batha, Abu Dhabi, and Dubai were all along our course line to Oman and had airports we could land at. The nearest one was almost an hour away. Would it make sense to land there? At this point how would it help us and what difference would it make? I had the plane under control and was actually having fun using the partial panel scan method. It was like a high stakes video game. Turning back to Riyadh would mean flying on instruments all the way back followed by a partial panel instrument approach, at night. And by the time we got to the first alternate airport along our route we would hopefully be out of the dust and into the clear sky making the partial panel situation less of an emergency. Plus if we continued on to Oman, we'd be poised to make the crossing to India once the vacuum pumps were replaced. Our decision? Keep going to Oman.

Pitch black outside the cockpit now. I could tell we'd left the dust behind because I'd seen a few lights here and there out in the desert. So we were technically in VFR flight conditions but my assumption that I'd be able to stop my partial panel scan once we cleared the dust had been incorrect. There were just not enough lights below to give me any sense of horizon. No matter, I had my scan routine down pat by then and was as comfortable as I usually was on a night flight over the desert.

Even though I was dealing with both vacuum pumps out I still had to do the normal things required to fly an airplane on a long cross country flight. Lee was manning the radios while I navigated, switched fuel tanks when needed and monitored our engine instruments which were on the other side of the cockpit in front of Lee. I glanced over at the engine instruments out of habit and noticed something out of place. I grabbed my small flashlight and shined the beam at the instruments for a better look.

"Lee, what does the right engine oil pressure and oil temperature read?"

"Right oil temp is running a little hot, getting close to the red line. Right oil pressure is way down. Close to the red too."

Christ, what now?

"Do me a favor, shine the light out at the right engine and tell me what you see."

Lee pressed his head against the window as he shined the flashlight out at the engine for a few moments before looking back at me.

"The engine is all covered in oil."

"Are you serious?"

Great, first we lose both vacuum pumps. Now we've got a major oil leak in the right engine. What's next?

"Keep an eye on the oil and cylinder head temperatures. I'm going to throttle back and see if we can baby that engine enough to make it to Oman."

I brought the right throttle back about halfway to try and ease the load on the engine. We only had a little over an hour left to go. Maybe there was enough oil left in the engine to make it. It was an optimistic approach but worth a shot I thought. While still using the partial panel scan to fly the Navajo we continued on into the night.

"Oil's getting pretty close to red line."

I glanced over at the gauges and confirmed Lee's assessment. Both oil temperature and pressure were bumping up against their red line limits. Time to shut her down. I closed the right engine throttle then pulled the propeller control all the way back over the stops and feathered the prop. I saw the blades of the right engine's propeller reflected in the cockpit lights quickly come to a stop. Then I trimmed up the plane for single engine flight and went back to my scan. I had to advance the left engine a little to maintain altitude but we were three hours into our flight and had burned off most of our heavy fuel so it didn't take much.

Okay, here's the situation. It was a dark and stormy night. Maybe not stormy but it sure was dark. Both vacuum pumps were out rendering most of the instruments used to control the plane useless. We had a major oil leak in one of our two engines forcing us to shut it down and we were landing at an unfamiliar airport in a foreign country. And just for good measure we had a cabin stacked high with avgas filled plastic containers ensuring that if we did crash we'd make a really big fireball. Did I miss anything?

No big deal though. I had my best friend at my side and he was doing a great job keeping the music flowing from his phone. On day one Lee had hooked up a splitter we could both hook our headsets into. That way we could listen to the same music as we flew across half the world. That night our heads were bobbing in unison as he played classic rock with a heavy load of STYX.

The approach and landing were anticlimactic. I'd gotten so used to the partial panel and single engine flying in and landing on the long runway at Muscat, Oman. I was more careful than usual to keep my speed up and not stall the plane but it turns out the most difficult thing I had to do that night was taxi in on one engine.

When we shut down and got out we were both a little shocked at how much oil was spread all over the right engine. When I checked, there were maybe two or three quarts of oil showing on the dipstick. We'd started with twelve. With nothing left to do we grabbed most of our gear and headed to the hotel. Once there we got our first lucky break of the night. They allow beer in Oman.

The first thing we did after calling Cory the next morning and telling him about the situation was to go back out to the Navajo and see what the damage was. Which was easier said than done. The security at the Muscat airport was so tight they only allowed pilots to go out to their aircraft if they were leaving. I tried to explain that we needed to do maintenance but that wasn't allowed.

"Okay, can you tow it to your maintenance facility then please."

"We don't have a maintenance facility on the field."

Right.

"So tell me then, what do you do if an aircraft is in need of maintenance?"

"They fly it to another airport where there is a maintenance facility."

"And if the aircraft is un-flyable?"

Blank stare.

After much wrangling and cajoling the head of security called the airport manager who, after making us wait for an hour, grudgingly allowed us access to the Navajo. When we got there we again pulled the cowling off the right engine and were greeted with an oil soaked mess. There was no way to determine where the leak was but it didn't seem to be coming from the valve cover I'd worked on in Greenland. So we grabbed a roll of paper towels from the cabin, wiped down the engine as best we could, put in all the last five quarts of oil we had with and started the engine. I could see the leak right away. Oil was actually spurting out from somewhere around the rear cylinder on the left side. But when we shut the engine down and looked we couldn't see an obvious hole in the cylinder or anything that would constitute a "smoking gun." It was pretty clear that the oil was coming from that rear cylinder though. Before I called Cory again I first called Darrell Gibson, my mechanic back home in Wisconsin. I told Darrell everything and asked him how long it would take to get to Oman and slap a new cylinder on the Navajo. Darrell said he could be on a plane with a new cylinder and all the necessary tools that afternoon. That sounded great to me and I told him to stand by but be ready to leave.

"Don't do anything for now. The owner is sending his own mechanics to check it out," Cory said over the phone.

"Are they bringing a cylinder?"

"I don't think so. I think they just want to see what's wrong."

"My guy can have that plane back in the air in twenty-four hours!"

But I was arguing with the wrong guy. Cory was just passing on information. If the Navajo's owner wanted to have me sit around while he had his own mechanics fix the plane then that's his call. I get paid by the day whether I'm flying or sitting by the pool.

Early the next morning I got a call from someone at Thai Regional to meet their mechanics at the airport. They'd flown in first thing and wanted to get started right away. I was encouraged by how fast they'd shown up. Maybe they could get the Navajo fixed quickly. However when I met the two gentlemen my positive mood quickly faded. Sitting in the airport security office were the two oldest mechanics I'd ever met. Larry looked like he was in his late seventies and Curly was at least eighty. Moe must have been on Vacation. At least they didn't speak English or have a new cylinder with them.

This should be productive.

After another grueling session of "Why do you want to go out to your aircraft if you're not going flying?" The four of us arrived at the Navajo. We pulled the cowling off the right engine again (I was getting good at that) and using international sign language I told, showed, pointed to the problem cylinder. They nodded appropriately and from what I gathered they wanted to see the leak for themselves. So once again we wiped the engine down, filled it with oil and ran it up. I had what I assumed was the chief mechanic in the cockpit with me and pointed out the spurts of oil coming from the rear cylinder. He gave me the thumbs up indicating that he saw the leak so we shut the engine down, put the cowl back on and went back into the terminal.

When we got back inside the head mechanic got on the phone to his boss and gave him a long account of what he had discovered. At least I assume that's what they were talking about. After a few minutes the mechanic handed the phone to me.

"Hello, Captain McCauley? Yes, my chief mechanic says you are all ready to go. Will you leave today?"

I was confused. What the heck? They hadn't done anything! We'd just put more oil in the plane and literally watched it shoot oil out of the engine!

"I'm sorry, there must be some misunderstanding. They didn't fix the leak. The engine needs a new cylinder before it can be flown."

"That's not what my mechanic says. He tells me that the engine runs well and he could see nothing wrong. So you will leave today, yes?"

I was beside myself. In as calm a voice as I could muster, I tried to explain that the Navajo had a major oil leak and there was no way it should be flown over seven hundred miles of open ocean in the condition it was in. The owner disagreed. He said that his mechanics were the best in the business and had worked for him for years running an entire shop full of mechanics who took care of his fleet of jet airliners. He also pointed out that I had just flown the same distance from Saudi Arabia to Oman with no difficulty. No difficulty? I told him all about the night flight from Riyadh and how when we landed there was almost no oil left in the engine. His solution? Put extra oil in the engine so even if it was leaking there should still be some left by the time we got to India!

I didn't know what to say. I couldn't believe what he was suggesting. Before I got even angrier I told him that I would call Cory and let him know my decision. Actually, I wasn't angry. I was confused. I couldn't believe what both the mechanics and the Navajo's owner were saying. It was like they had no aviation experience at all. What they were suggesting was madness.

I called Cory and told him what the owner had said and told him that there was no way I was going to fly that plane over the Arabian Sea in the shape it was in. I've flown a lot of planes with a lot of things wrong with them but even I have limits. I might be crazy but I'm not stupid. Well, not that stupid at least. Cory agreed with me and said if that's the case then pack up and go home. And just like that, we were done.

In thirty years of ferry flying this was the first time I'd failed to complete my mission. And even though it was through no fault of my own it still felt so … unsatisfying and unfinished. Which of course it was. All our hard work and flying was for nothing. Even worse was the fact that we wouldn't make it to play chess in Bangkok. When we found out we were going to Bangkok, Lee and I planned on playing a game of chess when we reached our destination because of the popular song "One night in Bangkok." The song was all about playing chess and we thought if we were going to be in Bangkok we had to play a game of chess. Lee and I had played a lot of chess growing up and thought playing a game there would be a cool way of celebrating our achievement. Now we were just tucking tail and running. I think I felt worse for the Navajo than for anything else. It felt like I was abandoning the plane that had faithfully brought us so far. Even though it had given me more challenges than normal.

We checked flights back to Minneapolis and found the cheapest one had an overnight layover in, of all places, Bangkok.

Lee and I got to play our chess game after all.

EPILOGUE

I wasn't retiring from ferry flying per se. I was just being a lot more picky about what flights I took. If the trip was to ferry a particular type of plane that I really wanted to fly or if it was going to a particular place that I wanted to visit, then sure, I'll take the trip. Other than that I really didn't have the time. The skydiving school in Wisconsin was getting busier every year and I needed to be on site more to make sure things ran the way I wanted them to. I also wanted to spend more time with Cathy now that the kids were all grown up and moved out of the house. One of the first trips Cathy and I took was a road trip from Wisconsin all the way down through the Baja Peninsula to Cabo San Lucas. It was a two week adventure with no schedule or destination in mind at all. We didn't intend to drive three thousand miles to the end of the Baja, it just sort of happened.

On the way back we stopped in and paid a visit to Pete Zaccagnino in Utah. We had a wonderful dinner with him. The next morning over coffee Pete hit me with a proposal. He had been hired to coordinate a trip around the world for six aircraft owners and their wives. We would all be flying an EPIC. The EPIC is a sleek, homebuilt single engine turbine aircraft that looks fast just sitting on the ramp. The trip was going to be a high dollar trip with no expense being spared. At each stop around the world the trip coordinators would have the most interesting and exciting thing they could find set up. We'd be staying in the best hotels in the area and eating at the best restaurants available. It was going to be literally the best trip around the world imaginable. And Pete wondered if I'd like to be one of the professional pilots hired to go along and assist the owners of the aircraft who didn't have the international experience to make the trip safely. I kept a straight face while Pete told me about the trip and what I'd be paid if I decided to go along. When he was done I told him that I'd probably be interested but that I'd have to check my schedule. Then Cathy and I said our goodbyes and headed back out to finish our road trip.

When we got in the car Cathy looked at me and asked, "What in the heck was that? When Pete started talking about that trip I figured you'd be jumping up and down begging to go along!"

I looked at her and smiled, "I was jumping up and down on the inside. But no matter how fun a trip might sound, a ferry pilot's gotta play it cool."

It looked like I wasn't going to retire just yet.

THE END?

ABOUT THE AUTHOR

Kerry McCauley grew up in central Minnesota. He began his career in aviation by becoming a UH-1H "Huey" helicopter crew chief and winter survival instructor in the Minnesota National Guard. He became a professional skydiving instructor and jump pilot before becoming an international ferry pilot. Kerry's career as a ferry pilot has taken him to 60 countries, over three oceans, and a dozen seas. Kerry has flown over 50 different types of aircraft, has accumulated over 9000 hours of flight time and over 20,000 skydives. He also starred in two seasons of the Discovery Channel series *Dangerous Flights*. Kerry lives in Wisconsin with his wife Cathy where they own and operate Skydive Twin Cities, along with their children, Claire and Connor. He still flies and jumps almost every day.

Works by Kerry McCauley:

Ferry Pilot: Nine Lives Over the North Atlantic.
Dangerous Flights: What Could Possibly Go Wrong?
Riskaholic: The Hobo Series.